PROFESSIONAL IDENTITY AND SOCIAL WORK

How are identities formed among social workers, many of whom perform complex, challenging and ambiguous public sector functions on a regular basis? Why does identity come to matter for professional social work? This book, the first of its kind in the field, examines professional identity in relation to social work by asking how practitioners think of themselves as a "social worker", a professional self-concept often entangled in a range of relations, beliefs, values and experiences.

Bringing together the perspectives of an internationally renowned group of specialists, the collection addresses a range of issues associated with professional identity construction and "being professional" in the context of a rapidly changing inter-professional environment. It introduces new concepts to social work, including materiality, enactment, performance, affect, entanglement, capital and worth, to consider the vexed issues surrounding matters of professional identity in social work.

This will be an essential guide to all those keen to debate the challenges and possibilities confronting contemporary social work through the lens of professional identity, whether they are students, educators, practitioners, researchers, managers, policy-makers or associated professionals. It will also appeal to those interested in social theory, organisational sociology and leadership as well as anyone working in related fields of health and education.

Stephen A. Webb is Professor of Social Work at Glasgow Caledonian University, Scotland. Previous to this he was Professor of Human Sciences and Director of the Institute for Social Inclusion and Well-being, University of Newcastle, New South Wales, Australia and Professorial Research Fellow at the University of Sussex, UK.

"This book is a very substantial contribution to the neglected topic of social work and its professional identity. Whilst retaining a clear and insightful focus, this collection ranges far and wide to incorporate key critical insights from a wide range of expert and knowledgeable commentators. This is an exciting addition to our underpopulated literature on professionalism in social work."

—*Roger Smith, Professor of Social Work in the School of Applied Social Sciences, Fellow of the Wolfson Research Institute for Health and Wellbeing, Durham University, UK*

PROFESSIONAL IDENTITY AND SOCIAL WORK

Edited by Stephen A. Webb

Routledge
Taylor & Francis Group

LONDON AND NEW YORK

First published 2017
by Routledge
2 Park Square, Milton Park, Abingdon, Oxon OX14 4RN

and by Routledge
711 Third Avenue, New York, NY 10017

Routledge is an imprint of the Taylor & Francis Group, an informa business

British Library Cataloguing-in-Publication Data
A catalogue record for this book is available from the British Library

Library of Congress Cataloging-in-Publication Data
A catalog record for this book has been requested

ISBN: 978-1-138-23442-0 (hbk)
ISBN: 978-1-138-23443-7 (pbk)
ISBN: 978-1-315-30695-7 (ebk)

Typeset in Bembo
by Apex CoVantage, LLC

Printed and bound by CPI Group (UK) Ltd, Croydon, CR0 4YY

This book is dedicated to my wife, Penni, the love of my life.

And in the spirit of inter-species companionship, to our dog Hegel, and kitten, Kore – the unspeakable girl – who did everything she could to stop this book being written by prancing around on the keyboard.

CONTENTS

ACKNOWLEDGEMENTS

As with all books, this one would not have been possible without the inspiration, support and knowledge of a great many people. It is always impossible to name everyone who has contributed to any book and the journey it takes. First and foremost, I would like to thank all the chapter authors for their excellent contributions. It was a great pleasure working with such a talented, stimulating group of international researchers. The innovative and original contributions will make a significant impact and contribution to the field of social work and more widely. I am grateful to the staff at Routledge, and particularly Shannon Kneis, Editorial Assistant, Sociology and Social Care, for her help and support. As before I have found Routledge to be such a great publisher to work with. Much discussion has taken place with colleagues and students at Glasgow Caledonian University (GCU). In particular, I would like to thank colleagues Ian Brodie, Brian Coyle, Scott Grant, Simon Gittins, Sharon Jackson, Martin Kettle, Barrie Levine, Pearse McCusker, David McKendrick, Louise Shanks and Lynn Sheridan, and doctoral researchers, Maura Daly, Natalia Farmer and Heather Lynch. In many ways this is a GCU social work book. Their progressive values continue to inspire. In various Scottish social work policy roles, people who helped me think about professional identity, I want to thank Mairi-Anne Macdonald, Pat McCowan, Brian Relph and Jane Devine for insights and discussion. Social work in Scotland is a healthier place with their policy and practice contributions. International research partners in Portugal provided support and discussion in developing this project, including Cristina Albuquerque at Universidade de Coimbra, and Inês Amaro, at Instituto Universitário de Lisboa. From Holland, an acknowledgement to my friend Willem Blok, a soul mate. As ever, I want to offer my deep gratitude for my wife, Penni, for her continuing support, patience, kindness and love. Finally, I would like to offer a dedication in the book to my old pal David Philpott. A steadfast "radical social worker" and piano man, who worked lyrically with people with head injuries, and died at the young age of 62 on the 12th September 2016. He is deeply missed.

NOTES ON CONTRIBUTORS

Liz Beddoe is an Associate Professor in the Faculty of Education and Social Work, University of Auckland, New Zealand. Liz's research interests include critical perspectives on social work education and professional supervision. Liz has published articles on supervision and professional issues in New Zealand and international journals. Recent books include the co-authored *Challenges in Professional Supervision* (2016, Jessica Kingsley Publishers) with Allyson Davys, *Social Work Practice for Promoting Health and Well-being: Critical Issues* (Routledge, 2014) and *Social Policy for Social Work and Human Services in Aotearoa New Zealand: Diverse Perspectives* (Canterbury University Press, 2016) with Jane Maidment.

Stewart Collins was Head of Social Work at universities in Scotland and Wales. He is Book Review Editor and Editorial Board member of the *Journal of Social Work*. He has co-authored and co-edited books on social work theory, language and discourse, and social work and alcohol problems. His research has focused on social work education, stress and well-being, voluntary counsellors and alcohol problems. Stewart has co-authored or authored more than 50 articles on these topics. In recent times his writing has concentrated more on probation work and positive perspectives surrounding social workers, such as job satisfaction, self-efficacy, resilience, coping, optimism and hope. He co-authored the classic *Social Work and Received Ideas* (Routledge, 1988) and the influential article 'Contract or Con-Trick' (1987) published in *British Journal of Social Work*.

Maura Daly is an experienced social worker, practice teacher and manager, having worked in the statutory and voluntary social work sectors for more than 30 years. She has previously published on direct social work practice and on practice teaching. She is currently researching for a PhD at Glasgow Caledonian University, where she is exploring the social work professional identity.

Mike Dent is Emeritus Professor, Staffordshire University, and Visiting Professor, Leicester University. He continues to research and publish widely on the comparative study of the professions within health care organizations, new public management, health care computing and user involvement. His articles have appeared in leading academic journals, including *Public Administration, Organization, Organizational Studies* and *Sociology of Health and Illness.* His recent research has been funded principally by the NIHR Service Delivery and Organisation and European Cooperation in Science and Technology (COST). He helps organize the annual International Dilemmas in Human Services Conferences as well as being on the committee RC52 Sociology of Professions Group of the International Sociological Association.

Julia Emprechtinger, MA in Social Work, is Senior Research Assistant at the Social Work Department of the University of Applied Sciences and Arts of Western Switzerland (HES-SO) and PhD candidate at the University of Education Freiburg/ Breisgau (Germany). Her research includes professionalization and professionalism in social work as well as the child and adult protection system in Switzerland. She is currently doing an ethnographic research project on the role of social workers in the interdisciplinary setting of the Swiss child and adult protection authorities.

Mark Erickson is Reader in Sociology and Director of Postgraduate Studies at the University of Brighton. He is the co-author of *Myths at Work* (Polity, 2000), *Business in Society* (Polity, 2009) and *Globalization and Work* (Polity, 2013) and author of *Science, Culture and Society: Understanding Science in the 21st Century* (Polity, 2016, second edition).

Melissa Hardesty is an Assistant Professor in the Department of Social Work at Binghamton University (State University of New York). Prior to this, she was an Assistant Professor with the North Carolina State University, Department of Social Work. Her ethnographic research of child welfare workers at a concurrent planning foster care and adoption agency in the Midwestern United States focuses both on the nature of the job and on the micro-politics of assessing parents on behalf of the state. Other research interests include feminist and anti-feminist selfies and the visual narrative content of prospective adoptive parent profiles. Melissa Hardesty also serves on the Board of Directors at the Stillwater Residential Treatment Facility in Greene, New York.

Elizabeth Harlow PhD, BA, CQSW, FHEA, has been involved with social work for 40 years, 28 of which have been spent in academia at Trent Polytechnic and the universities of Bradford, Salford and currently Chester. In addition to directing undergraduate and postgraduate programmes of study, she has led empirical research initiatives. Motivated by an interest in human relations, she researches the organization, management and delivery of services to children and families. Specializing in qualitative perspectives, she has published her work in leading social work journals and edited books as well as the journal *Social Work and Social Sciences Review*. She is currently an editorial board member of *Practice: Social Work in Action*.

Torben Elgaard Jensen is Professor in Techno Anthropology and Science & Technology Studies, Aalborg University, Copenhagen, Denmark. He is co-author of *The New Production of Users: Changing Innovative Collective and Involvement Strategies*, (Routledge, 2016); *Bruno Latour: Hybrid Thoughts in a Hybrid World*, (Routledge, 2011); and *Identity in the Age of the New Economy: Life in Temporary and Scattered Workplaces* (Edward Elgar, 2004). His research focuses on technical and social innovation practices. His work is broadly inspired by science and technology studies and the sociologies of innovation and organisation.

Emily Keddell is a Senior Lecturer in the Department of Sociology, Gender and Social Work, University of Otago. She has practiced in a variety of child and family social work positions in Aotearoa and the UK. Her research covers a number of areas of child and family social work policy and practice, including constructions of risk, decision making, the use of big data, and the relationship between inequalities and contact with the child protection system. She is involved in translational activities as a member of the Reimagining Social Work blog collective and as an Associate Member of Child Poverty Action NZ.

Martin Kettle is a Senior Lecturer in Social Work at Glasgow Caledonian University and programme lead for the MSc in social work. His recent publications include a study of the implementation of Self Directed Support in Scotland, a literature review of supervision, and an exploration of decision points and sense-making by child protection social workers. He is currently part of a research team working on a longitudinal study of social workers in Scotland from the point of qualification. His research interests include analysis and decision making in safeguarding work and professional identity.

Jadwiga Leigh has been a Lecturer in the Department of Sociological Studies, University of Sheffield since 2014. Prior to this, she practised as a social worker in statutory and voluntary settings. In 2013, Jadwiga completed doctoral research which focused on professional identity and organisational culture in England and Belgium. Her thesis will be published as a monograph entitled *Blame, culture and child protection* (Palgrave, 2017). Current research projects include an Economic and Social Research Council (ESRC)–funded project exploring child protection practice and organisational culture; an ESRC arts funded project called 'Re-humanising social workers'; and a study exploring social work regulation in England.

Jem Price is a Registered Social Worker and Principal Lecturer in Social Work at the University of Brighton, with a particular interest in international social work. Jem's published work has drawn on his research exploring the perspectives of social workers in the Philippines and of Filipino social workers in the UK, contributing, for example, to *Social work in East Asia* (Ashgate, 2014). He is a member of the Association of South East Asian Studies in the UK (ASEASUK) and of EN-SSPS, a European network of people in the social sciences whose work concerns the Philippines and its diasporic population.

Mark Smith was a practitioner and manager in residential childcare settings for almost 20 years and is currently Senior Lecturer and Head of Social Work at the University of Edinburgh. His first post in academia at the University of Strathclyde was to develop and deliver a Master's programme in residential childcare. He has written extensively on residential childcare. He moved to the University of Edinburgh in 2005. Mark completed an ESRC-funded Knowledge Exchange project on working with involuntary clients and has received further ESRC funding to work with the City of Edinburgh and East Lothian Councils to develop practice cultures in light of the findings of the Munro Review of Child Protection.

Tony Stanley is Chief Social Worker for Birmingham City Council, UK. He is the professional lead for quality social work and improving practice for vulnerable children and their families. Prior to this, Tony was the Principal Social Worker at Tower Hamlets for children, families and adults. Recent publications include problematizing the role of statutory services for cases of suspected radicalisation risk, and organisational cultures shaping practice. He promotes "child centred and family focused" social work, and the importance of children living relationally, supporting their connections with parents and wider family. He is researching social workers' constructions of "family" in radicalisation risk cases.

Peter Voll Dr. rer. soc., is Professor at HES-SO and head of the Institute of Social Work of the HES-SO Valais-Wallis. His current research projects focus on the relationship between social work and law, particularly on child and adult protection, and professional decision making in legal and organizational contexts.

Stephen A. Webb is Professor of Social Work and Academic Lead at Glasgow Caledonian University, Scotland. He previously worked at University of Newcastle, Australia, and the University of Sussex. Stephen is author of *Social Work in a Risk Society* (Palgrave Macmillan, 2006), and co-author/editor of *The New Politics of Social Work* (Palgrave Macmillan, 2013); *Evidence-based Social Work: A Critical Stance* (Routledge, 2009); *Ethics and Value Perspectives in Social Work* (Palgrave Macmillan, 2010); *Social Work Theories and Methods* (SAGE Publications, 2012, second edition, translated into Korean and Polish); *The SAGE Handbook of Social Work* (SAGE Publications, 2012); the major international reference work *International Social Work* (SAGE Publications, 2010, four volumes); and *Information and Communication Technology in the Welfare Services* (Jessica Kingsley Publishers, 2003).

Julia Wheeler is a Lecturer in Social Work at Plymouth University in the School of Health Professions. She completed her professional education in Social Work at the University of Bath. She is currently completing an Education PhD at Plymouth University concerning how social work students develop their professional identity, with a focus on aspects of professional socialisation. She is also interested in research with children and families social work and practice learning.

Fran Wiles works for the Open University, UK, as a Senior Lecturer and Assistant Head of Department (Social Work). She qualified as a social worker in the 1980s and remains registered with the Health and Care Professions Council. Her doctoral and subsequent research interests include social work professional identity and professional regulation. She is drawn to discourse analysis and narrative methodologies, as well as participatory research methods. She is currently researching how national boundaries impact on social workers' professional identities.

1

MATTERS OF PROFESSIONAL IDENTITY AND SOCIAL WORK

Stephen A. Webb

Introduction

Stuart Hall famously asked in a 1996 essay "Who Needs Identity?" Well, quite a few of us do, it seems from a quick glance at the issues of our times. No matter whether it is a discussion of nationhood, race, religion, popular culture or sexuality, identity has become a mainstay in everyday conversations about who we say we are and believe ourselves to be (Jackson, 2010). Today, people even talk about "identity theft" as the crime of the new millennium (Hoar, 2001).

Broadly speaking, identity and identification are root constructs in social sciences (Albert, Ashforth, and Dutton, 2000: 13). What helps root these concepts so centrally? I can think of three main reasons. First, they are tremendously versatile. As Alvesson et al. wrote of identity, it "can be (and perhaps has been) applied to almost any phenomenon" (2008: 7). Indeed, this has led some to caution against applying the term indiscriminately and dropping it into accounts unreflectively (Ashforth, 2016: 361). Second, the concept of identity helps to bridge analyses between levels of social life such as the personal, the group, the team and the organisation. This makes it a powerful device for connecting recursive links and understanding dynamic networks of association. Third, identity is all about definition. How we define ourselves, what we value and the collective relation to something or someone else *really does matter*.

So is there a starting definition that can help us think our way carefully into considerations about professional identity? Leary and Tangney (2003) offer a textbook guide to the distinction between identity and identification. Identity refers to the central, distinctive and more or less enduring qualities of an actor, while identification refers to viewing those qualities as self-defining (2). Identification stems from the Greek word *oikeion*, meaning "belonging", or "being part of". It implies advocacy of and alignment of interest with the profession of social work.

Leary and Tangney maintain that identity is a label, whereas identification refers to the classifying act itself. Thus identity is best construed as being both relational and contextual, while the act of identification is best viewed as inherently processual (2003: 3). As shown later this provides us with a standard, serviceable definition that can be built on and critically engaged with as we unpack matters of professional identity and social work.

Since Hall asked the question there has been a burgeoning literature on professional identity and social work, especially over the past 10 years. Within the field there has been an outpouring of interest and indeed speculation on matters of professional identity and identification. Some of the most compelling contributions over recent years have been made by authors gathered together in this volume. At the same time, within its short tangled history, the concept of professional identity has been subject to a searching critique. It appears to be more than a fad or even simply a productive line of research because it is a promising agenda for social work. This is because it offers a number of theoretical breakthroughs when drawing on the broader interdisciplinary social sciences. Perhaps, for social work, more so than other professions, it also gains significance in its pivotal relationship to a politics of location and worth (Hall, 1996; Stark, 2011). By politics, I mean both the various tensions for jurisdiction and territorial conflicts that are played out within and across professions and the difficult struggles that characterise the ongoing claims made for or against professional social work. At both individual and collective levels, activists, pressure groups and campaigners are mobilising around issues of identity. We have become accustomed to all kinds of "identity politics". To give an immediate feel for this we need only to look at the UK magazine *Community Care,* which has successively launched the "Stand Up for Social Work" campaign since 2006 to raise the profile of social work and showcase its signature identity. Across the Twitter online network supporters and activists have conscientiously added the brightly coloured "Stand Up for Social Work" badge logo to their profile photographs. All but a tiny fraction of perspectives on professional identity focus on its positive consequences. The darker side is rarely discussed. At a populist level it is seen as a good thing and therefore more of it must be better (see Chapter 16 in this volume). Indeed, in some important corners social work is worried about giving up too precipitously the "identity" of the profession. In the UK this is especially true in relation to concerns about the so-called loss of identity in the face of health and social care integration. It is felt that having a strong professional identity is likely to buffer the impact of threats to social workers' collective identity. In light of this, the ongoing generativity around matters of professional identity and the sustained concentration should not be that surprising.

The present book, the first of its kind in social work, examines professional identity – its nature, development and application – in social work through a social science lens. Indeed, throughout the book you will witness the way various authors draw on this rich interdisciplinary field to make sense of professional identity. The book demonstrates the significance of professional identity because of its links to a wide range of experiences, contexts, values and institutional locations that otherwise would not be associated in social work.

It has been indicated that identity has been subject to a searching critique in the social sciences. This is partly because there are so many diverse perspectives that have invoked it. It is also because of both the indiscriminate usage of the concept and its populist appeal. Once we dip into issues of professional identity in social work we soon discover they have been vexed by conceptual ambiguity, lack of consensus about core attributes and problems in identifying what counts in the constitution of identity. Studies have tended to focus on social workers' professional identity formation; the framing of key tensions around social workers' professional identity; issues which convey narrative representations of social workers in talking about their role, values and work; and the educational context in which professional identity is formed in preparation for front-line practice (Webb, 2016). All this makes it a kind of laboratory, then, for thinking about matters of professional identity.

I have deliberately chosen to underline the significance of "matter" in thinking about professional identity. Hence the chapter title "matters of professional identity and social work". The brilliant feminist physicist Karen Barad (2003), in 'Toward an understanding of how matter comes to matter', asked how matter came to be important, which led to an astonishing uptake of discussion in sociological circles. John Law (2004) took up her insights with great alacrity. He starts by putting a hyphen into Barad's opening play of words. "The world is an ongoing open process of *matter-ing*" (2003: 817). For Law, this concept of matter-ing leads to three crucial insights about the social world. First, the merging of two worlds: "the kingdom of facts, and the kingdom of values" (2004: 2). This is a move from what Bruno Latour (2004) calls "matters of fact" to "matters of concern". In the process, scientific facts, for example, become value-laden controversies. Fracking is a great example of this at work. Another example is the weapons of mass destruction justification used by the Bush administration for the war on Iraq. The UK government net migration targets is a more recent example of attempts to use scientific evidence to mask deeper matters of concern. Facts and values – natures and cultures – are enacted together; they transport and are all mixed up. Second, Law says it indexes the move from stability, things in themselves, *to things in process*. Third, as a part of this, it indexes a move to enactment (see Chapter 3 in this volume). Barad, Law reminds us, insists that worlds are being done, enacted into being, instance by instance (see Summerson Carr, 2010 for a discussion of expertise as enactment). Identity comes to resemble something like a series of concrete interactive episodes involving practitioners invested with specific goals, skills and linguistic capacities. Mattering becomes the frame through which social workers communicate their professional identity. So what does matter-ing mean if we bring it closer to social work and the focus of this book? The answer is: quite a lot. What is matter-ing about professional identity in social work? What is being made material, made relevant for social work? What is the business of social work all about when professional identity becomes a concern? How are "contributions" made to social work from other social sciences or professional fields, contributions that matter? Can we understand controversies and scandals involving social work, other professions and the public as fighting over matters of fact, and over the policies that might follow from those facts? And how does what matters get moved about when thinking about changing professional identity? As a side note for now: We will see how this concentration on "mattering" provides a very helpful corrective to those perspectives on professional identity which have a tendency to overemphasise the discursive, interactional and personal. Realities rather than opinions are being made. Reality is *being done* in professional (and other) practices of valuation (Law, 2004: 6).

There is no clear-cut acceptance of what is meant by professional identity. The muddled situation is further complicated by the fact that several competing theoretical perspectives are deployed to make sense of professional identity. For instance, at a practical level the extent to which front-line workers have to fulfil a narrow set of socially coded values, regulated by a professional body, as part of identity maintenance has been a troublesome and much debated matter for social work. Clearly, issues of professional identity in social work are contestable. A mix of competing rationalities and values are invoked in attempts to locate the specificities of front-line practice, at an individual and collective level, which generate debate about professional identity and social work.

Let's kick things off with some basic assumptions. At a practitioner level, professional identity – or how social workers think of themselves as social workers – is often defined as their self-concept based on attributes, beliefs and experiences (Ibarra, 1999; Schein, 1978). Here the focus is very much on the individual practitioner rather than the profession as a group collective. Despite a growing interest in matters of professional identity in social work, researchers know relatively little about how identities are formed among practitioners who carry out the complex, challenging and often ambiguous front-line functions (Baxter, 2011). The aim of this book is to examine the formative aspects of professional identity as it relates to social work. This will facilitate greater theoretical clarity and map possible alternatives to afford a better understanding of the field of social work. The book focuses on the significance of professional socialisation, workplace culture, boundary maintenance, jurisdiction disputes and inter-professional tensions with health, education and the police (Abbott, 1988). The book highlights the importance of beliefs as well as attachment and sense of belonging for the study of professional identity (Rothausen et al., 2015). Professional identification is often associated with increased personal accomplishment. The importance of identity formation as mainly social and relational in nature is attenuated. Here it is concerned with narratives of recognition, trust and organisational culture within hierarchal settings.

From these different perspectives we see the notion of professional identity as a complex one, and a cursory examination of the literature reveals that there is a great deal of contestability. Moreover, as will be seen, professional identity is not a stable entity: it is an ongoing process of accommodation and customisation shaped by contextual workplace factors. In this respect, identity formation is viewed as more interactive and more problematic than the relatively straightforward adoption of the role of "professional social worker". Given the increasing importance of professionals in all types of organizations (Wallace, 1995), and given the centrality of identity in how practitioners make sense of and "enact" their workplace environments (see

Weick et al., 2005), addressing issues of professional identity in this book is most timely. In the section which follows attention is drawn to the contestable nature of professional identity and the way this impacts on its various characterisations in social work.

Professional identity: background to a contestable concept

The literature on professional identity has consistently revealed its contestable and changing nature. This is in part due to the rapid changes that occur in organisational, workplace and professional life. As Dent points out in Chapter 2 (this volume) it is also related to wider matters of economic and political change, such as austerity and technology. Professional identity does not come ready-made. Many researchers think it is continually fashioned in temporary situations. We need consider this in terms of re-localization as practitioners get a grasp on the dynamics of professional identity. For example, what is the likely impact of agile working and hot desking in social work organisations? As Dent and Whitehead explain:

> Being professional becomes more than a means by which the individual navigates the increasingly choppy waters of organizational life. Being professional suggests a context of meaning and values, whereby the lawyer, judge, human resource manager, banker and so on is experientially located through the particular narratives and discourses which accrue with and around that identity position.
>
> *(2002: 5)*

The fact that individuals occupy multiple subject positions and shift, manoeuvre and negotiate within and across these adds to the complexity of thinking about professional identity. This leads Dent and Whitehead to conclude that "Identity is neither stable, nor a final achievement" (2002: 11).

The literature on identity and identification in organizational settings (Ashforth et al., 2008) suggests two core phenomena are at work in identity formation and maintenance: sense of belonging and attachment. This formulation is reflected in the institutional logics conception of identity discussed in the final chapter of this volume (also see Friedland, 2012; Thornton et al., 2012; Thornton and Ocasio, 2008). Ashforth and Mael's (1989) classic study summarises professional identity as consisting of three main factors: (i) distinctiveness; (ii) prestige; and (iii) the salience of out-groups. Distinctiveness refers to a profession's values and practices in relation to other comparable groups (teachers, nurses or occupational therapists); prestige, regarded by many as the hallmark of professional identity, is the second factor with an emphasis on status, reputation and credentials. The third antecedent factor, which again highlights the significance of relational factors, is identified as salience of the out-group, whereby awareness of the out-group – those who do not belong – reinforces an awareness of one's in-group (1989: 21).

As Payne notes

> The identity of the profession of social work has often seemed unclear and contested, and social workers in the UK have felt their identity to be bound up in specific roles provided for in legislation, rather than in broader conceptions of their potential role.
>
> *(2006: 138)*

There are plenty of examples of an increased uptake of the significance of professional identity for social work in statements across the international stage (Levy, Shlomo, and Itzhaky, 2014; Wiles, 2013). Most striking of all, perhaps, is the Scottish *Changing Lives: Report of the 21st Century Social Work Review* (Asquith, Clark, and Waterhouse, 2006), which makes explicit reference to the significance of professional identity. In 2004 the Scottish Executive commissioned an independent review of social work. *Changing Lives*, the Review Report, is described as the basis for "the biggest overhaul of social work in Scotland for 40 years" (Asquith et al., 2006: 3). The Report reflects the problems that beset social work and focuses particularly on issues of professional identity. It states "There is an urgent need for social work to clarify its professional identity in order to establish clear roles for individual social workers" (2006: 8.4: 39).

The Report goes further in identifying the core values and moral commitment in the make-up of social work's professional identity. The skills that social workers possess are underpinned by this shared set of values:

> The professional identity of social work need not be inextricably linked to specific organisational structures. Rather, professional identity should be based more on core values and principles in order to distinguish the nature of the social worker's contribution from that of individuals working within other agencies and to protect against the threat of boundary erosion as the result of development in other professions. Issues of recruitment and retention to social work are inextricably linked to the issue of professional identity.
>
> *(2006: 8.5: 39)*

The danger of boundary erosion is recognised here, but as shown later, the research literature tends to maintain that professional identity is intimately locked into aspects of organisational culture. The Scottish review dramatically concluded that *"the 'crisis' in social work is mainly a matter of professional identity* that impacts on recruitment, retention and the understanding of the profession's basic aims" (2006: 8; emphasis added). The crisis in social work *is* regarded a crisis of professional identity. Whether issues of professional identity actually constitute a crisis for social work, a moral panic or whether we are simply dealing with a matter of concern remains debatable (see Chapter 16 in this volume).

Professional socialisation, workplace relations and gender

Being labelled "unprofessional" is equivalent to striking the fear of God into many social work practitioners (Webb, 2016). Indeed, an accusation of being "unprofessional" is used as a powerful shaming device. Social workers who transgress risk bringing their credibility, reputation and integrity into question. They can be investigated for their "fitness to practice". In educational settings, social work students can be failed on fieldwork placements for "being unprofessional". "Professional misconduct" is an offence likely to be investigated by the Health and Care Professions Council in England and Wales. Indeed, Grant and Kinman (2012) reported that social workers regard it as "unprofessional" to admit that traumatic cases affected them emotionally. Not mixing one's personal life with work is considered as "being professional".

The significance of professional socialisation has been consistently acknowledged as a crucial factor in the formation of identity (Freund et al., 2014; Loseke and Cahill, 1986 and Chapter 13 in this volume). However, a major criticism is that it regards professionals as overly determined via processes of moulding, and as essentially passive recipients. Goldenberg and Iwasiw (1993) describe professionalisation as

> a complex and interactive process by which the content of the professional role (skills, knowledge, behaviour) is learned and the values, attitudes, and goals integral to the profession and sense of occupational identity which are characteristic of a member of that profession are internalized.
>
> *(4)*

Socialization – with role models and mentors, experiential learning and tacit knowledge acquisition – influences each learner, causing them to gradually think, act and feel like a social worker. Research has discussed how role models provide professional identities that one can "try on" to see if they fit (Ibarra, 1999). Helpful distinctions have emerged between *socialisation for work*, which corresponds primarily with experiences of qualifying professional education, and *socialisation by work*, which focuses on experiences in situ (Cohen-Scale, 2003). Protocols, rules and standards are learnt on a formal level (for example, work-based professional development) and informal context in contact with peer group, experienced role models and service users. This is a dynamic process whereby practitioners anticipate actions of other social workers. The transformation process of newly qualified social workers to professionals is an acculturation process during which the values, norms and performative rituals are gradually internalized (Grant, Sheridan, and Webb, 2016; Hodgson, 2005).

Identity work is pivotal in understanding how practitioners embed themselves into organizational life. It is through workplace cultures of socialisation that professional identities are developed in relation to discourses of recognition (practitioner competence and professional values). As Collins shows in Chapter 11 (this volume), newly qualified social workers display what they consider to be desirable professional identities of confidence, capability and suitability. Indeed, for some practitioners "being professional" and being oppositional are necessarily antithetical. Identity formation can act negatively and may not necessarily be a good thing when the possibility of organisational coercion comes into the frame. Workplace organisations exert influence on practitioners in part through identity work and identification but also through the regulation of professional conduct.

At a collective level, identity exhibits a logic which inscribes "autonomous" professional practice within a network of accountability and professional conduct which is governed at a distance. In social work, professionalism is autonomous to the extent to which the conditions of autonomy have already been inscribed in particular forms of conduct embodied in the notion of "professional competence" and regulation (Fournier, 1999). Professional conduct is deemed extremely important in social work, with accusations of being unprofessional having the effect of hardening an already risk-averse culture. As Fournier (2001) points out, the quest for professionalism reveals disciplinary control. Professionalism can be understood as a disciplinary technique, one largely exercised through the label "being professional". In the same way that no one wishes to be deemed incompetent, so no one wishes to be labelled unprofessional. Fournier argues that practitioners "will work harder and be more conscientious in the interests of the company if they believe themselves to be acting professionally, rather than as subordinates" (2001: 118).

Dent and Whitehead remark that "'being professional' appears to act in the interests of all concerned and so doing becomes a universal mantra" (2002: 3). Goffman noted that "being a professional" means adopting the "rhetoric of training which marks off the professional from the layperson" (1961: 46). He says that "the licensed practitioner is someone who is reconstituted by his learning experience and is now set apart from other men [sic]" (1961: 49). This in-group dynamic means engaging in impression management and forming a visible identity in dress, attitude and vocabulary. For Goffman, speech, expressive behaviour and demeanour embody intentions. In *Asylums,* Goffman (1961) discussed how organizations instil tacit acceptance and conformity through inducements. In his work on "face-saving", he emphasised how professionals are expected to use speech, with ritual care, to present an image of self-control and dignity (see Chapter 14 in this volume). Reflecting on this mix of cognitive and affective work, De Montigny claims that "Being a social worker is not just a job. It's a way of life" (1995: 57).

Barbour and Lammers contend the institutionalization of a professional identity can be conceptualized as "the emergence, establishment, and sedimentation of what it means to hold a particular position or engage in a particular activity in the context of the larger, generic notion of profession" (2015: 38). On-the-job learning activities are crucial in this respect. But there may be a dark side to professional identity. In emphasising the processual nature of power Alvesson and Willmott regard identity regulation as a restrictive feature of organisational control (Alvesson, 2001; Alvesson and Willmott, 2002). They demonstrate how employees are enjoined to develop self-images, narrative and work orientations that are deemed congruent with narrow, managerially defined objectives. The iteration of identity work regulation is likely to be keenly felt for middle and service managers in social work as they are squeezed between different constituencies. Alvesson and Willmott's focus on identity deepens themes developed within other analyses of normative institutional control. They develop empirical material to illustrate "how managerial intervention operates, more or less intentionally and in/effectively, to influence employees' self-constructions in terms of coherence, distinctiveness and commitment" (2002: 619). For Alvesson and Willmott (2002), organizational control is achieved through self-positioning of employees within managerially dominant discourses about work which they may become more or less committed to. Identity regulation is thus performed through micro practices, and is reflexively negotiated by practitioners.

We have seen how professional identity is a vehicle for understanding the interaction between work organisations and identity (Alvesson, Ashcraft, and Thomas, 2008; Thomas, 2008; Vough, 2012) and its consequences for the service users and organizations served by professionals (Korica and Molloy, 2010). Since professionals are organisationally situated, a better understanding of their identities needs to take differences in workplace culture, credentials and professional status into account. In social work, the differences between practitioners working in children and family teams may be significantly different from those working with disabled service users. Smith (2005), for example, considers the poor relation of residential childcare to the rest of social work (also see Chapter 12 in this volume).

It is important to recognise that gender divisions and gender bias play a significant role in this context. Throughout the 1980s and 1990s, certification, registration and licensure for social workers – but not social care assistants – marched rapidly throughout the developed Western world. The social workers were often women, who struggled to gain formal professional recognition and comparable pay conditions until bodies like the General Social Care Council in the UK and the Council on Social Work Education (CSWE) in the US were established. Men have been noticeably absent on the front line of services, but more prominent in managerial roles. According to the now-defunct General Social Care Council (GSCC) figures, more than 75% of qualified social workers in England are female (Galley, 2014). In a UK study that looked at student motivations to train as social workers, Furness (2007) found that between 2002 and 2005, 83% of total registrations for all pathways in social work were women. The idea that men's gendered identity is vulnerable and easily undermined when they do "women's work" might be a significant factor in this respect. A practitioner's gender will play a significant role in the formation of professional identity. Given the care ethics of social work and its welfare role, it's likely that female social workers understand their *gender and professional identities* as compatible (discussed in Chapter 16 in this chapter).

Boundaries, partnership and inter-professional work

Boundary work is important in mapping out professional identity and its tensions. In Abbott's (1995) study of professions, professional boundaries and turfs, he mapped fields of jurisdiction between those professions and turfs. Abbott's central insight is that it is the jostling for relative power and relative status between occupational groups that characterises the "system of professions" (Morrell and Tuck, 2013: 5). Professions pro-act and react by seizing openings and reinforcing or casting off their earlier jurisdictions. "Professions' claims for legitimate control are judged by various 'audiences': the state, the public, co-workers in the workplace. These external judgments ratify professions' claims, thereby making them efficacious against competitors" (Abbott, 2005: 246).

Social work as conceived by Abbott is a complex turf which needs to be defended against adversaries. He deploys a "network-constitutive approach" to examine the way it emerges out of a set of "boundary groups" with different types of jurisdiction claims at stake (1995: 546). Typical boundary conflicts and competing jurisdiction claims are tensions in child protection between the police and social work over access to national data on risk assessment of sex offenders. In the UK, multi-agency public protection arrangements (MAPPA) attempt to conflate professional roles but are often deferred by social workers because they impose a quasi–criminal justice role that results in risk minimisation. The police will typically informally control access to ViSOR (Violent and Sex Offender Register) – a computer system which provides a UK multi-agency information sharing tool – thus reducing the potential for sharing and storing critical information on sex offenders. The integration agenda between health and social care further tests the silo effect of professional territorial claims.

Professional territories of responsibility are delineated, privileges acquired and claims on material resources enforced. Nesting occurs within professions, but a danger for identity occurs when they lose their singular separation because of the overwhelming number of linkages binding them. Hudson (2002) observes there are three critical areas in which these rivalries are played out between different professions:

- professional identity, jurisdiction and territory;
- relative status and power of professions; and
- different patterns of discretion and accountability between professions.

Abbott (1995) focuses on the aspect of jurisdiction for social work which is related to exclusivity and exclusion, that is, the ability to make discrete claims for expert knowledge and assure authority over a certain professional realm, agent or object. Professional success for social work depends on the ability to maintain jurisdictional control over client-relevant expert knowledge and to expand legitimate spheres of intervention. Legitimacy comes from the power over particular work tasks and signature skills as well as external recognition. Boundaries between social work, counselling and mental health professions and psychology are examples of the contested and divided nature of jurisdictional claims (Heite, 2012).

In an empirical study of social work in health care, Beddoe (2013) is wary about the prospects for inter-professional harmony (see Chapter 9 in this volume).

Examining the credentials of health care social work in institutional settings, she shows how social work claims for knowledge are weak, which in turn impacts on professional identity and status in multidisciplinary settings (McMichael, 2000). Focusing on issues such as hospital discharge, Beddoe reports on how integration is dependent on organisational culture, including resource allocation and local perceptions of professional boundaries. Lymbery (2005) similarly argues that effective partnership within health and social care is hard to achieve, particularly in light of significant differences in power between various occupational cultures and the inherently competitive nature of professions jostling for territory in the same areas of activity. In the UK much of the policy thrust has been at the level of inter-organisational working rather than at the level of inter-professional partnerships. The extent to which identities can be forged which transcend the traits of particular professions and provide the most effective delivery of integrated provision and the achievement of organisational outcomes remains unclear. Abbott (1995) envisages pressures from other occupations that occupy a broadly similar position to social work – e.g. nursing, teachers and occupational therapy – in making jurisdictional claims on work that currently forms part of the social work role (see Harlow, Chapter 5 in this volume). In particular this is likely to be the case with assessments of older people and those with a disability that are currently undertaken by social work. Historically, as Abbott points out, "social workers have often conceded control to other professions, a cession that, for example, was quite explicitly made in psychiatric social work" (1995: 559). The main conclusion is that since its main area of jurisdiction is heavily dependent on state and government funding, "the profession is perpetually in a precarious position" (1995: 560).

In contrast to, say, nursing and teaching, the professional identity of social work continues to suffer in the public eye because of its association with clients of low status. Indeed, social work is often vilified because it does the "dirty work" of sorting out society's problems with stigmatised groups that some would prefer not to acknowledge existed (Morris, 2016).

Making sense of the terrain: how to use this book

Public perceptions of "social work" and "social workers" carry a powerful social charge. The image of social work often conveys stark ambivalence between, on the one hand, symbols of caring, nurturing and working with vulnerable people, to on the other hand, interfering "busy bodies" who perform a sort of moral policing and unnecessarily meddle in people's lives. This tension is inevitably reflected in issues of professional identity. While professional identity as it relates to social work is the unifying theme of this book, a range of material and themes from a variety of contexts are considered, allowing readers to reflect on this relation. In this sense it is a user-friendly book that allows readers to dip into and pick and mix the readings at their leisure. At the time of writing there is no dedicated text focusing exclusively on professional identity and social work currently on the market, although there are numerous of examples of an increased uptake and recognition of its significance in statements from associations, groups and researchers across the international stage (Levy, Shlomo, and Itzhaky, 2014; Wiles, 2013).

The book is divided and organised into three main sections:

1   Key concepts and perspectives.
2   Location, context and workplace culture.
3   Professional education, socialisation and readiness for practice.

The section divisions provide an intellectual map not only to the overlapping subject matter relating to professional identity but also to the significance of and the major themes in contemporary research on the way the concept of identity has developed as increasingly significant to social work. Not only will the book be a systematic resource on the leading research and practice-based trends in matters of professional identity for an international audience but it will also demonstrate the rich interdisciplinary nature of the field. The book is aimed at students, practitioners, policymakers and academic researchers. To this end it will provide an essential guide and reference work on contemporary issues around social work and professional identity. The aim is to reach an international audience – keen to debate the challenges and possibilities confronting contemporary social work through the lens of professional identity – who will find a focused set of ideas that resonate with or challenge the day-to-day experience of social work whether they are students, educators, practitioners, researchers, managers, policymakers or associated professionals.

The first section, *Key concepts and perspectives,* provides an overview of key perspectives, concepts and approaches that form around issues of professional identity. It shows how these have been adopted and critiqued within the field. The chapters in this section focus on the theoretical and conceptual matters of professional identity as it relates to social work. In providing fresh material that forges a connection between social work and professional identity through methodologically and conceptually driven considerations, the section is important for readers in making sense of the frameworks which contribute to the field of enquiry. It will help readers map a set of influences and trajectories, and compare them to each other. This assists readers in establishing key links and identifying relationships for or against different standpoints and the way these translate into practice settings. In Chapter 2, Dent offers some important ground-clearing work in critically reviewing the perspectives and approaches to professional identity, drawing on concepts of professional/professionalism, power, identity/identities, accountability and knowledge. He shows that gender diversity and intersectionality are integral to this process, and provides a helpful overview of their significance. In Chapter 3, Wiles discusses the different ways in which social work identity is conceptualised. For example, she shows how professional identity can be seen in terms of desired traits, or in conveying a sense of collective identity, sometimes focused around particular practice settings. She draws attention to international comparisons suggesting that social work identity should be seen in the political and socio-economic contexts of each country. Professional identity can also be thought of in subjective terms, whereby individuals come to identify themselves as social workers. The chapter concludes by exploring how the different meanings act as discursive resources for social workers to construct their professional identities, and suggests some skills and qualities which support social workers in this endeavour. In Chapter 4, Jensen offers a novel way of conceptualising professional identity. Drawing on Actor-Network Theory, the chapter provides a fresh perspective on professional identity and social work by challenging the traditional analytical separation of the so-called social and the so-called technical. The "techno-social" is proposed as a promising concept for social work and offered as an invigorated conception of professional identity. In Chapter 5, Harlow addresses some foundational conceptual matters about how changes to the core concept of "the social" is indicative of new understandings of professional identity in social work. Through the lens of a case study of supporting adoptive families, she closely examines the construction of social work, the meaning of the "social" component of "social work", and how emerging identity formation is hooked into broader social and economic contexts. This leads her to call into question any "fixed conception" of professional identity.

The second section, *Location, context and workplace culture,* is the most extended of the three. It foregrounds the importance of organisational context and significance of location for thinking about professional identity in social work. It does so by showing how it is situated within a rich and complex set of institutions, structures and processes that sustain the working life of professionals. The contexts of social work are wide ranging and dynamic, and they include the variety of institutional settings in which practitioners work or the types of service they implement. Social work occurs in a range of organisational contexts; its professional identity is likely to be shaped by public policies, service user perceptions, legal requirements and public expectations. Workplace culture and its mix of values, traditions, structures, beliefs, interactions and attitudes is considered significant in the treatment of professional identity. Its centrality is highlighted in the chapters in this section. In Chapter 6, Erickson and Price focus on the significance of the concept of vocation in considerations of the formation of professional identity. Using important insights from the sociology of Max Weber, they ask if the concept of vocation/calling help us to make sense of social workers' motivations and practices in the context of the Philippines and England. In a case study, they identify "strong inner motivations" and "a calling" to social work careers and practice connected to a sense of obligation and duty, and to other social work values.

In Chapter 7 Keddell and Stanley examine the impact of "risk work" on the formation of the professional in child protection social work. They discuss the way that an increasing faith in big data, nudge science and information flow in child safety reinforces an individualised view of professional identity and shapes practitioner and service user relations. In Chapter 8, Hardesty discusses identity formation, rationality, embodied knowledge, and objectification and the way tensions between these produce ethical dilemmas for social work. She demonstrates how professional identity is configured in tensions between different forms of knowledge that are articulated in front-line practice. The focus is on the context of child welfare. Hardesty argues that the construction of expertise in knowledge production is significant for the way practitioners understand themselves and ultimately plays a crucial role in shaping their professional identities.

In Chapter 9, Beddoe brings together innovative conceptual thinking with recent empirical research to explore social work identity in health care settings, arguably a significant field of practice in many parts of the world, including North America, Europe and Australasia. The influence of the French sociologist Pierre Bourdieu's philosophical framework is explored in a consideration of professional identity (Bourdieu, 1984). His concepts of "field" and "capital" are used to analyse the influence of power relations, utilising an emerging concept of "professional capital" for social work.

Inter-professional partnerships are now acknowledged by policymakers and strategists as critical for the health, social care and welfare of future generations in Europe. Emprechtinger and Voll turn attention to this important development in Chapter 10. The chapter critically examines how the increasing push towards inter-professional partnerships are likely to impact professional identity in social work, using the recently created interdisciplinary Swiss child and adult protection authorities or courts as examples and a field of observation. Commitment and resilience have long been regarded as important dispositional qualities for social workers. Collins, in Chapter 11, provides a detailed analysis of how commitment is decisive in shaping professional identities for social workers. He shows how it is important because of its association with motivation, values, recruitment, job satisfaction, job retention, job turnover, work performance, control and stress. He argues that social workers who are committed to their jobs are more likely to provide good-quality, committed service to their organisations and service users. In the final chapter in this section, Chapter 12, Smith asks what it would take to encourage a confident professional identity for residential social workers. The focus is on the relation between professional identity and the upbringing of children. Building on important earlier work, Smith considers the tensions that surface in seeking to conceptualise residential childcare within social work and argues that the tasks, the sites of practice and the means through which residential childcare is enacted mask fundamental differences between two players in the wider jurisdiction of child welfare.

The third and final section, *Professional education, socialisation and readiness for practice,* concentrates more explicitly on the formation or the making of professional identity. The identification question is at stake. The issue of how a social worker becomes socialised into the social work profession and prepared for practice is of critical importance. It is a process of learning the norms, education, signature skills and professional roles and values. This involves the internalization of the values and group norms of the profession in the practitioners or students own self-conceptions. Professional education and socialisation have been closely examined in related professional fields such as nursing, medicine, education and law. Thus far, little consideration has been given to its significance in social work. Using contemporary sociological concepts, this section explores different themes relating to professional socialisation and education. The authors in this section are concerned with how students reappraise their role perceptions and commitments during their educational preparation for practice. In transitioning to becoming qualified practitioners, students gain a greater understanding of their specialist role whilst becoming less rigid in their thinking. In this section the impact that social work education has on professional socialisation is examined. A focus on students' past experiences, the reflective nature of the process and the beliefs and values promoted in the training course of study is carefully examined.

Wheeler begins this section with an analysis of the role of professional education as a process whereby students develop a sense of self as members of a profession, internalize the values of their profession and exhibit these values through their behaviour. She presents empirical case study material in Chapter 13, maintaining that professional socialisation is a key aspect of social work pre-qualifying training, with practice fieldwork placement being a crucial element of this formative process. In Chapter 14, Leigh uses the seminal work of Erving Goffman to explore practitioners' "credible performances" as a feature of dramaturgical but situated practice in the making of professional identity in child protection work. She hints at the dark side of the potential straitjacket of the "professional" who is engaged in a type of empathic or tactical deception in making her performances convincing. In stressing the expansive affective dimension of organisational life, Leigh links this discussion to issues of prestige, recognition and professional reputation. In Chapter 15, Daly and Kettle examine what they call "fateful moments" in the shaping of professional identity in an educational context. Fateful moments occur when social workers are called on to take decisions that are particularly consequential or take a determinate stance in the face of adversity. Fateful moments often entail a *rupture*. Using rich case study material including reflective accounts written by social work students at the end of their graduate social work programme, the authors explore the issue of the development of professional identity.

Chapter 16 critically synthesises the key messages of the book chapter contributions using the lens of matters of concern. It draws on the institutional logics perspective to examine the way in which professional identity has become a matter of concern for social work. The chapter argues this because professional identity involves something inherently unsettled which needs to be investigated and explicated. Issues of professional identity permeate working life and exist, to a large extent, across all elements in social work. This final chapter focuses on the way that several logics of value and or evaluative work bring the concept centre-stage. The four logics are described as (1) a productionist rationality; (2) a sentimental politics of authenticity; (3) a dynamic stabilisation as a mode of professional reproduction; and (4) regimes of justification, worth and recognition. The chapter investigate theses "orders of worth" and the limitations and dangers associated with making professional identity a matter of concern.

In summary, the book aims to engage with students, practitioners, researchers, policymakers, service users and associated professionals to critically reflect on the importance of professional identity as a matter of concern for social work. It encourages readers to reflect on, compare and contrast the diverse dimensions of professional identity. The talented international contributors to the book aim to enrich our understanding of some of the central problems facing social work today and the ways in which these are intimately bound up with matters of professional identity.

References

Abbott, A. (1988). The System of Professions: An Essay on the Division of Expert Labor. Chicago: University of Chicago Press.

Abbott, A. (1995). Boundaries of Social Work or Social Work of Boundaries? *Social Service Review*, 69(4): 545–562.

Abbott, A. (2005). Linked Ecologies: States and Universities as Environments for Professions. *Sociological Theory*, 23(3): 245–274.

Albert, S., Ashforth, B. E., & Dutton, J. E. (2000). Organizational Identity and Identification: Charting New Waters and Building New Bridges. *Academy of Management Review*, 25(1): 13–17.

Alvesson, M. (2001). Knowledge Work: Ambiguity, Image and Identity. *Human Relations*, 54(7): 863–886.

Alvesson, M., Ashcraft, K. L., & Thomas, R. (2008). Identity Matters: Reflections on the Construction of Identity Scholarship in Organization Studies. *Organization*, 15: 5–28.

Alvesson, M., & Willmott, H. (2002). Identity Regulation as Organizational Control: Producing the Appropriate Individual. *Journal of Management Studies*, 39(5): 619–644.

Ashforth, B. E., Harrison, S. H., & Corley, K. G. (2008). Identification in Organizations: An Examination of Four Fundamental Questions. *Journal of Management*, 34(3), 325–374.

Ashforth, B. E. (2016). Distinguished Scholar Invited Essay: Exploring Identity and Identification in Organizations: Time for Some Course Corrections. *Journal of Leadership & Organizational Studies*, 23(4); 361–373.

Ashforth, B. E., & Mael, F. (1989). Social Identity Theory and the Organization. *The Academy of Management Review*, 14(1): 20–39.

Asquith, S., Clark, C., & Waterhouse, L. (2006). *The Role of the Social Worker in the 21st Century – a Literature Review*. Edinburgh: Scottish Executive Education.

Barad, K. (2003). Posthumanist Performativity: Toward an Understanding of How Matter Comes to Matter. *Signs: Journal of Women in Culture and Society*, 28(3): 801–831.

Barbour, J. B., & Lammers, J. C. (2015). Measuring Professional Identity: A Review of the Literature and a Multilevel Confirmatory Factor Analysis of Professional Identity Constructs. *Journal of Professions and Organization*, 2(1): 38–60.

Baxter, J. (2011). *Public Sector Professional Identities: A Review of the Literature*. Milton Keynes: The Open University.

Beddoe, L. (2013). Health Social Work: Professional Identity and Knowledge. *Qualitative Social Work*, 12(1): 24–40.

Bourdieu, P. (1984). *Distinctions: A Social Critique of the Judgment of Taste*, translated by R. Nice. Harvard: Harvard University Press.

Cohen-Scale, V. (2003). The Influence of Family, Social, and Work Socialization on the Construction of the Professional Identity of Young Adults. *Journal of Career Development*, 29(4): 237–249.

De Montigny, G. A. J. (1995). *Social Working: An Ethnography of Front-line Practice*. Toronto: University of Toronto Press, Scholarly Publishing.

Dent, M., & Whitehead, S. (2002). *Managing Professional Identities: Knowledge, Performativities and the 'New' Professional*. London: Routledge.

Fournier, V. (1999). The Appeal to 'Professionalism' as a Disciplinary Mechanism. *The Sociological Review*, 47(2): 280–307.

Fournier, V. (2001). Amateurism, Quackery and Professional Conduct: The Constitution of 'Proper' Aromatherapy Practice. In M. Dent & S. Whitehead (Eds.), *Managing Professional Identities: Knowledge, Performativities and the 'New' Professional* (pp. 116–137). London: Routledge.

Freund, A., Cohen, A., Blit-Cohen, E., & Dehan, N. (2014). Professional Socialization & Professional Commitment in Social Work Students – a Longitudinal Study. *Academy of Management Proceedings*, 2(1). Retrieved from http://proceedings.aom.org/content/2014/1/10679.

Friedland, R. (2012). Book Review: Patricia H. Thornton, William Ocasio & Michael Lounsbury 2012 The Institutional Logics Perspective: A New Approach to Culture, Structure, and Process. *Management*, 15(5): 582–595.

Furness, S. (2007). An Enquiry into Students' Motivations to Train as Social Workers in England. *Journal of Social Work*, 7(2): 239–253.

Galley, D. (2014). Why Are there so Few Male Social Workers? *The Guardian*, 26 July 2014. (Accessed 2 June 2016).

Goffman, E. (1961). *The Presentation of Self in Everyday Life*. New York: Doubleday.

Goldenberg, D., & Iwasiw, C. (1993). Professional Socialization of Nursing Students as an Outcome of a Senior Clinical Preceptorship Experience. *Nurse Education Today*, 13(1): 3–15.

Grant, L., & Kinman, G. (2012). Enhancing Well-being in Social Work Students: Building Resilience in the Next Generation. *Social Work Education*, 31(5): 605–621.

Grant, S., Sheridan, L., & Webb, S. A. (2016). Newly Qualified Social Workers' Readiness for Practice in Scotland. *British Journal of Social Work*, 46(2): 28–42. doi: 10.1093/bjsw/bcv146 First published online: March 12, 2016.

Hall, S. (1996). Who Needs Identity? In S. Hall & P. DuGay (Eds.), *Questions of Cultural Identity* (pp. 1–17). London: Sage.

Heite, C. (2012). Setting and Crossing Boundaries: Professionalization of Social Work and Social Work Professionalism. *Social Work and Society*, 10(2). Retrieved from http://www.socwork.net/sws/issue/view/22.

Hoar, S. (2001) Identity Theft: The Crime of the New Millennium. *Oregon Law Review*, 49(2): 1–13.

Hodgson, D. (2005). Putting on a Professional Performance: Performativity, Subversion and Project Management. *Organization*, 12(1): 51–68.

Hudson, B. (2002). Interprofessionality in health and social care: The Achilles' heel of partnership? *Journal of Interprofessional Care*, 16(1): 7–17.

Ibarra, H. (1999). Provisional Selves: Experimenting with Image and Identity in Professional Adaptation. *Administrative Science Quarterly*, 44(1): 764–791.

Jackson, R. L. (ed.) (2010) *Encyclopedia of Identity*. London: Sage.

Korica, M., & Molloy, E. (2010). Making Sense of Professional Identities: Stories of Medical Professionals and New Technologies. *Human Relations*, 63(12): 1879–1901.

Latour, B. (2004). Why Has Critique Run out of Steam? From Matters of Fact to Matters of Concern. *Critical Inquiry*, 30: 225–248.

Law, J. (2004). Matter-ing: Or How Might STS Contribute? Published by the Centre for Science Studies, University of Lancaster.

Leary, M. R., & Tangney, J. P. (2003). *Handbook of Self and Identity*. New York: Guilford Press.

Levy, D., Shlomo, S. B., & Itzhaky, H. (2014). The Building Blocks of Professional Identity among Social Work Graduates. *Social Work Education*, 33(6): 744–759.

Loseke, D. R., & Cahill, S. E. (1986). Actors in Search of a Character: Student Social Workers' Quest for Professional Identity. *Symbolic Interaction*, 9(2): 245–258.

Lymbery, M. (2005). United We Stand? Partnership Working in Health and Social Care and the Role of Social Work in Services for Older People. *British Journal of Social Work*, 36(7): 1119–1134.

McMichael, M. (2000). Professional Identity and Continuing Education: A Study of Social Workers in Hospital Settings, *Social Work Education*, 19(2): 175–183.

Morrell, K., & Tuck, P. (2013). Professions and Identity during Austerity: An Archaeological, Discursive Practice Perspective. *The Seventh Asia Pacific Interdisciplinary Research in Accounting Conference*, conference proceeding, July, sited Retrieved from 14th October, 2016, www.apira2013.org/proceedings/pdfs/K265.pdf.

Morris, L. (2016). AMHP Work: Dirty or Prestigious? Dirty Work Designations and the Approved Mental Health Professional. *British Journal of Social Work*, 46(3): 703–718.

Payne, M. (2006). Identity Politics in Multi-Professional Teams Palliative Care Social Work. *Journal of Social Work*, 6(2): 137–150.

Rothausen, T. J., Henderson, K. E., Arnold, J. K., & Malshe, A. (2015). Should I Stay or Should I Go? Identity and Well-Being in Sensemaking about Retention and Turnover. *Journal of Management*. Retrieved from http://jom.sagepub.com/content/early/2015/02/03/0149 206315569312.abstract.

Schein, E. H. (1978). *Career Dynamics: Matching Individual and Organizational Needs*. Reading, MA: Addison-Wesley.

Scottish Executive. (2006). *Changing Lives: Report of the 21st Century Social Work Review*. Edinburgh: Scottish Executive.

Smith, M. (2005). Applying Ideas from Learning and Teaching in Higher Education to Develop Professional Identity: The Case of the MSc in Advanced Residential Child Care, *Child and Youth Care Forum*, 34(4): 261–279.

Stark, D. (2011). *The Sense of Dissonance: Accounts of Worth in Economic Life*. Princeton and Woodstock: Princeton University Press.

Carr, E. Summerson (2010. Enactments of expertise. *Annual Review of Anthropology*, (39): 17–32.

Thomas, R. (2008). Critical Management Studies on Identity – Mapping the Terrain. In M. Alvesson, T. Bridgman & H. Willmott (Eds.), *The Oxford Handbook of Critical Management Studies* (pp.166–185). Oxford: Oxford University Press.

Thornton, P. H., & Ocasio, W. (2008). Institutional Logics. In R. Greenwood, C. Oliver, K. Sahlin & R. Suddaby, (Eds.), *The Sage Handbook of Organizational Institutionalism*. Thousand Oaks, CA: Sage.

Thornton, P. H., Ocasio, W., & Lounsbury, M. (2012). *The Institutional Logics Perspective: A New Approach to Culture, Structure and Process*. Oxford: Oxford University Press.

Vough, H. (2012). Not All Identifications Are Created Equal: Exploring Employee Accounts for Workgroup, Organizational, and Professional Identification. *Organization Science*, 23(1): 778–800.

Wallace, J. (1995). Corporatist Control and Organisational Commitment among Professionals: The Case of Lawyers Working in Law Firms. *Social Forces*, 73(3): 811–840.

Webb, S. A. (2016). Professional Identity in Social Work. In M. Dent, I. L. Bourgeault, J. L. Denis & E. Kuhlmann (Eds.), *The Routledge Companion to the Professions and Professionalism* (pp. 355–370). London: Routledge.

Weick, K., Sutcliffe, K., & Obstfeld, D. (2005). Organizing and the Process of Sense making. *Organization Science*, 16(4): 409–421.

Wiles, F. (2013). Not Easily Put into a Box: Constructing Professional Identity. *Social Work Education*, 32(7): 854–866.

PART I

Key concepts and perspectives

2

PERSPECTIVES ON PROFESSIONAL IDENTITY

The changing world of the social worker

Mike Dent

Introduction

Professional identity engenders a strong sense of meaning and worth for the individual and the collective as members of a profession; social work is no exception to this. Professional identity is often associated with a sense of vocation, reinforced by socialisation into the ranks of profession through the education and training process that all neophyte professionals go through, and the experience of working in the field (e.g. Bell, Nissen, and Vindegg, 2016). It is also the case, however, that what it means to be a professional will be somewhat different in different periods of time. The establishment of the welfare state after the Second World War (1939–1945) had a major impact on the work and status of public sector professionals, including social workers. Countries established what Esping-Andersen (1990: 26–34) calls 'welfare-state regimes'. He identified three dominant clusters: the 'liberal', corporatist and social-democratic. According to Esping-Andersen, the UK falls into the 'liberal' camp, for it is characterised by the 'modest' support it provided that was aimed at predominately low income, mainly working class, state dependents (ibid.: 26). This contrasts with the Scandinavian 'social democratic' model where support was generous and of a high standard that would meet the expectations of the new middle classes as well as the working class (ibid.: 27). The 'corporatist' variety is dominant within Continental Europe. Despite major differences between some of their organisational principles, particularly between France and Germany, they are all derived from the Bismarckian reforms of the later nineteenth century and represented a conservative response to the perceived threats of Marxism and Socialism at that time (Dent, 2003: 10). This response was very much shaped by the Church, supporting a strong traditional family rationale, which meant women were far more encouraged in being mothers than working. Esping-Andersen's (1990) analysis was strongly criticised from a gender perspective in the 1990s for largely ignoring for women's work across all three types (see particularly Lewis, 1992; Orloff, 1993), and Trifiletti (1999: 54) drew up a revised model of Esping-Andersen's model that takes these criticisms into account and relabels the 'corporatist' as the 'breadwinner' type, following Lewis's categorisation. Trifiletti(1999) also adds a category specifically for Southern European countries, labelled 'clientelistic', but it is not central to the argument in this chapter (see Dent, 2003: 17). These welfare systems have historically supported male breadwinners and assumed women as mothers will provide unpaid labour for the care of children, the elderly and the sick. This has implications for working women, including professionals, and their professional identities. Esping-Andersen (1999: 47–50, 2002) broadly acknowledges the criticism of the 1990 analysis, which reflected the theoretical blindness of his key argument (concerning 'de-commodification') to unpaid family labour (1999: 78). For the professional worker this relates to how much unpaid support lies behind the production of the professional role or identity, particularly – but not solely – in the case of women professionals (2002: 72–73).

This introduction has set the context for the discussion of professional identities within the public sector. Within the chapter I will discuss the broader concept of social identity before leading into a consideration of professional identities, including social work. In between the general and specific discussions on identities I will provide a sociological analysis of the professions, as it is crucial to understanding professional identity. Key here will be the argument that because the professions and professionalism has fairly radically changed in the wake of the dominant neo-liberal agenda that has permeated social policy since the 1980s.

Social identity

The concept of professional identity derives from the broader one of social identity. An individual derives from their lived experience as a member of social groups (e.g. family, community, occupation) or categories (e.g. gender, race, religion). This concept of 'identity' crosses several boundaries of the social sciences and is of particular interest to psychology, but for this analysis I am drawing on the sociological approach, for we are much more concerned with the interactional and institutional relations (or 'orders') of professions and professionalism than the individual practitioner (Jenkins, 2008: 17). Sociologists have become increasingly interested in the subject, given the growing emphasis on reflexive individualisation within late modern society that is most obvious in the growth and popularity of social media sites including Facebook. But it actually permeates almost every corner of our lives, eroding the traditional borders between public and private spaces. Gidden's (1991a) *Modernity and Self-Identity* has been influential in providing a relatively early analysis of this trend. In Gidden's scheme of things, this late-modern emphasis on identity has changed our understanding and experience of trust and trust relations, which goes beyond the personal and intimate to encompass our relationship with expertise, including those with the professions (see Chapter 15 in this volume).

In these relations, with professionals such as doctors, school teachers and social workers – and also science and technology professionals (e.g. airline pilots, computer professionals) – trust between the person and the professional is crucial, for it is rooted in the fact that we may often feel that 'other alternatives are foreclosed' (Giddens, 1991b: 90) or it may be because it is a 'leap of faith' as the problems faced are seen as too complex (Möllering, 2005: 295–296). Clearly, the role and identity of a professional embraces expertise, trustworthiness and being someone who can bear responsibilities. But first we need to look at our understanding of the professions and the place of social work within this institutional order, as well as how professions may have changed over recent years, for this has important implications for professional identities.

The professions

Simply stated, a profession can be seen as any occupational group that works with clients according to a publicly recognised specialist knowledge base and expertise (Larson, 1977). Moreover, it has a formal membership association and register of qualified members. It often regulates the workforce, as with the Scottish Social Services Council (SSSC). I could go on with a list of 'traits', but this would be unhelpful as earlier critics of this approach have pointed out (Johnson, 1972), for the approach is implicitly normative and ignores the issue of power relations. It has been reckoned that occupations which are able to monopolise a specialist expertise and knowledge could translate this into 'opportunities for income' (Macdonald, 1995: 9) in a way that reflects Weber's approach to social stratification.

Historically, the status of professions generally relied on aristocratic or royal patronage – although, as an organised force, the guilds also played a huge part in the emergence of the organisational form that professions followed with the craft model of career development via apprenticeship and journeyman onto master status. This model has continued well into the twentieth century in law and medicine (Krause, 1996).

The main dynamic shaping the professional identity of social work and similar occupations since the late nineteenth century has been the state, which has occupied a strongly heteronomous position relative to these professions. This was very different with the earlier establishment of law and medicine in their modern form in the nineteenth century, where the state needed these professions to ensure the governance of society (Johnson, 1995). These two professions have enjoyed probably the most autonomy of all the expert occupational groups, precisely because of these circumstances. Moreover, they became the established core within networks of occupations making up the division of labour associated with public order and health. Modern societies 'need' a disciplined and a reasonably healthy workforce; the professions of law and medicine play crucial roles in this, both directly and in 'shaping' the work of associated occupations and professions, including social work and nursing. In terms of Abbott's (1988) now classic analysis of the professions, law and medicine are examples of professions with full jurisdictional control:

> This is legitimated within the culture by the authority of the profession's knowledge . . . [and] established in law. It should determine the structure of referral that brings work to the profession. It should shape, indeed, the very public idea of the tasks that the profession does. Every profession aims not only to possess such a heartland, but to defend and expand it.
>
> *(Abbott, 1988: 71)*

But all professions exist within an interacting system, an ecology of competitive relations. Only some will gain and maintain full jurisdictional status. Other professions – including social workers, nurses and teachers – have had to settle for limited settlement of jurisdiction. These, nevertheless, are professions with public recognition and legal standing. They are not in any way semi-professions; moreover, they will never attain a dominant position within the system of profession without either some relative weakening in the power of the profession with full jurisdiction or changes in state regulation that directly impacts on the particular work arena. Within the health care arena, developments within nursing – with the development of specialist nurses and nurse practitioners (Dent, 2003: 105–107; Dent and Burtney, 1997) – are accepted by the medical profession within UK and North America, but less obviously so in Germany or Southern Europe (Dent, 2002), for reasons related to the nature of the professional jurisdictions within the different welfare regimes. Social work too varies in its forms between countries. Abbott (1988, 1995) gives the examples of England, USA and France in terms of their earlier development.

The challenge of new public management

Much of what we understand about the professions – and especially those professions working in the public sector – has been based on the welfare state model of professionalism. Since the 1980s, state policies and funding arrangements for welfare state services have been shaped by broadly neo-liberal thinking. This is not just a British phenomenon, but one found across Europe and beyond. The changes to professional work – and therefore identities – that ensued can be summarised in the term new public management (NPM). There were earlier indications of this development in the debates around deprofessionalisation, proletarianisation and deskilling (Freidson, 1994: 128–146). But the reality of NPM has been much more a reconfiguration of professional work and organisation rather than the professions becoming redundant. The professions have survived as a particular kind of organised work, characterised by longer periods of training and education than other occupations, as well as being substantially self-regulated and enjoying a high degree of work autonomy. The character of professional autonomy, however, has radically changed over recent decades (Lipsky, 1980). The professions, certainly in the public sector, are more regulated and publicly accountable than was the case previously.

What changed, as already indicated, was the neo-liberal revolution, which in the UK was closely associated with Thatcherism and with it the rise of NPM and subsequently the New Public Governance (NPG). These were designed to ensure the professions are more accountable to their clients/service users, employing organisations and the state.

The new managerialism of NPM was never a unified set of practices, but 'a theme which has distinct variations within the different sectors (e.g. health, education and social services)' (Dent, Chandler, and Barry, 2004: 1). What it has achieved overall, however, has been the establishment of a clear managerial jurisdiction around professional work that did not exist before. This, among other things, emphasised performativity and financial parsimony (Hood, 1995: 95–97). It also introduced, among other initiatives, competition and the real possibilities for the privatisation of public service provision. These different elements have had a profound effect on what being a professional means for many within the public sector. Previously, management – or administration – was seen as subordinate to professional work priorities. This is no longer the case. Following on the heels of NPM came NPG, which emerged partly because even management was concerned about the negative motivation and unintended consequences – primarily 'gaming' – that resulted from the mechanistic performative measures of NPM, with its emphasis on output measures. With NPG, the emphasis is on finding ways of coordinating the fragmented systems of service provision that NPM had brought about by 'promoting quality-led approaches to service redesign' (Ferlie, 2012: 240). This development was less of a direct attack on professional autonomy than NPM and crucially meant the professionals could – and needed to be – more centrally involved in the process of coordinating services. A good example of this are the patient care pathways within the UK National Health Service (NHS), which are primarily led by nursing and based on evidence-based medicine and practice (Allen, 2009; Dent and Tutt, 2013) – but there are examples to be found across the public sector, including social work. The examples impinge directly on professional work, for the assumption is that professionals will comply with the standards and protocols embedded within these systems. This evokes a rather different model of professionalism and occupational identity than was previously the case, before the introduction of NPM, for it assumes a more collective approach to professional practice than before. But now the nursing profession is more stratified between those who actively work on establishing the protocols and designing the systems and pathways, and the 'grassroots' or 'street-level' professionals who are intended to adhere to the guidelines (Evans and Harris, 2004).

This stratification is a development identified by Freidson (1994: 142) a few years ago, although his emphasis was on the distinction between 'rank and file' professionals and their colleagues who also served in a managerial role. This managerialised professional – hybrid – role is now well recognised and much debated (Noordegraaf, 2015). Hybrid roles within a profession can be very helpful in ensuring efficient and effective coordination between management and professionals. Professionals in this role can act as interpreters and translators across the management/professional boundary. Hybrid roles, however, can be ambivalent, for example, when their resources are limited and hard decisions concerning ways of working must be made. It is also a concern that experienced professionals spend considerable amounts of time dealing with managerial matters rather than using their expensively acquired skills and experience in dealing with cases.

Gendered and 'new' professionalism

Less obviously related to NPM and NPG is the issue of gender. The very concept of a profession, at least the classic varieties such as medicine and law, can be seen as essentially masculinist (Davies, 1996: 661; Hearn, Biese, Choroszewicz, and Husu, 2016). Those other professions such as nursing, teaching and social work are often viewed as somehow lesser, or semi-professions (Bolton and Muzio, 2008; Etzioni, 1969). This is an unhelpful term. While these professions do not have the power and influence of the classic professions of law and medicine, the status of these has more to do with professional jurisdictions (Abbott, 1988) than any sense of incomplete professionalisation that the term 'semi-profession' might indicate.

Famously, Flexner (Toren, 1969: 145) used the term 'semi-profession' earlier in the twentieth century within the US context to discuss social work. A primary justification was that the profession lacked a systematic theoretical knowledge base (Toren, 1969: 144). Even today the appellation is still being applied (Bolton and Muzio, 2008), but it is based on an unconvincing argument and suffers from the tautological weaknesses of the functionalist theoretical framework from which it is derived. Consequently, it ignores the issue of power relations (Johnson, 1972). Nevertheless, this assumption of being less than a full profession has impacted the construction of these occupations' professional identities. This can be further compounded where women make up a large proportion of the workforce (Bolton and Muzio, 2008), a situation that reflects the patriarchal structures within society (Hearn, Biese, Choroszewicz, and Husu, 2016; Macdonald, 1995: 124–156; Witz, 1990: 676–677). It is possible that the character of these patriarchal structures as they impact on the professions may be changing, for as Bolton and Muzio (2008: 291) point out, some female-dominated aspiring professions – including human resources/personnel – may pursue a professionalisation strategy to gain the autonomy and status independent of another profession (such as law). However, to achieve this these professions 'do gender according to masculine norms of conduct and exceed the cultural norms of managing like a man' (ibid.). Such masculinist approaches are unlikely to make much sense within the context of the people-oriented work that teachers, nurses and social workers carry out.

But to focus more on social work: the profession's recruits are predominantly female. For example, in 2009–2010 there were 5,130 female and only 925 male enrolments for social work undergraduate and postgraduate degrees (GSCC, 2010, cited in Furness, 2011: 3), and these figures are consistent with those throughout the previous decade. The under-representation of men in social work degree programmes and in the workplace may be related to the perceived lower status and earnings compared with similar graduate entry occupations, but equally, if not more so, it may be the perceived character and quality of social work. For example, dealing with disadvantaged families – often headed by single women – as well as child abuse allegations (see, for example, Galley, 2014) and more generally, working with vulnerable or 'damaged' individuals, has long been gendered female work (Hearn, Biese, Choroszewicz, and Husu, 2016). This reality, however, goes beyond the specific professions, for the pattern of male/female dominance across the system of professions is itself gendered (Davies, 1996) and masculinist too within patriarchal societies (Hearn, 1982; Hearn, Biese, Choroszewicz, and Husu, 2016).

It is important, however, to not elide the distinctions between women/men and our historically and culturally constructed femininities/masculinities (e.g. Brunni and Gheradi, 2002: 177–179; Butler, 1990; Davies, 1996: 663). It is not the consequence that, historically, men have, more or less, exclusively staffed the professions. Instead, the argument is that the professions reproduce patriarchal structures and relations within society and, for example, this to some extent has explained the relations between medicine and nursing. But one of the consequences of NPM for public sector services and the professions has been a shift from the traditional 'apprentice-journey(wo)man-"master"' guild-like patriarchal model to a much more competency-based learning model. The new curricula put far less emphasis on specific bodies of theoretical knowledge and more on practical scenarios thought to better equip new professionals for working in the field. Importantly, these scenarios are normally based on evidence-based practice (EBP), which provides the new legitimation for professional work. There is no clear evidence that this approach is gender-neutral, but it is a break with the patriarchy of the past. Nevertheless, it would be unwise to be sanguine. As Bolton and Muzio's (2008) study of HR professionals shows, once qualified and in post a woman may well find herself having to manage like a man, to adopt masculine subject positioning as a performative accomplishment (Brunni and Gheradi, 2002: 179) in order to succeed professionally at work.

Professionalism, social closure and responsibilisation

Bolton and Muzio (2008) rely on the Weberian 'social closure' model. This still informs much of the discourse around the subject (see Macdonald, 1995: 27–29), for it provides a very useful sociological lens with which to understand welfare state professions and professionalisation. Until the research of Witz (1990, 1992), its proponents were slow to address the issue of how to explain gender inequalities within the professions. However, with the entry of neo-liberalism and emergence of the NPM and later NPG reforms, the dynamics of professionalism and professionalisation have changed. Professionalism is no longer necessarily a vehicle of upward social mobility based on social exclusion. Public sector professions have become one particular kind of expert occupation, even though they are more formally regulated and subject to public scrutiny than others, in order to ensure the state has some control over the public services as well as encouraging a high degree of integrity among the practitioners for the benefit of the service users. But the discourse of professionalism is also employed by management to motivate non-professional employees (Fournier, 1999), as well as a wide range of occupations, to underpin their own claim to having expertise and trustworthiness, as for example in Fournier's (2002) example of aromatherapy. Such professional status is contingent upon 'maintaining cultural legitimacy in terms of prevalent social values and concerns' (ibid.: 117) far more than any Weberian 'social closure' process. This contemporary form of the professionalism discourse also reflects developments across a range of other 'new' occupations, ones not legitimated by – nor generally looking for – formal state recognition or registration. A good example would be management consultancy (Muzio, Ackroyd, and Chanlat, 2008).

Process driven vs. specialist professionalism

Within the public sector, the professions have new paths to legitimation via EBP (Webb, 2001). This seems to provide a more convincing legitimation than simply claiming expert status. EBP is part of NPG, which has led to the growing protocolisation of much professional work, particularly within health but also in social work. Within the UK we find protocol-driven care pathways the dominant model for designing and delivering efficient and effective care, which in theory brings together the professionals, managers and users of the service (Allen, 2009; Dent and Tutt, 2013), although in practice not all the professions are necessarily committed to the design and implementation of these care pathways (Allen, 2014). There are related, but even more contested developments within social work, too (Garrett, 2004). On the face of it, protocolisation would appear to be beginning to impose a new routinisation – or proceduralisation – on social work as well as nursing. However, within nursing, the protocols and the 'pathways' they underpin are principally designed and assembled by members within the profession. (See for example Dent and Tutt's (2013) account of care pathway design that I mentioned earlier.)

In the case of social work, at least within the UK, the experience of the profession has been that the government has been keener on restricting the autonomy of social workers rather than enhancing it (Garrett, 2004: 59). This contrasts with the case of nursing (Dent, 2003: 104–107) for many within the profession, proceduralisation is seen as primarily a mechanism for external control, but within social work it is seen as a mechanism that distracts them from their original purpose (Bauman 2000: 9 cited in Garrett, 2004: 56). Whereas, nursing broadly views protocols – or guidelines – and care pathways as enhancing the jurisdiction of nursing, in social work it's a different story. Social workers regard protocols and guidelines with suspicion. But in both cases, there are implications for professional identities.

The construction of professional identity

From the professional's perspective, her – or his – occupational identity is one that has been actively constructed during a period of education and training, a period of *proto-professionalisation* (Hilton and Slotnick, 2005) when the neophyte professional becomes socialised in the norms and values of profession. In other words, *proto*-professionalisation is a process of acquiring a professional identity. The concept has also been extended to patients regularly attending clinics, who become socialised often in very similar ways (de Swaan, 1988), a process that might also be applied to a range of different kinds of social-service clients. The development of proto-professionalism has implications for user involvement and the implications this may have on professional identity. The Hilton and Slotnick (2005) reference to proto-professionalism relates to medical education, but the analysis in identifying the following six elements seems to me to have remarkable continuities with other care professions too:

- Ethical practice
- Reflection/self-awareness
- Responsibility for actions
- Respect for patients/clients
- Teamwork
- Social responsibility

The training and education of professionals is followed by the ongoing experience of professional work, in which one's sense of professional identity will be further adapted and changed (Bell, 2015; Bell, Nissen, and Vindegg, 2016). This may be because of the disjunction between the training scenarios, case studies and the like. The actual experience of having responsibility for real-life cases is a different experience from classroom simulations. These experiences, Hilton and Slotnick (2005) propose, are part of the defining characteristic of a professional's practical wisdom, or *phronesis*, which one acquires only after a long period of experience, and reflection on that experience.

Professionals, collectively as well as individually, produce and reproduce 'identity' through discourse, narrative and representation. The construction, maintenance and any reshaping of a professional identity is a social process that will fully engage the individual social worker. Here I draw on the concept of discourse in order to better explain the connections between identity, knowledge and power. The notion of discourse being used here is a post-structuralist Foucauldian one (Foucault, 1980, 1984) wherein discourses are languages, representations, communications and practices that are available to the 'subjects' of discourse (e.g. social workers), or what Foucauldians refer to as 'fields of knowledge' (e.g. the work and organisation of social work within the public sector) (Dent and Whitehead, 2002: 9). Both 'subject position' and 'field' become realities as the outcome of certain processes through which certain knowledges – ways of understanding the world – become dominant (see Philip, 1979 for a classic study of this phenomenon in social work). For example, social work has a history in which the dominant knowledges have been grounded in various philanthropic and moral-based approaches to social reform as well as sociological and psychological informed approaches. Social work has early on in its modern history been much influenced by the scientific approach of Mary Ellen Richmond's social diagnosis method and today is much concerned with an evidence-based approach, but has also been much affected by radical perspectives too (see BASW, 2016). Today, the current emphasis on EBP and policy is now increasingly dominating the field (Gambrill, 2003, 2006, 2011). Taking EBP as our example, like any other discourse it is neither technically or morally neutral, however much its proponents wish it to be. It is a site of struggle and contestation, as social work (as other professions) is comprised of multiple knowledges and ways of knowing the world. The challenge for social workers, as an example, in terms of their professional identity, will be how far they try to accommodate the various discourses of social work as 'an embodied regulatory effect', and become process-driven social workers or, drawing more agentically on other knowledges available within social work, constitute themselves differently.

Relatedly, 'Discourse transmits and produces power; it reinforces it, but also undermines and exposes it, renders it fragile and makes it possible to thwart it' (Foucault, 1984: 100; quoted in Ramazanoglu, 1993: 19). For Foucault: '[T]here are no relations of power without resistances; the latter are all the more real and effective because they are formed right at the point where relations of power are exercised' (Foucault, 1980: 142). These power/resistance possibilities are central to our understanding of discourse. This can be clearly seen, for example, in the discourse around evidence-based practice in social work (Gambrill, 2010; Gray, Plath, and Webb, 2009). Moreover, this view of power relations is not hierarchical but circulatory, an enabling energy which can give rise to subjectivity, including crucially identity. Here it is important to note that we do not have a single identity – or set of discourses. Instead we have available to us multiple identities. A consequence of this is that we (the individual social worker as discursive subject) may well be riven with contradictory pressures – classically of home vs. work identities and roles, but possibly in terms of professional career as between, for example, being a 'pure' professional working directly with clients or taking on a more managerial/hybrid role.

Identity is always a process which is never finally completed. Nevertheless, for many of us a sense of professional identity does coalesce reasonably cohesively – however ambiguous and contradictory the process may feel at times. Only by engaging with the dominant professional discourses can the individual professional exercise power and have any influence – individually or collectively.

Foucault's post-structuralism is often seen as esoteric and unrelated to practicalities. But it does enable us to begin to understand the way professional expertise shapes the lives of others (clients) (Miller and Rose, 2008: 149). Their professional authority ('power'), however, lies in their own 'responsibilisation' (Fournier, 1999: 291), whereby they exercise their expertise essentially in the interest of the state to provide the management of normality (de Swaan, 1990). All of this could be summarised in the concept of 'governmentality' (Foucault, 1979; Fournier, 1999) so that professional work is in as Miller and Rose's (1990) terms 'government at a distance'. The professions, in short, make liberal government possible and vice versa.

Concluding discussion

Professional identity is an integral part of being a professional. It is both an individual and collective phenomena – and within a profession there will be several, possibly overlapping, identities coexisting and competing for dominance. As Abbott (1988) argued, the professions are related to each other within a system of jurisdictions that potentially could mean that the fortunes of different expert occupations will rise and fall. Generally speaking this has not been the case within the public sector, but if one adds into the equation, system or network of relations the state – a powerful player in the system of professions, and the user – traditionally a relatively weak player, but becoming less so – then the system of professions can be seen to be rather more fluid. This extended system reflects an Actor Network approach as developed by Bruno Latour and John Law (see Dent, 2003: 37–38 for a résumé), although I have no intention here in carrying out any extended analysis, only to use it as a way of explaining changes in professional identity. What we have seen since the 1980s has been the development and implementation of new technologies of control, driven first by NPM and subsequently through a possibly more benign NPG. An outcome of adjustment and contestation between the professions and the state has led to a radical remodelling of the public sector professions. This 'new' model has not completely driven out older professional identities, but it is much more technocratic and process driven – especially for the 'rank and file' – as well as trying to be user-friendly. This is a different world than the halcyon days of the welfare state in the mid-twentieth century. The professional identities that are shaped by the process of becoming and then being a professional are also rather different too.

References

Abbott, A. (1988). *The System of the Professions*. London: University of Chicago Press.

Abbott, A. (1995). Boundaries of Social Work or Social Work of Boundaries? *Social Service Review*, 69(4): 545–562.

Allen, D. (2009). From Boundary Concept to Boundary Object: The Politics and Practices of Care Pathway. *Social Science & Medicine*, 69(3): 354–361.

Allen, D. (2014). Lost in Translation? 'Evidence' and the Articulation of Institutional Logics in Integrated Care: From Positive to Negative Boundary Object? *Sociology of Health & Illness*, 36(6): 807–822.

BASW (British Association of Social Work). (2016). *The History of Social Work* (Jan Steyaert [ed.]). Retrieved from www.basw.co.uk/resource or directly at: http://www.historyof socialwork.org/eng/index.php.

Bauman, Z. (2000). Am I My Brother's Keeper? *European Journal of Social Work*, 3(1): 5–11.

Bell, L. (2015). Ethics, Values and Social Work Identity(ies). In L. Bell & T. Hafford-Letchfield (Eds.), *Ethics and Values in Social Work Practice* (pp. 37–46). Maidenhead, Berkshire: McGraw-Hill/ Open University Press.

Bell, L., Nissen, M. A., & Vindegg, J. (in press). The Construction of Professional Identity in Social Work – Experience, Analytical Reflection and Time. In Björn Blom, Lars Evertsson & Marek Perlinski (Eds.). *Welfare Professions in Europe*. Bristol: Polity Press.

Bolton, S., & Muzio, D. (2008). The Paradoxical Processes of Feminization in the Professions: The Case of Established, Aspiring and Semi-Professions. *Work, Employment and Society*, 22(2): 281–299.

Brunni, A., & Gheradi, S. (2002). Omega's Story: The Heterogeneous Engineering of a Gendered Professional Self. In M. Dent & S. Whitehead (Eds.), *Managing Professional Identities: Knowledge, Performativity and the 'New' Professional* (pp. 177–179). London: Routledge1.

Butler, J. (1990). *Gender Trouble*. London: Routledge.

Davies, C. (1996). The Sociology of Professions and the Gender of Professions. *Sociology*, 30(4): 661–678.

Dent, M. (2002). Professional Predicaments: Comparing the Professionalization Projects of German and Italian Nurses. *International Journal of Public Sector Management*, 15(2): 151–162.

Dent, M. (2003). *Remodelling Hospitals and Health Professions in Europe*. Basingstoke: Palgrave Macmillan.

Dent, M., & Burtney, E. (1997). Changes in Practice Nursing: Professionalism, Segmentation and Sponsorship. *Journal of Clinical Nursing*, 6: 355–363.

Dent, M., Chandler, J., & Barry, J. (2004). Introduction: Questioning the New Public Management. In M. Dent, J. Chander & J. Barry (Eds.), *Questioning the New Public Management* (pp. 1–4). Aldershot: Ashgate.

Dent, M., & Tutt, D. (2013). Electronic Patient Information Systems and Care Pathways: The Organisational Challenges of Implementation and Integration. *Health Informatics Journal*, 20(3): 176–188.

Dent, M., & Whitehead, S. (2002). Introduction: Configuring the 'New' Professional. In M. Dent & S. Whitehead (Eds.), *Managing Professional Identities: Knowledge, Performativity and the 'New' Professional* (pp. 1–16). London: Routledge.

de Swaan, A. (1988). *In Care of the State*. Cambridge: Polity.

de Swaan, A. (1990). *The Management of Normality: Critical Essays in Health and Welfare*. London: Routledge.

Esping-Andersen, G. (1990). *The Three Worlds of Welfare Capitalism*. Cambridge: Polity.

Esping-Andersen, G. (1999). *Social Foundations of Postindustrial Economies*. Oxford: Oxford University Press.

Esping-Andersen, G. (2002). A New Gender Contract. In G. Esping-Andersen with D. Gallie, A. Hemerijck & J. Myles (Eds.), *Why We Need a New Welfare State* (pp. 68–95). Oxford: Oxford University Press.

Etzioni, A. (ed.) (1969). *The Semi-Professions and Their Organization: Teachers, Nurses and Social Workers*. New York: Free Press, London: Collier-Macmillan.

Evans, T., & Harris, J. (2004). Street-Level Bureaucracy, Social Work and the (Exaggerated) Death of Discretion. *British Journal of Social Work*, 34(6): 871–895.

Ferlie, E. (2012). Paradigms and Instruments of Public Management Reform – the Question of Agency. In C. Teelken, E. Ferlie & M. Dent (Eds.), *Leadership in the Public Sector: Promises and Pitfalls* (pp. 237–251). London: Routledge.

Foucault, M. (1979). On Governmentality. *Ideology & Consciousness*, 6: 5–22.

Foucault, M. (1980). *The History of Sexuality, Vol. 1: An Introduction*. London: Penguin.

Foucault, M. (1984). Two Lectures. In C. Gordon (Ed.), *Power/Knowledge: Selected Interviews and other Writings 1972–1977 by Michel Foucault* (pp. 78–108). London: Wheatsheaf.

Fournier, V. (1999). The Appeal to 'Professionalism' as a Disciplinary Mechanism. *The Sociological Review*, 47(2): 280–307.

Fournier, V. (2002). Amateurism, Quackery and Professional Conduct: The Constitution of 'Proper' Aromatherapy Practice. In M. Dent & S. Whitehead (Eds.), *Managing Professional Identities: Knowledge, Performativity and the 'New' Professional* (pp. 116–137). London: Routledge.

Freidson, E. (1994). *Professionalism Reborn: Theory, Prophecy and Policy*. Cambridge: Polity.

Furness, S. (2011). Gender at Work: Characteristics of 'Failing' Social Work Students. *British Journal of Social Work*, 1–20. Available online. (Accessed 2 June 2016).

Galley, D. (2014). Why Are there so Few Male Social Workers? *The Guardian*, 26 July 2014. (Accessed 2 June 2016).

Gambrill, E. (2003). Evidence-Based Practice: Sea Change or the Emperor's New Clothes? *Journal of Social Work Education*, 39(1): 3–23.

Gambrill, E. (2006). Evidence-Based Practice and Policy: Choices Ahead. *Research on Social Work Practice*, 16(3): 338–357.

Gambrill, E. (2010). Evidence-based Practice and the Ethics of Discretion. *Journal of Social Work*, 11(1): 26–48.

Garrett, M. (2004). Have You Seen My Assessment Schedule? Proceduralisation, Constraint and Control in Social Work with Children and Families. In M. Dent, J. Chandler & J. Barry (Eds.), *Questioning the New Public Management* (pp. 55–70). Aldershot: Ashgate.

Giddens, A. (1991a). *Modernity and Self-Identity: Self and Society in the Late Modern Age*. Cambridge: Polity.

Giddens, A. (1991b). *The Consequences of Modernity*. Cambridge: Polity.

Gray, M., Plath, D., & Webb, S. A. (2009). *Evidence-based Social Work: A Critical Stance*. London: Routledge.

GSCC. (2010). *Raising Standards: Social Work Education in England 2008–2009*. London: GSCC. Retrieved from http://www.gscc.org.uk/cmsFiles/Education%20and%20 Training/SWEG%20Publications/Raising_Standards_08-09_web.pdf. (Accessed 2 June 2016).

Hearn, J. (1982). Notes on Patriarchy, Professionalization and the Semi-Professions. *Sociology*, 16(2): 184–202.

Hearn, J., Biese, I., Choroszewicz, M., & Husu, I. (2016). Gender, Diversity and Intersectionality in Professions and Potential Professions. In M. Dent, I. Bourgeault, J. L. Denis & E. Kuhlmann (Eds.), *The Routledge Companion to the Professions and Professionalism*. London: Routledge.

Hilton, S. R., & Slotnick, H. B. (2005). Proto-professionalisation: How Professionalization Occurs across the Continuum of Medical Education. *Medical Education*, 39: 58–65.

Hood, C. (1995). The 'New Public Management' in the 1980s: Variations on a Theme. *Accounting, Organizations and Society*, 20(2–3): 93–109.

Jenkins, R. (2008). *Social Identity* (Second edition). London: Routledge.

Johnson, T. J. (1972). *Professions and Power*. London: Macmillan.

Johnson, T. J. (1995). Governmentality and the Institutionalization of Expertise. In T. Johnson, G. Larkin & M. Saks (Eds.), *Health Professions and the State in Europe* (pp. 7–24). London: Routledge.

Krause, E. A. (1996). *Death of the Guilds: Professions, States and the Advance of Capitalism, 1930 to the Present*. London: Yale University Press.

Larson, M. S. (1977). *The Rise of Professionalism: A Sociological Analysis*. London: University of California Press.

Lewis, J. (1992). Gender and the Development of Welfare Regimes. *Journal of European Social Policy*, 2(3): 159–173.

Lipsky, M. (1980). *Street-level Bureaucracy; Dilemmas of the Individual in Public Services*. New York: Russell Sage Foundation.

Macdonald, K. M. (1995). *The Sociology of the Professions*. London: Sage.

Miller, P., & Rose, N. (1990). Governing Economic Life. *Economy and Society*, 19(1): 1–31.

Miller, P., & Rose, N. (2008). *Governing the Present*. Cambridge: Polity.

Möllering, G. (2005). The Trust/Control Duality. *International Sociology*, 20(3): 283–305.

Muzio, D., Ackroyd, S., & Chanlat, J-F. (eds.) (2008). *Redirections in the Study of Expert Labour: Established Professions and New Expert Occupations*. Basingstoke: Palgrave Macmillan.

Noordegraaf, M. (2015). Hybrid Professionalism and Beyond: (New) Forms of Public Professionalism in Changing Organizational and Societal Contexts, *Journal of Professions and Organization*, 2(2): 187–206.

Orloff, A. S. (1993). Gender and the Social Rights of Citizenship: The Comparative Analysis of Gender Relations and Welfare States. *American Sociological Review*, 58(3): 303–328.

Philip, M. (1979). Notes on the Form of Knowledge in Social Work. *The Sociological Review*, 27(1): 83–111.

Ramazanoglu, C. (1993). *Up against Foucault*. London: Routledge.

Toren, N. (1969). Semi-Professionalism and Social Work: A Theoretical Perspective. In A. Etzioni (Ed.), *The Semi-Professions and Their Organization: Teachers, Nurses, Social Workers* (pp. 141–195). New York: Free Press.

Trifiletti, R. (1999). Southern European Welfare Regimes and the Worsening Position of Women. *Journal of European Health Policy*, 9(4): 46–64.

Webb, S. A. (2001). Some Considerations on the Validity of Evidence-based Practice in Social Work. *British Journal of Social Work*, 31(1): 57–79.

Witz, A. (1990). Patriarchy and Professions: The Gendered Politics of Occupational Closure. *Sociology*, 24(4): 675–690.

Witz, A. (1992). *Professions and Patriarchy*. London: Routledge.

3

WHAT IS PROFESSIONAL IDENTITY AND HOW DO SOCIAL WORKERS ACQUIRE IT?

Fran Wiles

Introduction

The past decade has seen a growing interest in issues relating to social workers' professional identity. For students, it is increasingly viewed as an important outcome of qualifying education, to be developed and maintained throughout their social work careers. Being clear and confident about identity is considered to improve social workers' contribution in working with other professionals. A strong, positive sense of professional identity is said to bolster social workers' resilience to stress. Professional identity, when linked with the concept of 'professionalism', has become bound up with the regulation of practitioners and the avoidance of 'unprofessional' behaviour. These are just some of the ways in which the concept of professional identity has come to the fore; but are we all talking about the same thing? Understanding the different meanings and their usage is important for social workers, especially in the face of debate about the nature of social work and how it is best taught and regulated. This chapter discusses these meanings and suggests some ways in which practitioners – especially students and newly qualified workers – develop it. The chapter concludes by highlighting developments which have begun to emerge in the relatively short time since my original research was completed, and which might impact on further studies of professional identity (Wiles, 2010a).

I was initially doubtful about using the term 'professional identity', having observed it being harnessed to regulatory discourse in the language used by England's General Social Care Council (GSCC; Wardle, 2008). Anticipating some ambiguity in the interview data, I was nevertheless puzzled when final-year social work students consistently struggled to define professional identity; and their tentative efforts showed a wide divergence. Consulting the wealth of literature about teaching, nursing and social work, I saw the term 'professional identity' used to convey many different ideas. It is not surprising, then, that students' talk reflects a breadth of cultural meanings available within the social work community and in society more broadly.

Research parameters and methodology

The research, conducted between 2007 and 2010 in England, explored how professional registration affects the way that social work students talk about – and thus construct – their personal and professional identities. Social work regulation was established in 2001, with professional registers operational from 2003. When the research began, registration had only recently been extended to students in England, who were required to demonstrate their professional suitability both in and outside work (General Social Care Council, 2010). Acknowledging the importance of fitness to practise, I nevertheless wanted to discover whether this scrutiny had any impact on students' identities. In brief, the research found that professional registration does influence how students see themselves and how they behave; but this needs to be understood as part of broader identity work involved in learning to be a social worker. Since the transfer of regulation to the Health and Care Professions Council during 2012, students in England are not currently able to join the professional register; however, as universities are still required to investigate concerns about fitness to practise it seems a reasonable assumption that this finding holds good.

The research methodology was derived from a post-structuralist understanding of discourse and identity (Hall, 1996). Discourse analysis probes beneath the surface of policies and institutional practices to examine their complex, and sometimes contradictory, effects. In particular, I was interested in the discourse of professional regulation established by the creation of four UK care councils: one of the measures introduced in response to 'failings' catalogued in New Labour's 1998 white paper, 'Modernising Social Services' (Department of Health, 1998, discussed by Langan, 2000). Discursive meanings, conveyed through social, linguistic and institutional practices, define how people and their circumstances are viewed. Importantly, they have real and significant effects for the people concerned. So, for instance, the word 'professional' has many connotations in everyday language, but within the discourse of social work and regulation it often expresses normative expectations about practitioners' roles, skills and qualities.

Research process: obtaining the data

The students were all studying on a distance-learning Social Work undergraduate degree programme in England. Despite a cohort of some 500 students, recruiting participants proved to be surprisingly difficult. Once ethical approval was gained, I initially confined my invitation to 160 students living in three of the university's regions. Receiving only three replies, I extended the invitation to all students undertaking the second or final level of the degree. Eventually seven people volunteered: one second-year and six final-year students. This disappointingly low response may have been partly due to the sensitivity of the topic (Wiles, 2010b) or the considerable workload demands on the students.

Despite the self-selected nature of this small sample, the volunteers were reasonably mixed in terms of age, gender and ethnicity. Three men and four women, the participants were aged between their late twenties and early fifties; five had grown up in the UK and two had migrated from outside the European Union. While socio-economic data were not sought, three students depicted their family backgrounds as working class or economically disadvantaged. The degree programme is employment-based, and all participants were sponsored by statutory sector employers in adult social care, childcare, housing, education or mental health.

The study used semi-structured interviews lasting between sixty and ninety minutes, held at locations chosen by each participant. Consistent with the methodology, the aim of the interviews was to generate data about the discourses used in students' talk. Students drew on their experiences of social work education; examples from their practice placements which illustrated personal and professional identity; how they described themselves in private life and as developing professionals; the personal consequences of their transition from 'layperson' to 'qualified social worker'; and their experiences of professional registration and their understanding of its implications.

Discourse as a resource: the analysis

The interview data were submitted to a discourse analysis developed in social psychology (Edley, 2001; Potter and Wetherell, 1987). Drawing on both Foucauldian theory and conversation analysis, this method explores how people construct identity through spoken language. Unlike conversation analysis, however, this approach (hereafter referred to simply as 'discourse analysis') requires attention to the external context: cultural and social meanings are treated as 'discursive resources' for constructing identity through talk.

The first stage of discourse analysis involves searching the transcripts for recurring words, phrases, themes and ideas which signify 'patterns' – both commonalities and variations – in the data. Following the theoretical premise that people's talk draws on culturally shared meanings, it is important to search across the whole sample, rather than confining the analysis to each transcript in turn. A theoretical judgement then needs to be made about which patterns constitute appropriate themes or 'interpretative repertoires' to be analysed. Such decisions are based on the context of the interview and the researcher's familiarity with the external environment. Potter and Wetherell (1987) define interpretative repertoires as commonly used ways of talking about familiar phenomena or events, often revealed by speakers' assumptions that the context is obvious and needs no explanation. For example, an interpretative repertoire in the research data was 'social work values', which frequently and spontaneously arose in participants' talk with no attempt to quality or define its meaning.

The second stage of analysis examines how speakers use discursive patterns to construct and convey an identity in the interview context. The focus is therefore on the use of discourses as a resource, rather than on individual narratives, emotions or attitudes. This approach reflects the methodological assumption that individual talk is produced from a complex interweaving of the immediate context (the interview) and wider social debates (Billig, 1987). Further illustration will be evident as the data are discussed in this chapter (also see Wiles, 2010a).

Research findings

Perhaps due to my own caution about using the concept of professional identity, the research did not initially set out to explore its nature. It was both unexpected and fascinating, therefore, to discover that participants conceptualised professional identity in such different ways. The analysis showed students constructing their professional identity in relation to desired traits, or through developing a sense of shared identity with other social workers; alternatively, it was portrayed as a process of individual development. Each of these meanings is now discussed in turn; in practice, participants drew on an overlapping combination of discourses to describe their development as social workers. To further contextualise the research findings, I will interweave additional data from both my own and others' studies.

In this form of discourse analysis, it is usual to present a series of detailed extracts showing how each pattern is repeated and varied across the sample; economy requires, however, that I select mainly single illustrative examples. For ease of reading, some pauses and hesitations in the transcript have been omitted and explanatory text has been inserted between square brackets.

Professional traits

Although all participants struggled to define professional identity, their attempts drew to some extent on the sociological notion of professional traits. One student, for example, began by musing:

> Well it's so diverse, isn't it, that it's very hard to pigeon hole. They try and channel it into [occupational standards] and all the rest of it. It's not something easily put into a box is it?
>
> *(Student A)*

Despite the speaker's apparent uncertainty, the reference to occupational standards – used to assess students' progress while on their practice placements – formed a common pattern across all the transcripts. Similar findings are reported by Scholar et al. (2014), whose three-year study of a much larger sample of social work degree students found that, especially in the earlier stages of training, participants explained social work in relation to traits. Generic professional traits are summarised by Yam (2004: 929) as an 'extensive theoretical knowledge base', 'expertise in a specialized field', an 'altruistic commitment to service', an 'unusual degree of autonomy in work', 'a code of ethics and conduct overseen by a body of representatives from within the field itself' and 'a personal identity that stems from the professional's occupation'. These characteristics are easily recognised in the language adopted by policy and guidance documents, including those which set out the assessment standards for social work. Such documents act as powerful discursive resources which define 'good' and 'professional' practice (Nicoll and Harrison, 2003: 33; Watson, 2006); it is not surprising that students' talk is influenced by this way of describing professionalism.

An interesting example of how official documents both reflect and construct discourses is the UK government-commissioned review of the Diploma in Social Work (J.M. Consulting, 1999). Following close on the heels of 'Modernising Social Services', this report invoked and reinforced the government's rhetoric about the need to restore public trust, and explicitly drew on professional traits in the recommendations which influenced the introduction of a new Social Work Degree. Subsequently, the notion of traits as a mark of professionalism was further embedded into official discourse through the strategies which were introduced in the early 2000s to raise the status of social work in the UK: both professional registration and the enhanced qualification. At the time of the research, the English curriculum incorporated the National Occupational Standards (Topss, 2002: 55–63), which makes frequent reference to being 'professional'. Although the term 'professional' is not defined, certain traits are inferred. For example, social workers are expected to draw on theoretical and other knowledge, and demonstrate expertise in researching and critically analysing social work practice.

In my research, the traits of expert knowledge and autonomy were evident in the way participants talked about their social work learning:

> [I have gained] you know, the grounding in the theory and the knowledge. . . . And also the confidence to be able to talk about those things. I know that I've got that grounding now to give [my] opinions some sort of backing.
>
> *(Student B)*

> At this third level, we're expected to practice professionally with greater autonomy. So . . . I feel like I'm a professional social worker because I'm given a high degree of autonomy.
>
> *(Student C)*

Adherence to professional codes and boundaries was another recurring trait in most students' conceptualisation of professional identity:

> I was able to display my professionalism and form a working relationship with the [father]. But I have my line which I have to draw . . . I don't use my private mobile to text him – I borrow one of the manager's mobile phones. And there's no phone calls outside office hours.
>
> *(Student C)*

Meleyal's study (2014) found that media reporting of fitness to practise investigations left some social workers feeling vulnerable, worried about coming to the attention of the professional regulatory body. A similar finding occurred in my own study: while very few students had actually transgressed the codes of practice, most were able to recount a 'near miss' (such as a service user's complaint) which had caused them to worry about being reported to the regulator. As indicated earlier, however, a more common quandary was where to draw the line between personal and the professional life. In a similar vein, another recent study (Grant et al., 2014) revealed that social work students considered it 'unprofessional' to allow personal life to intersect with the job, or even to talk about the emotional impact of difficult, upsetting work.

Practising social work values – which can be linked with ethical codes of practice – was another recurring pattern in students' talk:

> The values [are] a big part of me considering myself a professional now. The grounding in the beliefs . . . you know, the bigger picture in terms of helping disadvantaged people.
>
> *(Student B)*

Some accounts invoked the idea of an 'altruistic commitment to service' referred to by Yam (2004); for example, Student C expressed difficulty in drawing a distinction between her personal and professional life because studying social work 'changes your whole being: you always want to help people, you know, as much as you can'.

These extracts provide a glimpse into one of the resources – the discourse of professionalism based on traits – which students used to construct their professional identities. A feature of discourse is that it remains powerful by successfully adapting and evolving. In the discursive language of the GSCC, professionalism had been promoted as a way of building public trust through regulating social workers' conduct (Blewett et al., 2008). An interesting development since the study reported on here is that the Professional Capabilities Framework, which replaced England's National Occupational Standards, gives a prominent place to developing professionalism in a broader sense which includes attention to one's own emotional resilience, support and learning. Overall, social workers are now expected to be able to 'identify and behave as a professional social worker' (The College of Social Work, 2012). This more dynamic conceptualisation of professional identity hints at the second usage of the term that emerged from the data.

A collective professional identity

Another way of talking about professional identity draws on a collective sense of being a social worker. In the data generated, this was evident in students' talk about particular practice settings, seen in the following attempt to tease out the meaning of professional identity:

> I know that you can go back to the values being the same [across different settings]. But the actual day to day work can be very different to do with what client group you're with.
>
> *(Student A)*

While the social work literature supports the idea that different kinds of collective identity are based around specialisms (Barnes et al., 2000; Moran et al., 2007; Judd and Sheffield, 2010), there is also a very strong interpretative repertoire which conveys the *loss* of identity caused by organisational restructuring and the impact of multidisciplinary practice. This is evident in the next extract in which the speaker invokes a sense of threatened professionalism and loss of role and identity, before taking up a position which asserts social work's particular value:

> Sometimes I've struggled with 'am I really making a difference, is there any purpose in this, is social work becoming un-professionalised?'. In the community mental health team . . . all the professionals seem to be doing very similar jobs as care coordinators. Does that mean that in five years' time social workers will be a mental health kind of professional rather than specifically a social worker? But I think at the moment social work definitely brings a unique sort of thing to mixed professional teams.
>
> *(Student B)*

Student B's reflections echo the concerns expressed by social workers in Barnes et al.'s study (2000) of Community Mental Health Teams, who feared that their professional identity, which they represented in terms of values and professional culture, was threatened by being located in a multidisciplinary team. While powerful, this cautionary interpretative repertoire is not the only one presented in the literature on multi-agency and multidisciplinary teams. Frost et al. (2005), writing about children and families work, found that diverse team members can work through conflicts and complexities to develop positive ways of working together. Walker (2010) argues that social workers employed in health or education settings sometimes have more opportunities than their local authority colleagues to use psychosocial and therapeutic skills, and to work creatively and holistically.

Leaving aside any evaluation of the advantages and disadvantages of multidisciplinary working, the point here is that these debates act as further discursive resources for social work students and newly qualified workers to construct their own professional identities. White and Featherstone's (2005) study of professional identity in a multidisciplinary team shows how practitioners construct shared narratives which uphold and reinforce occupational boundaries. For example, social workers reinforced their own sense of child protection expertise by frequently referring to the inferior knowledge of other professionals in the team. This study revealed a similar sense of collective narratives being used to emphasise occupational differences. Concerned about a service user's children, a student in a mental health team expressed frustration that her colleagues had not addressed the issue:

> I [met up] with the children and families social worker and said 'what's this all about?' See, I don't know if that would have happened if I hadn't done [it], because it was a very 'health' dominated team and most of the workers are nurses.
>
> *(Student A)*

A feature of the analysis method is to look for disruptions and 'trouble' in participants' talk (Wetherell, 1998), and this suggested tensions between social work identities in different settings. In particular, students expressed their perception that statutory child protection work holds a higher status than social work in older people's or preventive family support teams: similar tensions and findings are reported by other researchers (Moran et al., 2007; Scholar et al., 2014; Walker, 2010). This had an effect on students' sense of professional identity:

> It seems to be, in children's services where I work, that if you haven't worked in . . . the child protection arena . . . you're looked down on as not being a proper social worker.
>
> *(Student D)*

> I don't want to be working with older people . . . real social work [means] children and families to me.
>
> *(Student E)*

A variation of collective identity draws on social work as a unified category (rather than a setting-specific identity). This interpretative repertoire invokes social work's uniqueness, defined in opposition to other professions. Jones (2014: 485–486), for example, writes of social work's struggle to create a distinctive 'professional space' and 'core identity'. Scholar et al. (2014:1010) point out that the Professional Capabilities Framework 'implies that all social workers, no matter what setting they may work in, share a professional identity that transcends organisational structures, specific tasks and roles associated with particular service user groups'.

Another resource for collective identity is professional registration. In my study, participants frequently drew – sometimes implicitly – on regulatory discourses transmitted in publications such as codes of practice, which were also reinforced in teaching materials. Students referred to the positive effects of registration for the profession overall, and by implication for themselves as individuals:

> I think [registration] helps people to feel more professional. And when we feel more professional we act in a more professional way. I think it does build confidence, really, to be able to say 'well I belong to this professional body, therefore I am expected to conduct myself in a certain way'.
>
> *(Student F)*

Similar themes are evident in Meleyal's (2014, online) study, which found that 'the majority of social workers . . . welcomed being a registered profession. They spoke of hopes that registration would improve the status of social work and how it is perceived by the public and media'.

So far, then, I have discussed two broad ways in which research participants conceptualised professional identity, drawing on discourses of professionalism (in terms of desired traits and qualities) and a sense of collective identity. Also present in my data is a third way of understanding professional identity, concerned with how students were coming to 'identify themselves' subjectively as social workers or what is referred to as the process of identity work.

Identity work: becoming a social work professional

The interview transcripts capture a tentative sense of students' individual journeys towards professional identity. In addition to the notions discussed earlier, participants' talk conveyed something more fluid, personal and still in process:

> In your thinking, you're a social worker. Your understanding [and] knowledge you have gained as a social worker rubs [off] in your personal life as well. Even though it's your personal identity, your thinking has changed from your learning.
>
> *(Student C)*

> [Being a social worker is] part of your identity really; I suppose it is part of me.
>
> *(Student A)*

Personal experience is a significant resource for constructing professional identity (Watson, 2006). Understanding how and when to draw on personal history and experience – the use of self – is thus an important aspect of social work education (Harrison and Ruch, 2007; Seden, 2011): this does not mean that it is easy to learn. A recurring pattern in the data is that students present their professional identities as a source of contention in their personal relationships, requiring them to reconcile conflicting cultural discourses about issues such as child rearing, gender roles and political beliefs. The following extract, which arose relatively spontaneously in the interview, gives insight into students' changing relationships with family and friends:

> I get criticised . . . for being too like a social worker. My [friend] often says to me 'oh you're a typical social worker' because I have a view about something which he wouldn't have had. People have an image of me, you know. . . . Sometimes I don't get my friends . . . we can talk about football; we can talk about music. But then other issues, world issues, we just don't talk about because we can't. We're poles apart.
>
> *(Student G)*

Challenges of this kind are frequently reported in higher education research. Some working-class students experience an initial disjuncture in negotiating identity in the university setting (Reay, 2003; Reay et al., 2010). Family therapy trainees describe having to re-evaluate their personal and professional identities (Nel, 2006); and mature women undertaking nurse education have reported negative consequences for their personal relationships (Kevern and Webb, 2004). Newly qualified social workers can also experience the disruptive effects of emotionally demanding and stressful work on their personal lives (Jack and Donnellan, 2010)

Despite the considerable personal changes experienced in the student role, most participants represented their practice learning very positively:

> It's a very complex case but I'm working closely with the senior practitioner. So I feel very supported in this [student] role. And I feel like I have got a right to be doing this.
>
> *(Student F)*

Participants frequently described other practitioners in the practice setting as role models for professional identity:

> I learned a lot from the senior workers on our team, who were really good role models in terms of how you conduct yourself.
>
> *(Student F)*

> I had a really good Practice Assessor . . . and there was just something about the way he pulled his professional identity and his private identity together that made me feel I want to do that.
>
> *(Student E)*

The influence of the practice educator/supervisor is reported in other studies of students and newly qualified social workers (Grant, Sheridan, and Webb, 2016). Evaluating the impact of different variables on the development of students' professional identity, Levy et al. (2014) found the most important to be a satisfactory relationship with the supervisor who was seen as a role model. Similar findings are reported by Scholar et al. (2014), and in Kearns and McArdle's (2011) study of newly qualified social workers. It would appear that the assessment relationship is influential on professional identity, perhaps by offering novice practitioners close insight into how formal and tacit discourses are used by an experienced colleague.

Some writers (Frost et al., 2005; Watson, 2006) refer to the normative dimension of the agency setting as a 'community of practice'; in my research, this concept, developed by Wenger (1998), provided a useful perspective on the role of informal, non-assessed workplace learning (Kearns and McArdle, 2011; Nicoll and Harrison, 2003; Yam, 2004) in developing professional identity.

Wenger's theory builds on social learning theory and highlights the gradual adoption of professional values and norms through a process of socialisation and belonging. Through engaging in a joint enterprise, co-workers develop a shared 'repertoire' (Wenger, 1998: 153) of meanings and practices which both define and reinforce the community. This includes informal everyday interactions, ways of talking, shared narratives and even humour (Richards, 2006; White and Featherstone, 2005). In the practice setting, students and newly qualified social workers must synthesise different narratives and discourses about professional identity, both formal and informal. So, undertaking the role and responsibilities of a social worker – and being positioned by others in this way – is an essential vehicle for novices to construct their identities as they move from the community's periphery towards more central membership. A weakness in Wenger's work is its insufficient attention to unequal power relationships (Hughes et al., 2007). Nevertheless, the advantage of regarding the practice learning setting as a community of practice is that it highlights the continual *process* involved in becoming a professional. Indeed, this idea is reinforced in the requirement that 'to support the development of professional identity, students should not be the sole social work representative in a setting' (The College of Social Work, 2013: 16), and that they must work alongside a qualified and registered social worker in their final placement.

A cautionary note on the research findings

Discourse analysis provides a way of standing back and gaining a new and critical perspective on familiar social practices, and can suggest further questions for investigation. Attending to the nuances of talk makes visible the range of difficulties, often subtle and hard to express, faced by students in constructing professional identity. When interpreting the findings of discourse analysis, however, there are a couple of features which need to be taken into account.

First, interview data are not treated as a direct reflection of what people think. In this methodological approach, language is never seen as 'neutral' or merely descriptive, but constructs both the concepts being discussed and the identities of the speaker and others. It follows, therefore, that in an interview the initial meanings are co-constructed by the participant and researcher; and further meanings are produced during the subsequent interpretation of the data. Second, following the premise that *identities are fluid and multiple*, participants construct a particular version of professional identity in the interview situation. This does not mean that participants seek to present a misleading picture, but rather that the identities which are expressed in the interview context are not the only version. A good illustration of this argument is given in the observation that the people in their study were 'engaged in accomplishing a wide variety of identity positions. They were simultaneously constructing themselves as reasonable human beings, as individuals with certain reputations and histories and (usually) as cooperative and willing research subjects' (1999: 52).

In Chapter 14 of this volume Leigh discusses this in terms of social workers producing 'credible performances'. An interesting contextual detail is that almost all participants volunteered during the final six months of their studies when workload pressure would have been very high. Post-interview feedback indicated that participants had been attracted by the opportunity to discuss the topic of professional identity at this stage of their learning. Similar observations have been made by other researchers, including Moorhead et al. (2016) in their study of newly qualified social workers in Australia:

> professional identity was perceived as an important part of . . . early career experiences and participants greatly appreciated opportunities to critically reflect on it. Their motivations to participate in this study support

international literature from Kearns and McArdle (2011) and Campanini et al. (2012) who found exploring and maintaining a social work professional identity was an important dimension of early career experiences, and that newly qualified social workers appreciated opportunities to do so.

(8–9)

Taylor (2006) argues that social work practitioners construct a particular version of professional identity in the reflective writing that they submit for assessment and supervision. In this sense, participants had previous opportunities to 'rehearse' their professional identities; interviews provided a further reflective space in which these identities could be performed and enacted.

Further considerations: developments in the discourse

Before concluding, I want to briefly highlight some additional discourses which are relevant for social workers' identity development. They were not evident in my research data but are useful to consider for further study.

A current strand in the identity literature expands what is known about the effect of the employment context. One area of interest is the growing concern with training and supporting newly qualified social workers. In that context, having a strong professional identity is promoted as a source of resilience and strength (Kearns and McArdle, 2011; Moorhead et al., 2016). Harrison and Ruch (2007 online), for example, suggest that 'practitioners with integrated and attended-to professional identities are less likely to experience overwhelming stress, ill health or burnout'. They caution, however, that 'having a professional identity' – constructed in response to regulatory processes and prescriptive statements about social work tasks and competences – is far too narrow. More important, in their view, is 'being and sustaining a professional self': developing an internalised professional identity which acts as a source of strength. Recent government-led developments have raised concern that the greater focus on meeting employers' requirements may potentially encourage a narrow sense of professional identity (Rogowski, 2012; Scholar et al., 2014).

As noted earlier, the social work literature contains extensive discussion about the effect of multidisciplinary teams on professional identity. A recent development of this theme is the impact of working in 'non-traditional' settings (that is, agencies such as community projects which do not set out to offer a social work service). Despite advantages such as the opportunity to work holistically or therapeutically, Scholar et al., (2014: 1005) found that in their day-to-day practice, social work students 'faced the challenge of maintaining and developing their professional identity without immediately available social work role models'. In Australia, Harrison and Healy's (2015) study of social work graduates employed in generic non-government agency roles found that they were ambivalent about their professional identity, or in some cases rejected the social work title. Nevertheless, social work values – aligned with the ethos of the non-governmental organisation – remained an important part of these practitioners' identities.

Harrison and Healy's findings serve as a reminder that identities are sometimes formed in opposition to discursive norms (Foucault, 1994). There is a long history of resistance to the perceived elitism and conformity associated with the 'professionalisation' of social work. Despite social work's overall engagement with regulation and social work's protected title, some ambivalence about its professional status remains; indeed, this may signal a healthy criticality (Payne, 2013).

Finally, social work does not look the same in every country. Outside the UK, for example, it embraces community and development roles (Moriarty et al., 2011). Social work needs to be seen in the political and socio-economic context of each country (Weiss-Gal and Welbourne, 2008). With the increasing divergence of social policies, and of regulatory and educational frameworks, these considerations may even become increasingly true within the UK nations (Wiles, 2015). The influence of national meanings on professional identity, therefore, is an area requiring further comparative investigation.

Concluding discussion

In this chapter, I have argued that there is no single meaning of professional identity and suggested that it is more complicated than adopting certain traits or values, or even demonstrating competence. We need to exercise caution in using and teaching the concept of professional identity in a narrow way, without understanding the political, academic and professional discourses which underpin it. The slippery nature of the concept makes it open to appropriation by competing policy, regulatory, managerialist and professional discourses (Cribb and Gewirtz, 2015) which variously seek to control or empower social workers.

Alongside conceptualisations used within the curriculum, novice practitioners will be exposed to a range of additional meanings about professionals: in the workplace, university, their own families and society generally. Three main approaches have been outlined in this chapter. Professional identity can be thought of in relation to desired traits, and it can also be used in a collective sense to convey the 'identity of the profession'. We can also take a more subjective approach and regard professional identity as a process in which each practitioner comes to have a sense of themselves as a social worker. The different meanings of professional identity all have something to offer, providing resources as novices construct themselves as social workers. Practitioners are encouraged to develop a personal sense of *being* a social worker. This can emerge only through opportunities to articulate this identity in the workplace. The dynamic nature of professional identity highlights the difficult identity work which each practitioner must undertake, and prompts us to consider how this process might best be supported.

References

Barnes, D., Carpenter, J., & Dickinson, C. (2000). Inter-professional Education for Community Mental Health: Attitudes to Community Care and Professional Stereotypes. *Social Work Education*, 19(6): 565–583.

Billig, M. (1987). *Arguing and Thinking: A Rhetorical Approach to Social Psychology*. Cambridge: Cambridge University Press.

Blewett, J., Manthorpe, J., Tunstill, J., Harris, J., Hussein, S., Moriarty, J., Stevens, M., & Walton, A. (2008). Exploring the Use of the Codes of Practice for Social Care Workers and Employers across the UK. *Social Care Workforce Research Unit*. King's College London. Retrieved from http://www.kcl.ac.uk/sspp/policy-institute/scwru/res/knowledge/codes.aspx.

Campanini, A., Frost, L., & Höjer, S. (2012). Educating the New Practitioner: The Building of Professional Identities in European Social Work. *Revista de Asistenta Sociala*, 1(1): 33–47.

The College of Social Work. (2012). *Professional Capabilities Framework* [online]. Retrieved from https://www.basw.co.uk/pcf/. (Accessed 2 June 2016).

The College of Social Work. (2013). *Practice Educator Professional Standards for Social Work*. Retrieved from https://www.basw.co.uk/resources/tcsw/PEPS%20standards%20and%20guidance%20final%20Dec%202013.pdf. (Accessed 2 June 2016).

Cribb, A., & Gewirtz, S. (2015). *Professionalism*. Cambridge: Polity.

Department of Health. (1998). *Modernising Social Services: Promoting Independence, Improving Protection, Raising Standards*. London: Stationery Office.

Edley, N. (2001). Analysing Masculinity: Interpretative Repertoires, Ideological Dilemmas and Subject Positions. In M. Wetherell, S. Taylor & S. J. Yates (Eds.), *Discourse as Data: A Guide for Analysis* (pp. 189–228). London: Sage.

Foucault, M. (1994). An Interview With Michel Foucault. In J. D. Faubion (Ed.), *Power* (Vol. 3, pp. 239-297). New York: The New Press.

Frost, N., Robinson, M., & Anning, A. (2005). Social Workers in Multidisciplinary Teams: Issues and Dilemmas for Professional Practice. *Child and Family Social Work*, 10(3): 187–196.

General Social Care Council. (2010). *Codes of Practice for Social Care Workers*. London: GSCC.

Grant, L., Kinman, G., & Alexander, K. (2014). What's All this Talk about Emotion? Developing Emotional Intelligence in Social Work Students. *Social Work Education*, 33(7): 874–889.

Grant, S., Sheridan, L., & Webb, S. A. (2016). Newly Qualified Social Workers Readiness for Practice in Scotland. *British Journal of Social Work*. doi: 10.1093/bjsw/bcv146 First published online: March 12, 2016.

Hall, S. (1996). Who Needs Identity? In S. Hall & P. du Gay (Eds.), *Questions of Cultural Identity* (pp. 15–30). London: Sage.

Harrison, G., & Healy, K. (2015). Forging an Identity as a Newly Qualified Worker in the Non-Government Community Services Sector. *Australian Social Work*, 69(1): 1–12. doi: 10.1080/0312407X.2015. 1026913.

Harrison, K., & Ruch, G. (2007). Social Work and the Use of the Self: On Becoming and Being a Social Worker. In M. Lymbery & K. Postle (Eds.), *Social Work: A Companion to Learning* [Online], Sage. Retrieved from http://sk.sagepub.com.libezproxy.open.ac.uk/books/social-work-mark-lymbery. (Accessed 15 April 2016).

Hughes, J., Jewson, N., & Unwin, L. (2007). *Communities of Practice: Critical Perspectives*. London: Routledge.

Jack, G., & Donnellan, H. (2010). Recognising the Person within the Developing Professional: Tracking the Early Careers of Newly Qualified Child Care Social Workers in Three Local Authorities in England. *Social Work Education*, 29(3), 305–318.

JM Consulting Ltd. (1999). *Review of the Diploma in Social Work*. Bristol: JM Consulting.

Jones, R. (2014). The Best of Times, the Worst of Times: Social Work and Its Moment. *British Journal of Social Work*, 44(3): 485–502.

Judd, R. G., & Sheffield, S. (2010). Hospital Social Work: Contemporary Roles and Professional Activities. *Social Work in Health Care*, 49(9): 856–871.

Kearns, S., & McArdle, K. (2011). 'Doing It Right?' Accessing the Narratives of Identity of Newly Qualified Social Workers through the Lens of Resilience: 'I am, I Have, I Can'. *Child and Family Social Work*, 17(4): 385–394.

Kevern, J., & Webb, C. (2004). Mature Women's Experiences of Preregistration Nurse Education. *Journal of Advanced Nursing*, 45(3): 297–306.

Langan, M. (2000). Social Services: Managing the Third Way. In J. Clarke, S. Gewirtz & E. McLaughlin (Eds.), *New Managerialism, New Welfare?* (pp. 152–168). London: Sage.

Levy, D., Shlomo, S. B., & Itzhaky, H. (2014). The Building Blocks of Professional Identity among Social Work Graduates. *Social Work Education*, 33(6): 744–759.

Meleyal, L. (2014), Social Work Regulation: Help or Hindrance? *The Guardian*, 21 July 2014. Retrieved from http://www.theguardian.com/social-care-network/2014/jul/21/social-work-regulation-registration. (Accessed 2 June 2016).

Moorhead, B., Bell, K., & Bowles. W. (2016). Exploring the Development of Professional Identity with Newly Qualified Social Workers. *Australian Social Work*, 69(4): 456–467. Published online: 21 March 2016. doi: 10.1080/0312407X.2016.1152588.

Moran, P. Jacobs, C., Bunn, A., & Bifulco, A. (2007). Multi-Agency Working: Implications for an Early Intervention Social Work Team. *Child and Family Social Work*, 12(2): 143–151.

Moriarty, J., Manthorpe, J., Stevens, M., & Hussein, S. (2011). Making the Transition: Comparing Research on Newly Qualified Social Workers with other Professions. *British Journal of Social Work*, 41(7): 1340–1356.

Nel, P. (2006). Trainee Perspectives on their Family Therapy Training. *Journal of Family Therapy*, 28(3): 307–328.

Nicoll, K., & Harrison, R. (2003). Constructing the Good Teacher in Higher Education: The Discursive Work of Standards. *Studies in Continuing Education*, 25(1): 23–35.

Payne, M. (2013). Being a Social Work Professional. In J. Parker & M. Doel (Eds.), *Professional Social Work* (pp. 19–38). London: Learning Matters.

Potter, J., & Wetherell, M. (1987). *Discourse and Social Psychology: Beyond Attitudes and Behaviour*. London: Sage.

Reay, D. (2003). A Risky Business? Mature Working-class Women Students and Access to Higher Education. *Gender and Education*, 15(3): 301–317.

Reay, D., Crozier, G., & Clayton, J. (2010). 'Fitting in' or 'Standing Out': Working-Class Students in UK Higher Education. *British Educational Research Journal*, 36(1): 107–124.

Richards, K. (2006). *Language and Professional Identity: Aspects of Collaborative Interaction*. Basingstoke: Palgrave Macmillan.

Rogowski, S. (2012). Social Work with Children and Families: Challenges and Possibilities in the Neo-Liberal World. *British Journal of Social Work*, 42(5): 921–940.

Scholar, H., McLaughlin, H., McCaughan, S., & Coleman, A. (2014). Learning to Be a Social Worker in a Non-Traditional Placement. *Social Work Education*, 33(8): 998–1016.

Seden, J. (2011). The Use of Self and Relationship: Swimming against the Tide? In J. Seden, S. Matthews, M. McCormick & A. Morgan (Eds.), *Professional Development in Social Work: Complex Issues in Practice* (pp. 55–62). Abingdon: Routledge.

Taylor, C. (2006). Narrating Significant Experience: Reflective Accounts and the Production of (Self) Knowledge. *British Journal of Social Work*, 36(2): 189–209.

Training Organisation for the Personal Social Services UK Partnership (TOPSS). (2002). *National Occupational Standards for Social Work*. Leeds: TOPSS.

Walker, S. (2010). Back to the Future of Social Work: Child and Adolescent Mental Health and the Post Qualifying Curriculum in England and Wales. *Social Work Education*, 29(6): 616–632.

Wardle, M. (2008). Three-Year Anniversary of Protection of Title for Social Workers. *Community Care*, 1 April 2008. Retrieved from http://www.communitycare.co.uk/2008/

04/01/three-year-anniversary-of-protection-of-title-for-social-workers/. (Accessed 1 June 2016).

Watson, C. (2006). Narratives of Practice and the Construction of Identity in Teaching. *Teachers and Teaching: Theory and Practice*, 12(5): 509–526.

Weiss-Gal, I., & Welbourne, P. (2008). The Professionalisation of Social Work: A Cross-National Exploration. *International Journal of Social Welfare*, 17(4): 281–290.

Wenger, E. (1998). *Communities of Practice: Learning, Meaning and Identity*. Cambridge: Cambridge University Press.

Wetherell, M. (1998). Positioning and Interpretative Repertoires: Conversation Analysis and Post-Structuralism in Dialogue. *Discourse & Society*, 9(3): 387–412.

Wetherell, M., & Edley, N. (1999). Negotiating Hegemonic Masculinity: Imaginary Positions and Psycho-Discursive Practices. *Feminism & Psychology*, 9(3): 35–356.

White, S., & Featherstone, B. (2005). Communicating Misunderstandings: Multi-Agency Work as Social Practice. *Child and Family Social Work*, 10(3): 207–216.

Wiles, F. (2010a). *Professional Registration and the Discursive Construction of Social Work Students' Identities*. (unpublished EdD thesis). Retrieved from http://oro.open.ac.uk/view/person/fw6.html.

Wiles, F. (2010b). Blurring Private-Professional Boundaries: Does It Matter? Issues in Researching Social Work Students' Perceptions about Professional Regulation. *Journal of Ethics and Social Welfare*, 5(1): 36–51.

Wiles, F. (2015). Four Nations: How Has Devolution Affected Social Work Education and Discourses of Professional Identity across the UK. *Joint Social Work Education Conference*, The Open University, July 2015. Retrieved from http://jswec.net/2015/sessions/four-nations-how-has-devolution-affected-social-work-education-and-discourses-of-professional-identity-across-the-uk/.

Yam, B. (2004). From Vocation to Profession: The Quest for Professionalization of Nursing. *British Journal of Nursing*, 13(6): 978–982.

4

MATERIALITY, PERFORMANCE AND THE MAKING OF PROFESSIONAL IDENTITY[1]

Torben Elgaard Jensen

Drawing on Actor-Network Theory, this chapter introduces the notions of translation and performativity to provide a novel perspective on professional identity and social work.[2] The first part of the chapter presents observational data of an interactional event between a social worker and a client. The second part elucidates the techno-social heterogeneity of the event through an analysis based on the Actor-Network Theory of translation. The third part discusses the precarious and temporary natures of the techno-social hybrids in social work through the concept of performance. Finally, the chapter discusses how an actor-network-inspired analysis of socio-technical performance may contribute to discussions about professional identity in social work.

Introduction

In Stephen Webb's first chapter in this book, he outlines some of the well-established ways of conceptualizing professional identity. From this account it is possible to summarize identity as describing 'how a social worker thinks of herself or himself as a social worker', as 'a key cognitive and affective resource' and as 'practitioners' professional self-concept based on attributes, beliefs, values, motives, and experiences'. These descriptions of what professional identity is clearly invite a broad range of investigations of identity. Amongst other things one is inspired to think about how social workers' self-conceptions come into being and change over time, and how different connotations and nuances of meaning become attached to statements such as 'I am a social worker' or 'being a social worker, my task is . . .'. Yet, despite the broadness of the identity-as-self-conception agenda, there is also something which is conspicuously absent – at least from the perspective of the present chapter, and from the perspective of Actor-Network Theory by which it is informed.

To get a sense of what might be added to identity as self-conception, let us imagine two clients sitting on a bench outside the building where they occasionally go to meet with their social workers, and let us also imagine that the two clients are talking about what their social workers *are like*. We may note here that although the term 'are like' sounds a bit commonsensical, it quite precisely brings up a question of identity: to say that X *is like* Y is to say something about the identity of X. So what approach to the identity question might we imagine in the conversation between two clients? My guess is that clients would rarely discuss how the social workers 'think' or 'conceive' of themselves. What is far more likely is that clients would discuss what their social workers do, or perhaps what they don't do. Does she accept my arguments? Is he signing me up for the course I want? Is she making recommendations which allow me to have benefits? With the clients' interest in 'doing', I would also imagine that they would include a concern with other material and organizational aspects of the social work institution, such as waiting times, changes in rules and protocols, and the trajectories of their cases. The clients would therefore not uphold a clear distinction between the inner beliefs of the social worker and the technical and material circumstances of her or his workplace. In short, my guess is that the clients would look at the social worker as a *package deal* and that they would look at *what they actually get out of it*.

The perspective on identity of my two imaginary clients is close to the performative view of identity that I will introduce in this chapter. In a performative view, the identity of the social worker is nothing more and nothing less than what she does and is able to do when meeting the client.[3] Although this may sound simple, the description of 'doing' is anything but simple. To say that we should describe 'doing' doesn't answer any of the most immediate questions that will face any social scientist who embarks on a description. What aspect of doing should we focus attention on? What is an adequate description of doing? In grappling with these questions, Actor-Network Theory is – not exactly a solution – but a resource. Actor-Network Theory can be described as a set of empirical sensitivities and inspiring case studies that provide resources for making good descriptions of practices as they unfold and of the entanglement of social and material entities that generate these practices (Latour, 2007; Law, 2001). In this chapter, I will begin by introducing a small empirical case, which I will then analyze by means of two concepts from Actor-Network Theory that may assist us in thinking about the identity of social workers. The first concept, *translation*, will help us develop a richer description of doing by deliberately blurring the line between the social and the technological. The second concept, *performance*, will help us describe how several different patterns of practices simultaneously unfold when social work is taking place. In the final part of the chapter, I will attempt to summarize how Actor-Network Theory may contribute to studies of identity in social work.

An observation of social work

As a part of my PhD research, I spent quite a lot of time observing and interviewing social workers in a social centre in Copenhagen (Elgaard Jensen, 2001b). On one particular day, I was making observations of the work at the counter. The counter is in the reception area where clients are serviced when they come in directly from the street. Participant observation is the term that social scientists might casually use for this type of endeavour – but participation would have been a nightmare for me. I have very little knowledge of the daily business of social work, so I would have made a fool of myself in seconds if I had to take part in the work at the counter. To protect me from participation the caseworkers had created a cover: they assigned me a desk and gave me a pile of case files to hide behind. If a long queue of clients was building up, and the clients started wondering why *I* didn't do any work, then I could easily duck behind my pile of cases and pretend that I was busy. So there I was, sitting at the desk behind my cover, overhearing conversations and frantically writing field notes.

After a little while, the following event occurred (extracted from field notes):

Client: I have applied for a sewer worker education. *[He is clearly angry and almost yelling.]*

Caseworker: What is your social security number?

Client: You don't have to find my case. I'm running around to all the different offices. Why don't you send me a letter about what is happening?

Caseworker: You want to get an answer!

Client: Yes.

Caseworker: I'll just find your case and see if something has happened.

[The client agrees and states his social security number.

The caseworker walks to a file cabinet, finds his case and reads for a little while. She returns and informs him that nothing has happened.

The caseworker offers the client an appointment with the caseworker in charge of the case.

The client agrees.

She finds the meeting schedule, and they set a date and a time. The client leaves. He appears to be less angry than earlier.]

I believe most people would agree that this is a rather trivial event. It is highly unlikely that the client would go home and write a complaint. The caseworkers wouldn't reflect much on the encounter, and it wouldn't be a topic in their lunch break conversations. Even the most imaginative tabloid journalist couldn't make a story out of it. This is simply the kind of mundane event that everyday life in the social centre is full off.

So what should we make of it? What might this event tell us about the performance of identity and the roles played by materiality and technology?

To begin, I would like to make three straightforward observations about the event:

1   *It works.* The event is somehow functional. Whatever technological or social there is in this event, it plays together in a rather seamless way.

2   *Transformation.* Something happens to the identity of the client. He isn't quite the same in the end as he is in the beginning.

3   *Redirection.* The client – a big, angry man – articulates his complaint loudly, but this is somehow deflected by the social worker, who is very small and very calm in comparison.

Translation

The first analytical tool that I will apply to this event is the concept of *translation*. I will use it in the specific sense in Actor-Network Theory (e.g. Callon, 1986; Latour, 1987; Law, 1986). Following the lines of French semiotics, Actor-Network Theory takes all actors[4] or entities to be relational. Entities take their form and acquire their attributes as a result of their relations with other entities (Law, 1999). 'Translation' is a broad term covering the processes by which two entities become related in such a way that one entity replaces or speaks in the name of the other. By definition, a translation changes the attributes of the two entities because it changes (some of) the relations that constitute them. Furthermore, a translation redistributes power in the actor network: one entity is made less powerful in its role as an ally, while another entity is rendered more powerful.

The perhaps strangely neutral language of entities and translations suggests an important difference between Actor-Network Theory and the vast majority of social science. Actor-Network Theory is a move away from the types of analyses that take the world to be populated with things that have certain essences in and of themselves, such as technical objects, natural objects, social objects or psychological objects. On the contrary, Actor-Network Theory claims that these apparently essential differences are results of continual and ongoing negotiation processes in the world.

So in order to study practice, and the performance of identities in practice, we do not need these ontologies that separate 'the social' from 'the technical' from 'the material' and so on. We simply need to follow the flow of how entities become associated or disassociated, and how some entities substitute for others and come to speak in their name literally or metaphorically.

If we apply this mode of analysis to the empirical case, we can describe a chain of translations. As a starting point we can pick the arrival of the client with a complaint, and as the end point we can pick the exit of the client with an appointment. Between these two points, we can pinpoint a series of translations:

1   The complaint ('Why don't you send me a letter?') is translated into a wish ('You want to get an answer!')
2   The wish is translated into the verbal stating of the social security number.
3   The stating of the social security number is translated into the retrieval of the case file.
4   The case file is read and compared to the wish. This comparison translates into the fact that nothing has happened.
5   The fact that nothing has happened is translated to a wish for meeting.
6   The wish is related to the meeting schedule and is then translated to an appointment.

In this series of translations, a whole number of different entities are at play. A client and a caseworker, wishes and complaints, social security numbers and meetings, case files and schedules. If the goal was simply to unfreeze the rigid boundaries between the technical and the social, then it is quite obvious that the notion of translation is already doing the work that it was supposed to.

Now, the fact that one thing changes into another that changes into yet another is of course only moderately interesting. What is more interesting is the *pattern* of translations. What aspects of the world are produced and reproduced through this event?

To analyze these matters, actor-network theorist Michel Callon has invented a number of terms to describe how certain entities manage to persuade others to undergo translations (Callon, 1986).

One term is *interessement* (Callon, 1986: 205–211). This is when one entity attempts to redefine the interests of others. When you are complaining that we haven't sent you a letter, you define yourself as an accuser of the system. But we – the system, the social worker and the way we normally go about things – suggest that you want an answer.

If interessement is accepted, the actual translation can begin to take place. One entity is now substituted by another. The complaint is replaced by the wish for an answer.

Finally, by actively participating, the 'entity' (as client or caseworker) lets itself *enrol* and *mobilize* as a part of network (Callon, 1986: 211–219). When the client replaces a complaint with a wish, he is playing his part in a network that ascribes him a particular role. A key element of this is to state his social security number; an action he refused just a little while ago. A mandatory, standardized action such as stating the social security number is called an *obligatory passage point* in Actor-Network Theory (Callon, 1986: 205–206). Entities that are enrolled in the network are persuaded to move through these points and thus contribute to the solidification and routinization of the network. It almost goes without saying that the entities that successfully define and control obligatory passage points become indispensable and grow in strength. To take one very obvious example: most of us are contributing to the strength of Bill Gates because we are persuaded that purchasing Microsoft products is an obligatory passage point. Of course, 'persuaded' should be taken in the broadest possible sense of the word. Entities become translated by other entities through anything from brute force and 'rational argumentation' to trickery and seduction.

So the more detailed description of the broader process of translation is this: interessement, enrolment, mobilization. One possible consequence is the establishment of a certain geography of obligatory passage points.

I will use these concepts on one more part of the event in the social centre. At a certain moment it is realized that nothing has happened in the case, so the wish for an answer is blocked. Will the client get the sewer education he applied for? No answer can be given. At this point, the caseworker makes another attempt to redefine the interest of the client. She suggests that he wants a *meeting* with the caseworker in charge of the case. The client seems to accept this interessement move. Then the caseworker finds the meeting schedule and makes a move to enrol the client into a particular slot in the calendar. The wish for a meeting is thus connected with the obligatory passage point of accepting an appointment with another caseworker at another time. The client accepts this move. So now he lets himself enrol in a network where he is an element in the scheduling of work in the social centre. When (or if) he arrives on the agreed time, we may say that he has become mobilized into the network.

I have sketched two translations: from a complaint to the wish for an answer, and from the wish for an answer to the wish for a meeting. These two translations can be depicted as a disciplinary process. Giving the analysis a Foucauldian twist, we could say that critique of 'the system' is turned into an individual problem. Resistance to stating the social security number is turned into compliance. Impatience with the system is turned into waiting for an appointment. Finally, a certain distribution of mobility is re-enacted; initially, the client protested to running between the offices and demanded that they sent him a letter instead. But at the end he accepted that he must physically move to see the social workers, while the social workers will stay at the centre.

All this is achieved not by the social worker herself but through the intricate choreography of relations between her, the client, the social security number, the case files, the meeting schedule and numerous other elements. In this process, relations change through translations, but the actors of the actor-network change are changed or re-formed as well. The part of the network which we might call 'the bureaucracy' is solidified by once more being successful. The part of the network which we might call 'the client' is now partially redefined by its new connections to obligatory passage points such as a social security number and an appointment-making device.

Performance

If entities are what they are because of their relations, then it also follows that entities are performed or enacted into being, and that they are somehow temporary and precarious. Whatever the efficiency of the judo trick–like translations, the outcome is *not* a client with a coherent, stable essence to be held inside forever after.

A number of authors within the Actor-Network Theory tradition,[5] notably John Law (1994, 2006) and Annemarie Mol (1999, 2002), have tried to develop concepts and empirical analyses that are sensitive to different, precarious and complexly related performances.

In one study, John Law investigated the work of a large British research organization, and he developed the concept of *modes of ordering* to describe its complex practices (Law, 1994). John Law is partially inspired by Foucault. In this vein, he describes how certain 'regimes' of doing things make it hard to do otherwise. The organization is thus full of entrenched practices and strategies. However, Law departs from Foucault by arguing that several different and partially conflicting 'regimes' or 'epistemes' are in operation at any given time. None of these modes of ordering, as Law calls them, will ever grow into an all-encompassing episteme, nor will they be able to instate their version of 'good order' on all practices in the organization. A mode of ordering is a certain pattern of network that entails a certain form of subjectivity, a certain way of going about things and a moral tale about why this is the right way to do it.

Administration is one such mode. This is the bureaucratic mode of ordering. It strives for routinization, formalization and consistency. It is about defining roles, procedures, rules and hierarchies. The ideal agent is systematic, planning and meticulous. The ideal morality is to process cases without regard to personal or emotional considerations.

A second and very different mode of ordering is called *Enterprise*. This is about opportunism, pragmatism and achievement. The ideal agent is an entrepreneur who is sensitive to the shifting opportunities and demands – and this might well include bending or breaking the rules set up by bureaucrats. Enterprise is about seizing the day and making the most of it.

These two modes of ordering might also be imputed to the event in the social centre. Towards the end of the event, the client is properly processed as an element in the meeting schedule. This seems to be the Administration mode of ordering.

In the beginning of the event something resembling Enterprise is performed. The client comes across as a free agent, accusing the system and suggesting a quick and unorthodox fix for the problem: 'Why don't you send me a letter about what is happening?'

It can be quite fascinating to try to pinpoint the modes of ordering or logics that are played out in an organization. Quite evidently, modes of ordering imply technologies of various sorts. How could Administration sustain itself without file cabinets, social security numbers and meeting schedules?

It would, however, be a mistake to see the modes of ordering as disconnected universes, or to picture the client as irrevocably split into an Enterprise-client and an Administration-client. Over and over again Law and Mol make the point that there are intricate links and partial connections between performances. It is therefore a good empirical strategy to look for connections, disruptions and interferences between different modes of ordering. In this specific case, we might delve into the connections between the Enterprise-client and the Administration-client. At a quick glance, it may seem that an iron curtain is pulled down at the moment the bureaucratic wheels start to spin and that the client is completely transmogrified from a critic to a docile follower. How can there be any connection between such antagonistic projects as Enterprise and Administration? This question is broader than I can handle in the present chapter, but we can make some modest beginnings by looking again at the unfolding events in the social centre.

First, we might notice the sequence of events.[6] In the *beginning* the client complains; *later* he is processed. It might be that Administration is somehow dependent on Enterprise to have taken place. Thus, we might speculate that ventilating anger is necessary before calm procedures can be carried out. So Administration may work best when it waits a little while before it eventually takes over.

Second, if we look at the efforts of the caseworker, they all seem to be very much by the administrative book. There is only one proper way to find a case, only one conclusion about it and only one proper way to book an appointment. But there are also cracks in the surface. One of them is the time of the appointment. In cases of routine check-ups, clients often have to wait for several months. In this case, the client gets an appointment within weeks. So through the discretion of the social worker Enterprise enters Administration. The social worker and a meeting schedule in the middle of a bureaucratic procedure now perform the impatience that was earlier performed by a client with an angry voice.

As a third attempt to find connections between Enterprise and Administration we might search the Internet and find the ethical rules of social workers. One of them might read: *Clients are acting individuals – not objects for treatment and help.* So here we have a rule – the hallmark of bureaucratic functioning – and this rule prescribes that clients are acting individuals, something much more in line with Enterprise. This is yet another example of how the different modes of ordering are related in complex ways. The main point is that the ordering operations of the Enterprise are comprised of the simultaneously enactment of rule-following coupled to the agency of the individual client or caseworker.

The conclusion is quite simply that there are no iron curtains between modes of ordering. Modes of ordering do more work than clients to achieve purity.

Professional identity as a matter of socio-technical performance

In this chapter, I took my starting point in some of the more well-established conceptions of identity as self-conception and as a cognitive and affective resource. As several authors have pointed out, questions of identity come to the fore in situations where identity becomes uncertain and contested, when our lives and practices change rapidly, when institutions and people around us are on the move and when others make numerous and sometimes conflicting claims and demands on us (Calhoun, 1994; Hall and du Gay, 1996). These situations of change, movement and conflicting demands are widespread in contemporary societies, and social workers are undoubtedly a professional group which is heavily subjected to these identity pressures. To assist us in understanding and navigating this situation we need good tools in the form of concepts and ways of thinking about identity.

The well-known conceptions of identity serve important purposes and articulate important discussions. However, as I have suggested throughout this chapter, we may turn to Actor-Network Theory for a novel and broader view of what we might discuss under the topic of professional identity.

One impetus for rethinking our approach to identity is the fact that information systems and technologies of social work are changing rapidly. If the tools of the trade are important for constituting it, then we may do well by attending theoretically and empirically to the material and technological dimensions of social work. The concepts and cases made possible by Actor-Network Theory are resources for describing agency as an effect of associations and translations between social and technical matters. The incessant technical changes are therefore articulated well through Actor-Network Theory, but increasingly also by a number of other socio-technical strands of social science.[7]

Another crucial feature of Actor-Network Theory is the insistence on perfor-mance. As I have attempted to show, this insistence breeds an empirical attention to the minutiae of interaction and subtle complexities of managing daily work. Iden-tities, in this perspective, become the somewhat fragile and temporary formations that are pieced together in the course of organizing the ongoing flow of interac-tions between materialities, people and technologies. This way of understanding identity is in part an empirical approach, but it also implies distance to any notion of identity as some kind of 'stable core' that social workers should or could hold within themselves. The attention to performance does not rule out that stabilities can be achieved in practice, but insists on treating this question as an empirical matter.

On a final note, I would like to emphasize another positive side effect of study-ing professional identity by means of Actor-Network Theory. Our ability to think about a topic is to a large extent limited by our 'conceptual technologies' and our habits of allowing particular objects into our analyses, while relegating others to the realm of the irrelevant. The rather abstract and minimalist conceptual apparatus of Actor-Network Theory implies an ambition to be relatively open and curious with respect to the size, shape and composition of the analytical objects. By following the actors, *their* association of the matters at hand and the evolving flow of events, new analytical objects may come into view. In the present chapter, I have described at least two somewhat strange objects:

- a client entity flowing through a series of translations and performing in a number of media, and
- a neutral administrative mode of ordering with client anger folded into it.

My sense is that strange objects of this sort may stimulate our sociological imagina-tion and assist us in finding new ways to understand and engage with professional identity in social work.

Notes

1 Parts of the material in this chapter was published in a special issue on Technology in Social Practice (Nissen, 2001) in the journal *OUTLINES:Critical Social Studies*. I thank editor Pernille Hviid for allowing me to use the original material (Elgaard Jensen, 2001a) in the present context.
2 See Bruno Latour's (2007) *Reassembling the Social: An Introduction to Actor-Network-Theory* for a thought-provoking introduction to Actor-Network Theory and its differences from mainstream sociology.
3 There are striking parallels between the performative view of identity described here and what Summerson Carr (2010) calls the 'enactment of expertise' in social work. She main-tains that professional expertise is not something one has but something one does. 'Exper-tise is performative expertise in that it is enacted in the real-time course of communicative

practice, which is never insulated nor isolated from institution and ideology' (22). Against the prevailing discursive preoccupation with identity, she goes on to say it is

> all too easy to presume that expertise is a matter of people interpreting, establishing the value of, and thereby managing, if not totally mastering, the objects of their expert interest. However, as anthropologists have elegantly shown, the culturally ascribed qualities of the things that engage experts profoundly shape the manifestation of expertise.
>
> *(26)*

4 ANT employs a semiotic definition of an 'actor'. An actor is anything that acts or receives activity from others. Actors are generally defined as anyone or anything that makes a difference in the course of some other agent's action. The scope of actors is thus extended far beyond individual humans (Latour, 1996).
5 This move towards performance, enactment and multiplicity is often referred to as 'After ANT' (see Law, 1999).
6 This attention to the sequence of practices is inspired by Mol (2002).
7 For a review of socio-material approaches, see Fenwick et al. (2015). For a review of practice theory, see Schatzki (1996) and Miettinen et al. (2009).

References

Calhoun, C. (1994). Social Theory and the Politics of Identity. In C. Calhoun (Ed.), *Social Theory and the Politics of Identity* (pp.9–36). Oxford: Blackwell.

Callon, M. (1986). Some Elements of a Sociology of Translation: Domestication of the Scallops and the Fishermen of Saint Brieuc Bay. In J. Law (Ed.), *Power, Action and Belief: A New Sociology of Knowledge?* Sociological Review Monograph (32, pp. 196–233). London: Routledge and Kegan Paul.

Elgaard Jensen, T. (2001a). The High Impact of Low Tech in Social Work, *OUTLINES Critical Social Studies*, 3(1): 81–87.

Elgaard Jensen, T. (2001b). *Performing Social Work: Competence, Orderings, Spaces, and Objects.* (PhD dissertation). University of Copenhagen.

Fenwick, T., Edwards, R., & Sawchuk, P. (2015). *Emerging Approaches to Educational Research: Tracing the Socio-Material.* London: Routledge.

Hall, Stuart, & Paul du Gay (eds.) (1996). *Questions of Cultural Identity.* London: Sage.

Latour, B. (1987). *Science in Action: How to Follow Scientists and Engineers through Society.* Cambridge, MA: Harvard University Press.

Latour, B. (1996). On Actor-Network Theory: A Few Clarifications. *Soziale Welt,* 47(4): 369–381.

Latour, B. (2007). *Reassembling the Social: An Introduction to Actor-Network-Theory.* Oxford: Oxford University Press.

Law, J. (1986). On the Methods of Long Distance Control: Vessels, Navigation and the Portuguese Route to India. In J. Law (Ed.), *Power, Action and Belief: A New Sociology of Knowledge? Sociological Review Monograph* (pp. 234–263). London: Routledge and Kegan Paul.

Law, J. (1994). *Organizing Modernity.* Oxford: Blackwell.

Law, J. (1997). *Traduction/Trahison: Notes on ANT.* Retrieved from www.comp.lancs.ac.uk/sociology/stslaw2.html. Department of Sociology, Lancaster University.

Law, J. (1999). After ANT: Topology, Naming and Complexity. In J. Law & J. Hassard (Eds.), *Actor Network Theory and after* (pp. 1–14). Oxford and Keele: Blackwell and the Sociological Review.

Law, J. (2001). *Aircraft Stories: Decentering the Object in Technoscience*. Durham, NC: Duke University Press.

Law, J. (2006), 'Disaster in Agriculture, or Foot and Mouth Mobilities', *Environment and Planning A*, 38, 227-239.

Miettinen, R., Samra-Fredericks, D., & Yanow, D. (2009). Re-Turn to Practice: An Introductory Essay. *Organization Studies*, 30(12): 1309–1327.

Mol, A. (1999). Ontological Politics: A Word and Some Questions. In J. Law & J. Hassard (Eds.), *Actor Network and after* (pp. 74–89). Oxford and Keele: Blackwell and the Sociological Review.

Mol, A. (2002). *The Body Multiple: Artherosclerosis in Practice*. Durham, NC and London: Duke University Press.

Nissen, M. (2001). Beyond Innocence and Cynicism: Concrete Utopia in Social Work with Drug Users. Outlines: *Critical Practice Studies*, 14(2) 54–78

Schatzki, T. R. (1996). *Social Practices: A Wittgensteinian Approach to Human Activity and the Social*. Cambridge: Cambridge University Press.

Summerson Carr, E. (2010). Enactments of Expertise. *Annual Review of Anthropology*, 39: 17–32.

5

CONSTRUCTING THE SOCIAL, CONSTRUCTING SOCIAL WORK

Elizabeth Harlow

Introduction

Over the last decade social work and social work education in England have been subject to intensive government review resulting in a number of reports (for example, Croisdale-Appleby, 2014; House of Commons Education Committee, 2016; Munro, 2011; Narey, 2014; and Social Work Task Force, 2009). Any 'body of practice' might benefit from improvements, but it may be argued that over recent times the profession of social work has been scrutinized excessively, beyond the purposes of improvement alone. Furthermore, there is a view that the media have presented social work in a negative light, with instances of individual professionals, and the profession in general, having been scapegoated by being held responsible for the failings of others (for example, see Jones, 2014). This context, together with the complex role and difficult working environments, has contributed to problems in retaining experienced practitioners (House of Commons Education Committee, 2016; see also Harlow, 2004). Additionally, economic austerity and spending cuts have led to the closure of the profession's regulatory body, the General Social Care Council, as well as the College of Social Work. Against this landscape, the question of social work's professionalism, identity and future is uncertain.

This chapter does not focus on these specific issues, but takes them into account when giving consideration to the construction of social work in general and the welfare regime of which it is a part. In giving consideration to these constructions, the meaning of the 'social' component of 'social work' is deemed to be important to the identity of the profession, along with the socio-economic context from which it emerged and to which it currently belongs. This calls into question the essentialism of a fixed professional identity. A chronological approach to the construction of social work is taken and then a case study is offered. A concluding discussion follows on from the case study.

Constructing the 'social' over time

According to the *Concise Oxford English Dictionary,* 'social' has a variety of meanings, two of which are as follows: first, 'of or relating to society and its organization', and second, 'concerned with the mutual relations of human beings or of classes of human beings'. These general definitions are important to the overall content of this chapter and the construction of social work, but there is also a meaning of 'the social' that has arisen from a distinct body of scholarship: from a particular socioeconomic perspective, the social might be understood as a sector in which diverse problems and special cases are grouped together, and then assisted by a qualified body of personnel (Deleuze, 1980). Born out of a specific power/knowledge complex, the social or social sector is therefore a hybrid domain consisting of connecting lines between entities such as wealth and poverty as well as families and professionals.

Drawing on the writings of Foucault (either directly or indirectly), Donzelot (1980; 2008), Doran (2004) and Rose (1996) articulate the rise of the social and its power/knowledge underpinnings. Foundational to their arguments (which concerns Europe, but particularly France) is the principle that sovereign power was associated with the control of territory. With the rise of liberalism and the transition towards government, attention was refocused on the population as a commodity or resource. This meant that there was benefit in growing a large population, but also a population that constituted a labour force. This large labour force would produce goods that could be bought and sold on the market. Rather than control the population, the government assumed the responsibility of managing it. This role of managing the population was encouraged by the sociological ideas of Durkheim, who introduced the concept of solidarity. Within this theoretical configuration, the importance of 'society' overshadowed the individual, and interventions to protect the whole population from the uncertainties and excesses of the market were considered appropriate (see Doran, 2004). During the twentieth century, ideas concerning the importance of the social domain persisted and influenced governments to pursue policies to do with solidarity, social protection, social justice and social rights (Rose, 1996).

In practice this meant that when in poverty or experiencing a crisis, families may be provided with financial and professional assistance. These family failings or crises may vary over time and place, as well as with economic development and class position. Assistance or tutelage for families (which was also fluid and variable) facilitated compliance with societal and family norms and had the potential to both liberate and regulate. Although Donzelot described the ways in which families were 'policed', this term was broad and encompassed 'all the methods for developing the quality of the population and the strength of the nation' (Donzelot, 1980: 6–7). For Donzelot, the social was:

> the set of means which allow social life to escape material pressures and politico-moral uncertainties; the entire range of methods which make the

members of a society relatively safe from the effects of economic fluctuations by providing a certain security which gives their existence possibilities of relations that are flexible enough, and internal stakes that are convincing enough, to avert the dislocation that diverges of interest and beliefs would entail.

(Donzelot, 1980: xxvi)

Within this configuration, social work took its place alongside other regulatory entities such as psychiatry, education and the judiciary.

Although there was always a liberal (and later neo-liberal) fear of totalitarianism that required the power of the state to be contained, more recent developments have eroded a commitment to the interventions that constituted the social. Whilst the twentieth century witnessed a harmony between Durkheim's sociological ideas and those of the economist Keynes, this harmony has now been undermined: it has been argued that profits are required for investment in business and enterprise as opposed to the financing of ever-increasing welfare consumption. Globalization is an important new dynamic that has altered the relationship between the social and economic domains (Donzelot, 2008; Jordan and Drakeford, 2012). Garrett (2013) acknowledges that although the economic crisis could have given rise to a shift in dominant thinking, after the initial shock and attempts to resolve the immediate concerns, there has been in general a return to 'business as usual'.

Given the demise of Keynesian economics and the rise of neo-liberal globalization, questions have been raised about the ongoing provision of the social or the social sector, but also of the continuity of society itself (see Baudrillard, 1983 and Rose, 1996). Rose (1996) considers this to be a new era of 'advanced liberalism'. National governments no longer have to think about solidarity and social cohesion as foundations for economic security; instead, economic security is brought about by an increased emphasis on economic performance with a particular emphasis on markets, competition and individualism. It is argued that governments should intervene only in favour of the market and encourage competition and enterprise. For Stoesz (2002 cited in Arnd-Caddigan and Pozzuto, 2008), the 'social model' of problems and solutions has been replaced with an 'economic model' by which individuals are understood to be competing in terms of their own interests. To paraphrase Donzelot (2008: 124), this thinking is so dominant that individuals are required to become entrepreneurs of themselves and wage earners are expected to exploit their own human capital. The emphasis on individualism brings with it new responsibilities (Beck and Beck-Gernsheim, 2002).

Although Baudrillard (1983) and Rose (1996) have questioned whether globalization, the changed approach to the economy and this reduced emphasis on 'society' has led to the end or the death of the social, in this new era the state is not withdrawing entirely from its supportive and policing role, but the power/knowledge complex has altered, and the technologies with which the power/knowledge complex is carried out have changed accordingly (see Rose, 1996). In the past there was a notion of universal social citizenship, now, however, this notion has been supplanted with two categories of citizens: the included and the excluded. The included are full economic contributors and the excluded receive various forms of assistance and curtailment as a consequence of failing in their individual responsibilities. Specialist interventions aim to rehabilitate individuals in order that they might regain as swiftly and as economically as possible their enterprising and competitive capabilities: dependency is discouraged vigorously (see Froggett, 2002 for a psychosocial perspective on this).

It can be seen therefore that the principle of the market remains ascendant. Although all members of society should be included and should contribute as functioning members, there is no desire to eradicate inequality between individuals, as inequality serves to encourage competition: 'In short, social policy is no longer a means for countering the economic, but a means for sustaining the logic of competition' (Donzelot, 2008: 124). If the power/knowledge complex has shifted, and the social has mutated as described earlier, what are the implications for the organization and identities of social workers? The following section traces the emergence and transformation of social work as it reflects the evolution of the power/knowledge complex and policy imperatives in England from the nineteenth to the twenty-first centuries.

Constructing social work over time

According to theorists such as Donzelot (1980, 2008), Doran (2004) and Rose (1996), social work was one component of the social. That is, a particular power/knowledge complex gave rise to the welfare state and social work. The way in which social work has been organized in England over the twentieth and twenty-first centuries illustrates some of the arguments made above. Consideration will now be given to this, firstly to organizational configurations then to some recent key shifts in the responsibilities and features of social work practice.

Organizing social work

In England, in the middle of the twentieth century practitioners became state employees in three specialist departments: Welfare, Mental Health and Children. Principles of solidarity and optimism for the contribution that might be made by social work were evident in the Seebohm Report (1968), which recommended the merging of the three departments, and the creation of one department that offers holistic services to all:

> We recommend a new local authority department, providing a community-based and family oriented service, which will be available to all. This new department will, we believe, reach far beyond the discovery and rescue of social casualties; it will enable the greatest possible number of individuals to act reciprocally, giving and receiving service for the well-being of the community.
> *(Seebohm, 1968: para 2 quoted in Powell, 2001: 62)*

Legislation was passed and Social Services Departments were created in England (Powell, 2001). The Barclay Report followed in 1982 and built on the foundations laid by the Seebohm Report. This report encouraged the continuation of the Social Services Departments but recommended their decentralization, giving a further emphasis to the geographical communities and a holistic approach to problems and their solutions. Social Services Departments, whether decentralized or not, represented the significance of social work at the time, which for some commentators was the profession's zenith (see Rogowski, 2010).

This organizational arrangement was short lived, however. In an attempt to reduce costs and drive up standards by means of market competition, there developed a preference for services to be provided by others as opposed to the state: Local authority Social Services Departments were expected to become enablers rather than providers. The government encouraged individual and family self-help and the provision of services by private and voluntary sector organizations (Siddall, 2000). In consequence, many Local Authority functions were devolved to others or 'contracted out'. These developments were primarily associated with the NHS and the Community Care Act (1990) which related to services for adults. In addition, local authorities began to pursue a similar approach in relation to children and their families, even though there was no legislative requirement (Petrie, 2010). The drive for services to be provided by others rather than directly by the state led to the creation of regional trusts – Care Trusts for adults under the remit of Health or Children's Trusts under the remit of Education (see Birrell, 2006). This approach continues to be encouraged, partly because it may facilitate liaisons between different professional groups, but also because there may be economies of scale: it is expected that regions will combine children's services and/or create partnerships with relevant voluntary and community sector organizations (see DfE, 2016: 45). Furthermore, it has been proposed that independent trusts should take over statutory services where local authorities have been deemed to be failing in their role (for a reflection on this, see House of Commons Education Committee, 2016).

Organizational reconfigurations have meant the dismantling of Local Authority Social Services Departments, the separation of adult and children's services and the ongoing drive to deliver services by organizations other than the state. This may be considered important given the previously holistic approach to the support and control of the population: to some extent these changes may be considered symbolic of the erosion of solidarity and the mutation of the social. Referring to those in need, the users of social services, Nikolas Rose argues that:

> They are no longer seen as part of a single group with common social characteristics, to be managed by a 'unified social service' and 'generic social workers' who can recognize the common roots of all social problems. The marginalized, the excluded, the underclass are fragmented and divided; their particular difficulties thus need to be addressed through the activities of a variety of specialists each of whom is an expert in a particular problem.
>
> *(1996: 346)*

Practicing social work

Methods of doing social work were articulated by Howe (1987), and Payne (1997) summarized these methods into three different overarching approaches to practice: the reflexive therapeutic, the socialist-collectivist and the individualist-reformist. From the early part of the twentieth century, these approaches gained ascendency in succession (according to Lymbery, 2001), with the socialist-collectivist most significant during the 1970s. However, it is important to note that eclecticism occurred, and specific approaches were overshadowed rather than redundant: there was a shift in emphasis or popularity. Following the Barclay Report described earlier, and in keeping with some of the key principles of the socialist-collectivist approach, community social work was encouraged. This meant a widening of the practitioners' attention in an attempt to prevent the development of problems. Whilst there was a recognition that the detail of community social work would vary, the emphasis was on the 'individuals in their communities or networks of which they are a part' (Barclay, 1982: 13.23–13.25 quoted in Powell, 2001: 63). Particularly evident in community social work is a feature that underpins all of the social work approaches described earlier: the understanding of, and response to, 'the person-in-environment' (Gibelman, 1999). As approaches to the social have moderated, these relational features of social work do not appear to be as important as they once were. Social work has become increasingly administrative, managerial and technicist in content (Harlow, 2003).

A reduced emphasis on relationship-based practice or understanding the person-in-environment may be attributed to two of the interconnected trends that were introduced earlier: the trend towards individualism and the trend towards instrumentalism (see Pozzuto and Arnd-Caddigan, 2008). Instrumentalism might be associated with the economy, efficiency and effectiveness of market competition and managerialism, but also the relatively new emphasis on 'what works' (or evidence-based practice). The emphasis on 'what works' means that all professionals contributing to the social are expected or required to practice in accordance with the available evidence. Whilst the intent to benefit the recipients of interventions is positive, questions concerning the construction and measurement of evidence arise. Academic debates concerning evidence and knowledge generation have persisted for some time, and the implications for social work have been raised (for example, see Butler and Pugh, 2004 ; Webb, 2001). Within this context, social work's concern with a sociological analysis of problems together with relationships and feelings makes it appear 'vague and woolly', and the requirement for quantified evidence of the success of practice may put it at a professional disadvantage (Rogowski, 2010 drawing on the work of Jordan, 2007). Alternatively, the content of social work practice may be changed in order that it might be quantified and measured in accordance with the drive to draw evidential conclusions about 'what works'.

Instrumentalism is in keeping with principles of individualism that underpin the current policy initiatives in England (see Houston, 2010). These ontological principles assume that human beings are independent, rational and calculative (as opposed to intersubjective social beings). Instrumentalism and individualism are evident in services to adults, where there has been a shift away from social work to care management. Rather than provide a service themselves, social workers as care managers facilitate assistance in accordance with specified budgets. Over time, care management is giving way to the personalization approach, which aims for service users, as independent rational individuals, to assess their own needs and directly choose and purchase services for themselves (for further discussion on the personalization agenda, see Jacobs et al., 2011 and Needham, 2011). By means of these policies, the provision of a service based on relationship and appreciation of a person in his/her own specific context is deemed irrelevant, and social work with many adult service users becomes redundant. As Lymbery (2014) concludes: 'It seems that the core mission of social work has been heavily compromised by the long-term "administrative" work undertaken under community care combined with its apparent irrelevance to the user-dominated world of personalisation' (306). Although these developments have occurred mainly in relation to practice with adults, they are also gaining momentum in the care of children – in the case of children with disabilities, for example. In accordance with a budget, parents and children can choose and purchase services that meet their needs (see Crosby, 2010). The role of social workers in assessing the needs of children was also reduced by means of the Common Assessment Framework. By means of this measure an assessment of a child's needs could be led by any professional who already had contact with the family. For example, an assessment might be led by a teacher, a childcare provider or a health care visitor. However, as Rogowski (2010) asks, with professionals such as teachers and health care visitors taking on this role, what is left for the social worker? Since Rogowski made his comments, the Common Assessment Framework has been superseded by the Single Assessment Framework, but the principle concerning the lead profession remains in place (see, for example, Bristol City Council, 2014).

Social workers with a responsibility for children and families have been concerned increasingly with child safeguarding and corporate parenting (Harlow et al., 2013). Even within this domain, however, after making an assessment, they find themselves planning a timetable of interventions, then recruiting and coordinating the specialist services of others. This shift, which jettisons the professional knowledge and skills of practitioners, has been identified as problematic when the safeguarding of children is at issue. According to Munro:

> The professional account of social work practice 'in which relationships play a central role' appears to have been gradually stifled and replaced by a managerialist account that is fundamentally different. The managerialist approach has been called a 'rational-technical' approach where the emphasis has been on the conscious, cognitive elements of the task of working with children and families, on collecting information and making plans. This focus has led to 'a curious absence . . . of any considered attention to the core dynamics, experience and methods of doing the work'.
>
> *(Munro, 2011: 86 drawing on the work of Ferguson, 2011)*

Munro then goes on to say:

> The responses collected by Community Care and the British Association of Social Workers (BASW) to the review's questions about practice echoed a picture of a managerial focus on process rather than practice, with reduced time for providing help to children and families themselves so that, after assessment, children and families are generally referred to other services.
>
> *(Munro, 2011: 87)*

Munro concluded that professionalism (particularly associated with systems theory and relationship-based practice) should be retrieved and social work should be reinvigorated. Whilst this goal was positive, largely welcomed and gave rise to a variety of changes – such as the revision of the Common Assessment Framework identified earlier and a new emphasis on innovative frameworks for practice (see for example, Goodman and Trowler, 2012) – it may have been impossible for her report to fundamentally alter the overarching trends that have shifted the contribution of social work in the construction of the social. What follows is a case study of current practice that illustrates some of the policy trends identified earlier and also shows how some social workers are still able to practice in accordance with principles established previously, even though the linguistic descriptors might have changed.

Supporting adoptive families: a case study

The provision of support to adoptive families is relatively new in England, with introductory legislation being passed in 2002 and implemented in 2005 (Luckock and Hart, 2005). In England, adoption support services are defined in the Adoption Support Services Regulations 2005, and Local Authorities are required to draw up an adoption support service plan and to monitor its implementation (Rushton and Monck, 2009). Services are being made available as the needs of adoptive families change. In the past, it was predominantly babies that were adopted, but now children across the age range are in this position, and given their earlier experiences, they may have complex physical, emotional, developmental and emotional needs (Scott and Lindsey, 2003). These may challenge the abilities or commitment of adoptive parents, who may require assistance in order that placement disruption is avoided. Services to be made available include financial support; discussion groups; mediation relating to contact arrangements; therapeutic services to adoptive children; assistance following disrupted adoption; and the provision of counselling, advice and information (Pearce and Banks, 2013). Although social workers are the leading group of professionals in facilitating and supporting adoptions, the term 'social work' does not appear in this list of potential services.

A Centre for Adoption Support was created in England in 2013 by two charitable agencies working in partnership, along with a cluster of local authorities. The Centre and the services it offers were established by means of short-term funding won competitively from the National Prospectus Grants Programme (see www.gov.uk).

Given this source of funding, the performance of the service was audited by the Department for Education against a set of (predominantly quantitative) indicators. The aims of this new initiative were to improve the facilitation of adoption orders and support families where disruption was at risk of occurring. This latter component of the service was subjected to a commissioned illuminative evaluation (Hall and Hall, 2004), which took place from February 2014 to March 2015 (see Harlow et al., 2015). A mixed-methods approach was used and the organizational, managerial and practice components of the service were taken into account. The Chief Executives and Project Manager participated in a series of reflective management group meetings where the progression of the project was discussed. Documents were analyzed, whilst question-naires and interviews with parents, teachers and social workers enabled the research team to examine the progress of the children and their families, and the services that had been received.

When asked to specify the services provided, the response from the manage-ment team was: consultancy (the opportunity for adoptive parents to seek advice from a professional member of the new team in her office), life story work, training workshops, activity days, newsletters and therapy. The specific contents of training packages (which aimed to improve parenting, for example) were sourced from else-where, as was therapy. This facilitative role that was demonstrated by the practition-ers might be described as social brokerage (Dartington, 2010). Social brokerage is not the same as care management, as it does not require social workers to manage budgets, nor is it the same as referral. Writing about this process in relation to adult care, Dartington says: 'Social brokerage, unlike referral which tends to fit the indi-vidual to the resource, is about the integration of resources around the individual and maintains the individual in relation to his environment' (Dartington, 2010:108). Research respondents were appreciative of the facilitative role undertaken by the practitioners.

All services provided by the Centre were elaborated upon in a paper written at the end of the project by the Project Manager and a medic and published under the journal heading of 'Health Notes' (see Evans and Dickenson, 2015). As with the promotional material and website, there is no mention of social work in the Cen-tre's provision of services. However, the key team members who staffed the Centre for Adoption Support were qualified social workers. When prompted to describe the professional foundation of provision, one of the Chief Executives stated clearly that it was traditional social work of the kind associated with the work of Florence Hollis (1972): that is, relationship-based social work as it is known today, which is based on the psychosocial casework articulated by Hollis. Furthermore, the Project Manager described the professional foundation of the service as social work along with dyadic developmental psychotherapy.

From an interpretation of the data generated from the evaluative research pro-ject, it was clear that social work was practiced. For instance, the community of adoptive families was developed and maintained by means of newsletters and activ-ity days. The activity days may also be understood as a form of relational practice known as 'group work'. Direct work with children was undertaken by means of life story work and principles of relationship-based social work appeared to provide a foundation for all activity. Informed by their knowledge of child development and attachment theory (particularly the work of Hughes, 1999, 2004), practitioners made assessments of need and used their relationships with parents and children to bring about positive change. In keeping with some of the key characteristics of relationship-based social work (see Hennessey, 2011 and Ruch et al., 2010), practitioners communicated in ways that encouraged trust; they enabled parents and children to express emotion; and they were supportive. Because practitioners became 'emotionally intelligent' after participating in training on dyadic therapeutic interventions, it might also be argued that the social work practice was 'emotionally intelligent' (see Howe, 2008). Service users appreciated the help they received from their social workers, and the following anonymized quotations offer an illumination of this.

Mrs Black: You know when someone comes with the intention to help. It just oozes out of them. She [the social worker] was just one of those people, who I felt safe [with], and you know this is going to get better.

Mrs White: The social worker was somebody [you] just trusted. She seemed calm . . . [with] good experience and very wise. She got to know Hannah a little bit at that stage and Hannah liked her. [They] just seemed to click.

Mrs Grey: Every few weeks, we make an appointment [to see the social worker]. Robert's going to Rock and River [activity day] and we'll see her there, and she's coming to see me the following week. It does help talking to her. A few weeks ago she took Robert for a walk and Robert pointed everything out to her. I don't know where we would be without the help now.

Overall, the work service was well received by the research respondents. Crucially, however, as indicated earlier, the service was known as adoption support rather than social work, with key components of provision being training and therapy.

Concluding discussion

The case study provides an up-to-date illustration of many of the policy trends identified earlier. For example, the Centre was created by means of a partnership between five different agencies with the founding principle that the Local Authorities would be purchasing the services provided by the charities. Furthermore, the funding for the Centre was won competitively; it was short term; and it was made available on the basis of quantifiable outputs that were audited by the Department for Education. The Centre was constructed in response to a specific community with an emergent focus of need: adoptive families. Social workers, trainers and therapists provided 'tutelage' in order to avert risk: that is, help was offered in order that family norms and adoptions were sustained, and young people with a range of difficulties would be less likely to find themselves amongst the category of 'the excluded'.

Although the Centre was staffed by social workers who delivered good quality relationship-based practice, the terms 'adoption support', 'training' and 'therapy' were predominantly used to describe service provision. One might question why the social work that was practiced was not more explicitly acknowledged, and that the term 'social work', if not completely absent, was cast into shadow. The two theoretical themes of individualism and instrumentalism which were introduced earlier may have some bearing here. What the service offered was not a generic social service, but targeted, with the specialist focus giving rise to a specialist nomenclature. Related to this, problems and their solutions were increasingly constructed as individual (to do with health or education), with individual solutions framed as therapy or training. In terms of instrumentalism, practitioners in the Centre for Adoption Support were drawing on the current knowledge concerning the cause of adoption disruption and the recommended solutions, these being predominantly concerned with therapy or parental training. Although there is relatively little evidence about 'what works' in supporting adoption, evaluations and reviews of therapeutic and parental training interventions (as opposed to social work) are under way, with some being funded by the government (see Stock et al., 2016). Even when social work is practiced, and is appreciated by recipients (as earlier), if it cannot be articulated by means of a positivist approach, then it will not officially 'count' (see Chapter 8 in this volume). Over time, an unintended consequence may be the demise of relationship-based practice.

Cost effectiveness also informs the drive towards evidence-based practice. The dominant thinking requires scarce resources to be invested in only that which is likely to show positive reward, particularly in an era of austerity. Financial considerations, though not the only drivers, also encourage the trend towards self-help, personalization and assessments made by others, as with the Single Assessment Framework. In this example, the requirement for social work is diminished. Professionally qualified social workers are expensive resources; if their role can be undertaken by alternative professionals or unqualified others, then savings may be made. Malin (2015) articulates this principle in relation to social work and the *Troubled Families* initiative, whereby work with families is undertaken by unqualified personnel rather than registered social workers.

However, the case study in this chapter shows the existence of diversity in service provision in England and the continuity of professional social work in some settings: this small third-sector organization shows practitioners assessing families, acting as brokers, attending to relational needs and pursuing positive change. Nevertheless, social workers in general are said to be beleaguered, and it has been argued that the loss of an organizational base together with a relatively weak identity may lead to the profession's demise (Rogowski, 2010: 148 acknowledging the contribution of Clarke, 1996). Although Gibelman (1999) reminds us that social work has always demonstrated flux, and that there is no fixed entity called 'social work', the quantity and quality of change in England over recent times may be significant and extraordinary. It might be concluded that the stature of social work has diminished: social work has lost its place in the current configuration of the 'social' (as symbolized by the dismantling of the Social Services Departments, the reduced use of the title and in the changed construction of problems and their solutions). Put another way, social work is being written out of the social. However, this does not mean that the social as articulated by Donzelot (1980) is dead – the social continues, but in a reframed and different guise. By comparison to previous decades this guise may be reduced, fragmented, audited and individualized, but the very same methods of 'policing' and regulating the population continue to be exercised.[1]

Note

1 Thanks go to John Lawler and David Cracknell, who commented upon an earlier draft of this chapter.

References

Barclay, P. (1982). *Social Workers: Their Roles and Tasks*. London: Bedford Square Press.

Baudrillard, J. (1983). *In the Shadow of the Silent Majorities or 'The Death of the Social'*. New York: Semiotext(e).

Beck, U., & Beck-Gernsheim, E. (2002). *Individualization*. London: Sage.

Birrell, D. (2006). The Disintegration of Local Authority Social Services Departments. *Local Government Studies*, 32(2): 139–151. doi: 10.1080/03003930600586134.

Bristol City Council. (2014). *Guidance to Completing the Single Assessment Framework: For Professionals Assessing Needs of Families for Early Help*. Bristol: Bristol City Council. Retrieved from www.bristol.gov.uk.

Butler, I., & Pugh, R. (2004). The Politics of Social Work Research. In R. Lovelock, K. Lyons & J. Powell (Eds.), *Reflecting on Social Work Discipline and Profession* (pp. 55–71). Aldershot: Ashgate.

Clarke, J. (1996). After Social Work? In N. Parton (Ed.), *Social Theory, Social Change and Social Work* (pp. 36–60). London: Routledge.

Croisdale-Appleby, D. (2014). *Re-visioning Social Work Education: An Independent Review*. Retrieved from www.gov.uk/government/uploads/system/uploads/attachment_data/file/285788/DCA_Accessible.pdf.

Crosby, N. (2010). *Personalisation: Children, Young People and Families*. Wythall: In Control.

Dartington, T. (2010). *Managing Vulnerability: The Underlying Dynamics of Systems of Care*. London: Karnac Books.

Deleuze, G. (1980). The Rise of the Social. In J. Donzelot (Ed.) *The Policing of Families* (pp. ix–xii). London: Hutchinson.

DfE (Department for Education). (2016). *Putting Children First: Delivering Our Vision for Excellent Children's Social Care*. Retrieved from www.gov.uk/government/publications.

Donzelot, J. (1980). *The Policing of Families: Welfare Versus the State*, translated by R. Hurley. London: Hutchinson.

Donzelot, J. (2008). Michel Foucault and Liberal Intelligence. *Economy and Society*, 31(1): 115–134.

Doran, N. (2004). Re-writing the Social, Re-writing Sociology: Donzelot, Genealogy and Working Class Bodies. *Canadian Journal of Sociology*, 29(3): 333–357. Retrieved from www.web.b.ebscohost.com.

Evans, G., & Dickenson, K. (2015). Northwest England Post-Placement Adoption Support Service, 2013–2015. *Fostering and Adoption*, 39(2): 179–183. doi: 10.11770308575915588717.

Ferguson, H. (2011). *Child Protection Practice*. Basingstoke: Palgrave Macmillan.

Froggett, L. (2002). *Love, Hate and Welfare: Psychosocial Approaches to Policy and Practice*. Bristol: Policy Press.

Garrett, P. M. (2013). *Social Work and Social Theory*. Bristol: Policy Press.

Gibelman, M. (1999). The Search for Identity: Defining Social Work – Past, Present, Future. *Social Work*, 4(44): 298–322. Retrieved from www.web.b.ebscohost.com.

Goodman, S., & Trowler, I. (2012). *Social Work Reclaimed: Innovative Frameworks for Child and Family Social Work Practice*. London: Jessica Kingsley Publishing.

Hall, I., & Hall, D. (2004). *Evaluation and Social Research: Introducing Small-scale Practice*. Basingstoke: Palgrave Macmillan.

Harlow, E. (2003). New Managerialism, Social Services Departments and Social Work Practice Today. *Practice*, 15(2): 29–44. Retrieved from http//:dx.doi.org/10.1080/09503150308416917.

Harlow, E. (2004). Why Don't Women Want to be Social Workers Anymore? New Managerialism, Postfeminism and the Shortage of Social Workers in Social Services Departments in England and Wales. *European Journal of Social Work*, 7(2): 167–179. doi: 10.1080/1369145042000237436.

Harlow, E., Barry, J., Berg, E., & Chandler, J. (2013). Neoliberalism, Managerialism and the Reconfiguration of Social Work in Sweden and the United Kingdom. *Organization*, 20(4): 534–550. First published on-line in 2012. doi: 101177/1350508412448222.

Harlow, E., Mitchell, A., Doherty, P., & Moran, P. (2015). *Constructing and Delivering Services of Support: An Evaluation of the Northwest Post-Placement Adoption Support Service* (p. 2). Chester: University of Chester.

Hennessey, R. (2011). *Relationship Skills in Social Work*. London: Sage.

Hollis, F. (1972). *Casework: A Psychosocial Therapy* (second edition). New York: Random House.

House of Commons Education Committee. (2016). *Social Work Reform: Third Report of Session*, 2016–2017. Retrieved from www.publications.parliament.uk/pa/cm201617/cmselect/cmeduc/201201.pdf.

Houston, S. (2010). Beyond *Homo Economicus*: Recognition, Self-realization and Social Work. *British Journal of Social Work*, 40: 841–857. doi: 10.1093/bjsw/bcn132.

Howe, D. (1987). *An Introduction to Social Work Theory*. Aldershot: Ashgate.

Howe, D. (2008). *The Emotionally Intelligent Social Worker*. Basingstoke: Palgrave Macmillan.

Hughes, D. A. (1999). Adopting Children with Attachment Problems. *Child Welfare*, 78(55): 541–560. Retrieved from www.web.b.ebscohost.com.

Hughes, D. A. (2004). An Attachment-Based Treatment of Maltreated Children and Young People. *Attachment and Human Development*, 6(3): 263–278. doi: 10.1080/14616730412331281539.

Jacobs, S., Abell, J., Stevens, M., Wilberforce, M., Challis, D., Manthorpe, J., Fernandez, J., Glendinning, C., Jones, K., Knapp, M., Moran, N., & Netten, A. (2011). The Personalization of Care Services and the Early Impact on Staff Activity Patterns. *Journal of Social Work*, 13(2): 141–163. doi: 10.1177/1468017311410681.

Jones, R. (2014). *The Story of Baby P. Setting the Record Straight*. Bristol: Policy Press.

Jordan, B. (2007). *Social Work and Well-being*. Lyme Regis: Russell House.

Jordan, B., & Drakeford, M. (2012). *Social Work and Social Policy under Austerity*. Basingstoke: Palgrave Macmillan.

Luckock, B., & Hart, A. (2005). Adoptive Family Life and Adoption Support: Policy Ambivalence and the Development of Effective Services. *Child and Family Social Work*, 10: 125–134. doi: 10.1111/j.1365-2206.2005.00358.x.

Lymbery, M. (2001). Social Work at the Crossroads. *British Journal of Social Work*, 31: 369–384. Retrieved from www.web.b.ebscohost.com.

Lymbery, M. (2014). Understanding Personalisation: Implications for Social Work. *Journal of Social Work*, 14(3): 295–312. doi: 10.1177/1468017313477326.

Malin, N. (2015). Editorial: Austerity and Some Contemporary Challenges for Professionalism. *Social Work and Social Sciences Review*, 18(1): 3–14. Retrieved from https://journals. whitingbirch.net/index.php/swssr/article/view/845.

Munro, E. (2011). *The Munro Review of Child Protection: Final Report: A Child Centred System*. Norwich: The Stationary Office.

Narey, M. (2014). *Making the Education of Social Workers Consistently Effective: Report of Sir Martin Narey's Independent Review of the Education of Children's Social Workers*. Retrieved from www.gov.uk/government/publications.

Needham, C. (2011). Personalization: From Story-line to Practice. *Social Policy and Administration*, 45(1): 54–68. doi: 10.1111/j.1467–95152010.00753.x.

Payne, M. (1997). *Modern Social Work Theory*. Basingstoke: Macmillan.

Pearce, J., & Banks, A. (2013). Adoption Support Services in England and Wales. *Community Care Inform*. Retrieved from www.ccinform.co.uk.

Petrie, S. (2010). The 'Commodification' of 'Children in Need' in Welfare Markets: Implication for Managers. *Social Work and Social Sciences Review*, 14(1): 9–26. doi: 10.1921/095352210X495104.

Powell, F. (2001). *The Politics of Social Work*. London: Sage.

Pozzuto, R., & Arnd-Caddigan, M. (2008). Social Work in the US: Sociohistorical Context and Contemporary Issues. *Australian Social Work*, 61(1): 57–71. doi: 10.1080/03124070701818732.

Rogowski, S. (2010). *The Rise and Fall of a Profession?* Bristol: Policy Press.

Rose, N. (1996). The Death of the Social: Re-figuring the Territory of Government. *Economy and Society*, 25(3): 327–356. Retrieved from www.web.b.ebscohost.com.

Ruch, G., Turney, D., & Ward, A. (2010). *Relationship-based Social Work: Getting to the Heart of Practice*. London: Jessica Kingsley Publishers.

Rushton, A., & Monck, E. (2009). *Enhancing Adoptive Parenting: A Test of Effectiveness*. London: British Association of Adoption and Fostering.

Scott, S., & Lindsey, C. (2003). Therapeutic Approaches in Adoption. In H. Argent (Ed.), *Models of Adoption Support: What Works and What Doesn't* (pp.16–27). London: British Association of Adoption and Fostering.

Seebohm Report. (1968). *Report of the Committee on Local Authority and Allied Personal Social Services*. London: HMS, Cmnd. 3703.

Siddall, A. (2000). From Beveridge to Best Value: Transitions in Welfare Provision. In E. Harlow & J. Lawler (Eds.), *Management, Social Work and Change* (pp. 24–35). Aldershot: Ashgate.

Social Work Task Force. (2009). *Building a Safe, Confident Future: Final Report of the Social Work Task Force Report: November 2009*.

Stock, L., Spielhofer, T., & Gieve, M. – The Tavistock Institute of Human Relations (TIHR). (2016). *Independent Evidence Review of Post-Adoption Support Interventions Research: Research Brief*. Department for Education. Retrieved from www.gov.uk/government/publications.

Stoesz, D. (2002). The American Welfare State at Twilight. *Journal of Social Policy*, 31: 487–503. doi: 10.1017/S0047279402006669.

Webb, S. A. (2001). Some Considerations on the Validity of Evidence-based Practice in Social Work. *British Journal of Social Work*, 31(1): 51–79. Retrieved from www. web.b.ebscohost.com.

PART II

Location, context and workplace culture

6

VOCATION AND PROFESSIONAL IDENTITY

Social workers at home and abroad

Mark Erickson and Jem Price

The concept and practice of vocation

The concept of 'vocation' and its cognate, 'calling', has a long, if discontinuous, history in the social sciences. Whilst it is absent in the works of Karl Marx, the founder of the sociology of work, it plays a prominent role in Max Weber's writings, underpinning his most famous work, *The Protestant Ethic and the Spirit of Capitalism* ([1905] 1958), and reappearing at the end of Weber's career in two influential essays. Later writers on the sociology of work and the professions underplayed the concept of vocation in favour of more structured and measurable aspects of employment, a trend that itself was indicative of Weber's predication of increasing rationalization of all aspects of modern society. But vocation never wholly disappeared nor retreated back into its origin point in theology; the idea of a vocation really had escaped from the cage (Weber [1905] 1958: 181) and embedded itself in our everyday lives and discourse (Dawson, 2005). This, if for no other reason, should make it an object worthy of our attention. Yet there is another very significant reason why we should consider the idea of vocation or calling (the distinctions/similarities between these will be explored more fully in this chapter)[1] and that is that vocation takes us away from a purely capitalistic conception of what work entails; it takes us beyond the horizon of the cash nexus and the demands of efficiency.

Very little work has been done on examining the role of calling and vocation in professions other than those with an avowedly religious dimension; this itself is perhaps a reflection of a disquiet at using the concept due to its clear connection to the practice of religious faith. However, one further thing contributes to this lack of attention for calling and vocation: vocation is a concept that is firmly established in everyday discourse with a clear constellation of meanings that are mundane and secularized. Put simply, our everyday usage of the word 'vocation' is deployed in a straightforward way to indicate a career or occupational trajectory. Social scientists may want to distance themselves from such mundane definitions, and that may be appropriate, but doing so uncritically may serve to occlude something very important about vocation and its role in contemporary society. Further, we need to recognize the wide constellation of meanings that 'vocation' attracts inside social scientific discourse; the concept has 'ambiguous and varied connotations' (Dawson, 2005: 222).

Our examination of the concept of vocation and our consideration of its useful-ness and applicability in understanding aspects of professional life for Filipino social workers at home and abroad begins with the classical sociology of Max Weber. Weber's *The Protestant Ethic and the Spirit of Capitalism* ([1905] 1958) provides an historical account of the emergence of calling and vocation at the time of Luther, the subtle changes to this idea through the Reformation and into the industrial period, and the continuing role that this has in contemporary society. Weber voca-tion's roots are found in religious discourse: "Now it is unmistakable that even in the German word *Beruf*, and perhaps still more in the English *calling*, a religious conception, that of a task set by God, is at least suggested" (1958: 79). All three words – *Beruf*, vocation and calling – relate to an active process of being called to a duty; this initially meant by God but, later, by society's norms of the necessity and redemptive value of work itself (Nietzsche, 1969). This is a crucial shift Weber identifies: from the calling to a religious, perhaps even monastic, career, to the calling to a vocation of earthly work where the work itself was an expression of spirituality and indicative of the possibility of salvation. Luther, and Calvin later, in their formulation of vocation 'democratized' the concept by showing that not only were those in formal religious roles (monks, nuns, priests) called to a vocation, but everyone who was involved in useful work was also called and therefore eligible to be chosen for the Kingdom of God. The modern concept of vocation thus has its roots in the Reformation's reformulation of what it meant to be called: all work could be a vocation as long as it was 'good' work and the executor of that work expressed pietism and asceticism.[2] Weber returned to the concept of vocation later in his career in two seminar lectures delivered in 1919 (Weber, 1948a, 1948b). Here, and especially in *Science as a Vocation* (1948b), Weber considers quite how it is that we articulate our sense of vocation and what it is that social scientists may look for when examining this concept.[3]

Weber, in considering what it means to have the vocation of 'scientist' in mod-ern society, identifies two distinct components. The first is what he calls the external aspects of science as a vocation: how it is organized as a career, how it is funded, how it develops a structured hierarchy of visible institutions of professional locus and identity. He moves on to consider the second component: the inner vocation for science. Here Weber discovers a 'passionate devotion' for science that is the inner motivation of the scientist, a desire to serve the goal of the scientific community and the adoption of a value system that includes self-sacrifice and a recognition that no recognition for one's efforts may be forthcoming.[4] This distinction is a useful one for us: where we may agree with many commentators, and indeed with the original Lutheran idea that all forms of work can be a calling or vocation in that we can identify *external* characteristics whereby they display value – be that through the formation of professional guilds or institutions, through attachment to formal training and qualifying routes or simply through the attachment of pecuniary value to them – it is the *inner* calling that distinguishes some forms of work from others. Here we can say that it is only some occupations and/or social roles that include this sense of inner calling, of being called to a duty that is other-directed. For this reason, and notwithstanding our earlier comments concerning the translation of the word *Beruf*, we propose separating the idea of *vocation*, the idea of a career, from that of a *calling*, the inner feeling of duty to serve something other than the self in one's career, occupation, profession or simply everyday actions. This separation of the two concepts has been used by others, notably Dik and Duffy (2009); we depart from their analyses of the vocation of counsellors in that where they consider 'calling' to be a "transcendent summons, originating beyond the self" (2009: 427) and 'vocation' to be "an approach to a particular life role that . . . holds other-oriented values and goals" (2009: 428). We consider such distinctions to be less significant than that between the inner and outer understandings of calling and vocation as expressed by the research participants in our study. For us, the inner sense of motivation towards duty must be understood in terms of the external conditions of vocation that the individual is embedded within.

In summary, tensions and contradictions between the usage of the concepts of vocation and calling provides the sociology of the professions and social work theory useful insights on the formation of professional identity with an additional framework to help understand motivations for work and considerations of worth. The need to move beyond simple 'cash nexus' incentive models to consider motivations has long been recognized in the social sciences (from Baldamus, 1961 to Noon and Blyton, 2007) and vocation/calling clearly does this without reverting back into an 'ideological' model (Althusser, 1971; Willis, 1977) or relying on a psychological model of substitution (Casey, 1995). We can agree with Bauman, up to a point, that as capitalism and globalization have expanded work has taken on a more meaningless aspect, leaving only a few in a situation where they have a 'vocation', whilst disagreeing with him that these few are a 'privileged elite' (Bauman, 1998: 34). Quite the opposite: it is likely, as Dik and Duffy suggest (2009: 431), that those who really are the elite of our societies will endorse values of power, privilege and wealth accumulation rather than other-directed and duty-bound aspects of calling and vocation.

In the following section we will consider what it is that calling and vocation bring to our understanding of social work as a vocation in the Philippines and in England. Specifically, we will focus on the place of calling and vocation in the lives and practices of social workers before going on to explore the tensions that emerge around this when Filipino social workers make the transition from the Philippines to England. At the outset we must make it clear that Filipino social workers' motivations to work, and their reasons for entering the profession in the first place, are diverse and complex. As mentioned in the 'Research design and process' section later in this chapter, a small empirical study was carried out using qualitative methods, mainly semi-structured interview schedules. Given the size of the sample here (33 in total: 24 in the Philippines, 9 in England), and the complexity of the topic, we are wary about overgeneralizing and overstating the role of vocation/ calling in social workers' motivations and orientations to work. Having said that, it was a very striking feature of this research that almost all participants articulated some, often many, aspects of their professional career and practice in terms of a calling, and almost every participant noted the significant role of religious faith and structure in their professional practice and professional identity.

Before looking in detail at this group of Filipino social workers it is important to consider the historical and sociopolitical context that our research participants are located within. The recent history of the Philippines, the rise of the profession of social work and the transnational movement of Filipino social workers are inextricably linked.

Social work in the Philippines

The Philippines has one of the highest rates of population growth in Asia. From 2007 to 2015, the estimated population grew from around 88 million to 102 million. Most are people of faith: around 90% of the population is Christian, with 80% Roman Catholic, whilst 5% are Muslim. Although more than 80 languages and dialects exist, most speak Filipino and many speak English. Poverty is a prevailing issue and around 10% of the population work overseas (Price, 2014). However, economic growth in recent years has been strong and was projected to reach 6.4% in 2016 and 6.2% in 2017 (Cruz et al., 2016).

Whilst the 'humanitarian impulse' was present in the Philippines before colonial rule, the development of social work began during Spanish occupation, when missionaries converted most of the population to Christianity and developed schools, hospitals and almshouses to support this (Almanzor, 1966: 27). The period of US rule (1898–1946) saw the continued growth of charitable provision alongside increased public sector coordination and direct provision of welfare. Filipino writers such as Viloria and Martinez (1987) and Landa Jocano (1980) have been accused of presenting benign accounts of this story: "The early Spanish missionaries not only 'watched over' the spiritual well-being of the people but also administered in the maintenance of hospitals, asylums, and orphanages for the natives" (Landa Jocano, 1980: 190).

After independence, social work developed as a profession, initially influenced by aid workers from the USA and later by a handful of Filipinos trained as social workers in the USA (Almanzor, 1966; Yu, 2006). Thus, the two key influences on social work in the Philippines might be seen as Christian philanthropy and American social work practice. Yu asserts, however, that histories of Philippine social welfare have failed to engage critically with the nature of foreign rule: "The austerity of the Spanish colonial government and the omnipotence of the clergy created a model of social welfare that was dominated by the religious orders, with minimal government involvement" (Yu, 2006: 561). The potential for faith to limit expectations and individualize deservedness for support was a striking feature of the data gathered for this study. Again, for Yu (2006: 562), these beliefs "hold perseverance in suffering as a virtue, fate as the will of God and misfortune and poverty as punishment for sin or a test of character". Notions of individual failings and salvation, within welfare and broader society, were a key legacy of Spain's colonization of the Philippines. Meanwhile, under US rule,

> welfare initiatives only had value if they facilitated colonial subjugation and assimilation. An individualist perspective also came with the restrictive colonial environment that would also have provided penalties for anyone who suggested structural attributions to social problems.
>
> *(Yu, 2006: 565)*

For Yu, therefore, colonial rule brought a functional, residualized and individualist form of welfare. It could be argued that the Spanish and US influences complemented and reinforced each other in this regard.

In 1946, the Philippines became a republic and state welfare provision grew. Schools of social work were established and the Philippine Association of Social Workers was formed in November 1947. In 1965, regulation of social work and social work agencies was introduced. The formation of the Schools of Social Work Association of the Philippines in 1969 was further evidence of a growing presence and formal recognition. Meanwhile, in 1965 Marcos was elected President and was to remain so until 1986. This period witnessed growing UN focus on a development agenda. Marcos, however, faced growing opposition and in 1972 declared martial law, which remained, tellingly, until a visit of the Pope in 1981. The 1970s saw a "shifting emphasis from the traditional, often institution-based social welfare to community-oriented programs and services which underscored people's own capacities for problem-solving" (Lee-Mendoza, 2008: 31). Social work became increasingly linked to social and economic development, working with communities to develop small businesses and skills for employment. In 1986, mass 'people power' demonstrations drove Marcos into exile and Corazon Aquino became President. She, too, emphasized development rather than relief, creating the Department for Social Welfare and Development (DSWD). From the 1990s onwards, social work continued to operate within local government units, nongovernmental organizations (NGOs), faith-based charitable providers and some private sector agencies (such as private hospitals and industrial settings). To a much greater extent than in parts of the 'west', the work of NGOs is seen very much as part of social work and a place for social workers (Price and Artaraz, 2013).

Today's social workers in the Philippines work in a wide range of agencies including NGOs (international and national), central and local government, business, charities and faith-based organizations. Areas of practice include child welfare and family support, work with older people, women, disabled people and those with mental health problems, disaster management, community development and sustainability, community organizing, and advocacy and social action (Price, 2014).

Practice is often generic but may equally focus on 'sectors' of the population, such as street children, farmers, the urban poor or migrant workers. The Philippine Government has in recent years shifted emphasis towards poverty reduction through models of social protection, and high numbers of social workers are engaged in these efforts. The DSWD's 2009 Annual Report, for example, set out some areas of attention within the sector, including, "the expansion of the Pantawid Pamilyang Pilipino Program (4Ps) or the conditional cash transfer program ... from 337,416 in 2008 beneficiaries to 1 million in 2009" (DSWD, 2009, p3). Under this programme, grants are made to poor households "upon compliance to conditions set by the program" (ibid., p4). "The conditionalities include sending their children to school and bringing them to health centres on a regular basis, and providing pre and post-natal care and delivery by a skilled birth attendant to pregnant women" (ibid., p24). However, Raquiza (2010) noted that 1 million beneficiaries constitute only a quarter of those in poverty in the country.

Furthermore, with a focus on education and health to break inter-generational poverty, the more direct issue of a regular income was, Raquiza (2010) suggested, being overlooked. The Report also highlights the growth of emergency employment measures, 'economic resiliency' assistance, disaster relief and rehabilitation. Also striking in the Report is the extent of reliance upon agencies outside the Philippines. The 4Ps was supported by UNICEF, projects in poorer regions (day centres, irrigation and infrastructure projects, health stations, livelihood centres, schemes to reduce 'gender violence') were funded by the Spanish government and assistance to those affected by conflict in Mindanao was supported by the UN World Food Programme. A further high-profile programme, partly funded through loans from the World Bank (Raquiza, 2010) and overseas grant aid, was called Kapit-Bisig Laban sa Kahirapan: Comprehensive and Integrated Delivery of Social Services (KALAHI-CIDSS). Under this scheme, now the National Community-Driven Development Program, funds support community initiatives including basic infrastructure, community enterprise, skills training and health/day centres. Part of this programme, in urban poor communities, was supported by a US$3 million grant from the Japanese government through their Social Development Fund (DSWD, 2011).

Research design and process

Primary data were gathered in a 5-week study visit to the Philippines (during which 'indigenous' literature was gathered, study visits made and semi-structured interviews undertaken with 24 participants in the Philippines: 11 social workers; one social worker in training; seven social work academics; five policymakers) and also via semi-structured interviews with nine Filipino social workers in England. The analysis was thematic, employing a combination of inductive and deductive coding, the development of comparative categories and second-level coding.

Prior to visiting the Philippines, contact was made by email with social workers, policymakers, educators, academics and representatives of other key social welfare agencies in the Philippines. Access was in part facilitated by the Philippine

Association of Social Workers, Inc. (PASWI), in advance and during the study visit. However, an online search of agencies and universities also yielded a good number of participants, as did word-of-mouth suggestions when in Manila. Indeed, when in the Philippines, PASWI members assisted in accessing a wider range of interviewees. Thus, the sampling strategy was a realistic combination of convenience and snowballing (Bryman, 2012; Robson, 2011) with clear categories from which it was anticipated that interviewees would be drawn (social work academics and educators, social workers in practice and other persons engaged in welfare policy development).

Interviews were ultimately conducted with 24 people in the Philippines. The sample was as follows:

- 19 were female and five male;
- all but two (senior staff of an international NGO) identified as Filipino; and
- nine participants might be described predominantly as practising social workers, six as social work academics, five as holding welfare policy and planning positions, two as current social work students and two others (the aforementioned NGO staff); there was, however, some overlap between these categories.

All nine interviewees in England were Filipino social workers trained in the Philippines and all but one was female. Eight of the participants were employed in statutory social work settings and one was retraining as a nurse.

Social work as a calling: the inner world of Filipino social workers

As we have seen, the roots of the Weberian conception of calling and vocation are in religious faith and the sense of duty or obligation to God, but we can distinguish inner and external aspects of this calling. In this section we will consider the inner motivation for social work that can be identified as a calling, rather than the *Beruf* aspect of career and occupation. It is worth noting that it is participants themselves who are applying this label to their own accounts of why they entered social work and how they practice their social work.

Weber and others argue that this inner calling, this sense of duty, has been secularized in contemporary society. This may be the case, but personal religious faith was a significant motivating factor for entering the profession for many Filipino social workers. Indeed, for some, social work was an alternative route to following an avowedly religious calling. For example:

> I'd been wanting to go to . . . a religious organisation, so I said I can still serve without going to that road . . . so probably that's my ultimate purpose. Angel
> *(FSW UK 40–49 F)*

> Personally, I enrolled in social work because of my faith. Mark
> *(FPOL P 18–24 M RC)*

Faith was a key motivating factor towards social work for most participants. As well as using faith to explain their motivation for entering the profession, participants spoke often about religion and faith in terms of their everyday social work practice:

> the fact that . . . I have this religious upbringing, is there and you cannot set aside about fate, about God's plan. . . . So I was growing up thinking that sometimes you are not the one who is maneuvering your life. There is always someone up there, a supreme being or a God basically leading your way. Jay
>
> *(FSW UK 30–39 M RC)*

> In helping you are walking, going to paradise, in God . . . our priests, so they teach us or they are helping me to be more effective and be more responsive to people. So it guides me to do what God wants me to do . . . in the Bible there are lots of readings that where God helped different . . . the blind, the poor, the disabled. Leah
>
> *(FSW P GOV 30–39 F RC)*

This religious orientation to social work was considered entirely appropriate by our participants. This was, after all, simply an expression of an aspect of a worldview that was nearly always shared by their service users:

> in doing our helping process the spiritual aspect is also included like what we did in our youth, in our street children. We basically teach them the values, they're . . . learning how to call God in times of crisis, so that they may know the right and wrong . . . how to follow their parents, how to follow the rule of God so that they may be a good person. Yes, and also that in crisis, one of our, maybe many of our clients are losing their faith because of their problem and we try to let them back the faith. Leah
>
> *(FSW P GOV 30–39 F RC)*

It was religiosity, not Christianity, that was the norm for this group of social workers in the Philippines; they expected it in their colleagues and in their service users. When asked if Christian values underlie social work in the Philippines, Marissa commented as follows:

> not just Christian teaching but its universal values about human life and like . . . our colleague in social work, she is Muslim and in their own context, the situation in Mindanao, they are also human beings. They have the concept of whose responsibility is welfare and I would like to respect them and I think that what is good about Filipino social workers . . . we understand that culture as well. Marissa
>
> *(FAC P 50–59 F RC)*

Given this norm and expectation, the lack of religiosity in England – indeed the rejection and exclusion of religiosity in social work practice – was a very significant difference and contrast to the experience of Filipino social workers who came to work in England.

Social work as a vocation: external professional identities

Filipino social workers in England encounter a very different world of social work practice from their home country, but also a different professional ethics and structure attached to social work practice. The role of religious belief in everyday life and practice was the starkest difference encountered, and many participants commented on this dramatic 'culture shock'. For example, a Filipino social worker based in England tellingly reflected upon the acceptability of 'overt' reference to religious practice within social work:

> In my country, if they have a problem, why don't you pray? . . . You can't do it here . . . it's a no-no . . . although I did it once when a person was really, really down and she had no hopes at all this mum and I said maybe it's time for you to pray? I did it once but I was scared to do that at the time. Ella
>
> *(FSW UK 40–49 F C)*

Much was said by participants about the public image of the profession, but this was often couched in religious terms when describing the case of the Philippines:

> In the Philippines, they see you as a saviour. Nina
>
> *(FSW UK 25–29 F RC)*

> They thought you are just like a Good Samaritan or a nun. Ella
>
> *(FSW UK 40–49 F C)*

In contrast, participants in England described practice in much more formal and structured ways. For example:

> In the Philippines, you deal with families . . . but here you don't have that . . . if it's a mental health issue, then you have the . . . mental health social worker . . . it's very, how do you call it, compartmentalised . . . I like this model but then I find it difficult as well because your role is not, is not seen as, as a helping person . . . your role is like managing the case . . . in the Philippines it's different because you are there, you help them, you talk to them, you go to this, you take them there . . . here, you become, you are managing the case and, umm, tapping all these resources . . . every time they ask after we did assessment, did your social worker help you? And they said no because they will not see your role clearly, because they don't know that when I ask somebody to help them, that's my role, that I'm helping them. Grace
>
> *(FSW UK 30–39 F RC)*

Filipino social workers in England, of course, became accultured to their new environment, their new role as social workers and the different relationship they have to service users. They learnt, perhaps, to hide their personal and religious beliefs and to maintain a professional distance that was quite different from that deployed in the Philippines:

> So now I'm more careful with not putting in my own belief in working with families in the Philippines maybe because they're all Filipinos. I can speak straight to them . . . like a mum . . . but here . . . I just don't feel too confident to be, you know, saying those things . . . they would say you're . . . going beyond your boundary . . . I remember a family saying 'You don't tell me what to do with my family because it's my family' and I was thinking but you're asking for some help and I'm . . . just trying to give you the bigger picture . . . it's like giving them one of your arm and then they would still want more. Emily
>
> *(FSW UK 40–49 F RC)*

> If you see the clients outside your office, if you have a chat with them, that's kind of unprofessional. . . . In the Philippines . . . it's alright if they ring you any time. Bridget
>
> *(FSW UK 40–49 F RC)*

In these examples we can see the conflict between the inner conditions that participants expressed in the Philippines – the sense of calling, the role of religious faith in motivating them towards this career and inspiring their everyday practices – and the external and formal aspects of 'vocation' (by which we mean here professional career and occupational structure) in England. Not only did participants describe how they hid and bracketed their religious faith and practices from their colleagues and services users, but they also learnt to enact a professional identity that was actually in conflict with their personal belief system and considerably at odds with how they were used to, and would prefer to be, practising. These examples illustrate the tensions between a mode of practice that the Filipino social workers would have preferred and the strictures that professional identity, role and statutory responsibilities required:

> Yes, like my first child protection . . . my manager said . . . 'when do you think we are going to remove this child? She has a chaotic substance misuse, lifestyle and everything', and I said 'But mum now is engaging . . . why don't we give her a chance?' I can work with them . . . enhancing the social functioning of mum . . . yes this baby needs protection . . . so focus on mum. . . . My manager said 'Alright but you need to have a timeframe'. It goes initially alright but she started undoing everything . . . so I just then have to say 'No I am

not happy with what you are doing'. To the point where I said, alright, if she doesn't meet this one then I would agree that we remove the child. Bridget
(FSW UK 40–49 F RC)

Bridget's line manager was clearly alert to statutory responsibilities and deadlines, which meant responses could not be as fluid as the social worker wanted. Nina explores a similar point:

> I was telling my senior practitioner . . . we normally do this like this . . . and she, she acknowledged that. . . . It's different because it is very statutory. . . .You don't have that flexibility as a worker . . . we are binded with what is statutory and what needs to be done. Nina
>
> *(FSW UK 25–29 F RC)*

Angel talked of having greater freedom to make decisions in the Philippines:

> more freedom in terms of decision-making and that makes you more creative . . . if you have limited resources, it makes you more creative. Angel
>
> *(FSW UK 40–49 F)*

The suggestion was that creativity is stifled by a regulated and proceduralized approach to practice in England. Administrative paperwork and bureaucracy in general were often identified as being one of the biggest differences between social work practice in England and the Philippines. Given these significant differences and, in particular, the need to hide aspects of self and rein back, to say the least, one's creativity, we might expect the Filipino social workers in England to be quite critical of social work practice in England. This was not the case. All Filipino workers in England identified things that provided a sense of job fulfilment or professional worth:

> I think the things that keep me going . . . probably there's a lot . . . there are times when, because I live locally as well . . . you come across your clients and you know, they tell you thank you very much for helping us . . . once that, umm, you've learnt that, umm, your biggest piece of work is to protect the child . . . that's a relief, that's a reward. Third . . . money. You know, I'm able to support my family back home, umm, I manage to assist my brother who basically graduated from a very prestigious university . . . I managed to build a house for my family. Jay
>
> *(FSW UK 30–39 M RC)*

Sheila was motivated to support people in thinking and talking through their difficulties:

> I just feel that, at the end of the week when . . . for example I have a . . . single foster carer who needs to support her grandson because her daughter has

been sectioned . . . so just liaising with the social worker, you know, talking about what is the problem, how can we support this. . . create good outcome. . . . I think those kind of . . . simple things . . . how they appreciate your work, you know, your effort in terms of helping them. Sheila

(FSW UK 40–49 F C)

Sheila, therefore, conveyed satisfaction at using skills of engagement to achieve positive outcomes for people with whom she had developed a relatively trusting relationship. However, also present was a desire to be appreciated and valued. The following worker saw strengths in the approach to child protection in England and had shifted towards a position of deriving satisfaction from small outcomes:

I can see my role now . . . appreciate my role . . . you don't expect a big result but you just appreciate what you can do at that time. Grace

(FSW UK 30–39 F RC)

Grace appeared to have found value in work at a micro level, seeking small changes in behaviour. The following quote also indicates a growing understanding and appreciation of the often one-to-one and 'personalized' form of social work in England:

if a child or a person has disability, they give a lot of attention, which is another difference. . . . Here, I see, social workers they are committed to their work. . . . I really admire their commitment and the other difference is . . . each child has different needs and they try to fit in and identify what kind of appropriate service you could offer them . . . an individual plan, which is really very good. In the Philippines, you know, we cannot . . . if we have children with severe disability and the parents cannot cope, we have an institution for that. . . . That's why, when they say we lack resources, I cannot . . . oh my god, I cannot accept that. Bridget

(FSW UK 40–49 F RC)

Bridget saw real positives in services tailored to individual need but suggested this simply could not be afforded in the Philippines, where families were forced either to 'manage' or 'abandon' their children. Many participants expressed appreciation of the value of well-targeted and well-resourced support for individuals, of supervision and of structured processes for the protection of vulnerable individuals.

Filipino social workers conveyed a strong sense of work as their mission and as a core aspect of their identity in the world. Such indications were, it has to be said, more evident in the data collected in the Philippines than in England. Having said that, it was clear that many of the Filipino social workers in England still maintained the value set and attachment to their profession of their Philippines-based colleagues.

Social work is everyday life and we are privileged. . . . It is a profession that, I would say, that taught me basically what is life. Jay

(FSW UK 30–39 M RC)

Concluding discussion

Does the concept of vocation/calling help us to make sense of social workers' motivations and practices in the Philippines and England? Whilst not in any way exhausting explanations of why individuals entered the profession and how they maintain their professional identities in the Philippines, it certainly conveys significant elements of this. The participants in this study all identified strong inner motivations – a calling – to social work careers and practice that were firmly connected to a sense of obligation and duty, to other-directed values. The role of personal faith in both motivation and practice was palpable in almost all of our participants' self-descriptions of themselves as social workers; in addition, they themselves often used the word 'calling' to explain their world to us. The one worker who identified as 'irreligious' described a very strong calling to advancing forms of social justice.

Similarly, our participants also expressed a firm commitment to a vocation as professional social workers both in the Philippines and in England. The role of social workers and the career structure were significantly different in the two locations, but the connection of external professional identity to career was visible across all our participants. However, it is in considering the transitions between the Philippines and England that social workers experienced that the concept of calling and vocation becomes particularly revealing. It reminds us that motivation towards career is not only pecuniary or authority driven, but is attached to personal and group values; we see the adherence to a value set that is formed in the context of the Philippines being transported into the England social work setting.[5] But the focus on the *Beruf* side of this coupling calling and vocation is most telling. The Filipino social workers who made the transition to England were forced to hide their internal (faith-based) calling and they did this by promoting their external (secular) vocation through a new assumed and ascribed professional identity. They all expressed some degree of difficulty in managing this process – almost a sense of guilt that they needed to do this – but recognized that the exigencies of the society and its institutions that they now inhabited insisted upon it.

Notes

1 Subtle differences in emphasis occur in translating the word 'calling', with its more religious and spiritual overtones, when reading the German *Beruf*, from the deployment of the more secular 'vocation'.

2 The connection between this idea and the anti-capitalism of some of the social movements emerging in this period is quite clear.

3 The Gerth and Mills translation of *Science as a Vocation* is curious in a number of ways and not, it can be argued, particularly accurate. Irving Velody and Peter Lassman's reappraisal of this essay (Lassman and Velody, 1989) included a new translation by Michael John (Weber, 1989).

4 In our previous work we found that such attitudes were still remarkably prevalent amongst scientists working in UK higher education at the turn of the millennium (Erickson, 2002).

5 Further research will benefit from exploring professional identity in relation to the sociology of worth literature. See Sayer, 2005; Stark, 2011.

92 Mark Erickson and Jem Price

References

Almanzor, A. (1966). The Profession of Social Work in the Philippines: Historical Background. *International Social Work*, 9(4): 27–34.
Althusser, L. (1971). *Lenin and Philosophy and Other Essays*. London: NLB.
Baldamus, W. (1961). *Efficiency and Effort: An Analysis of Industrial Administration*. London: Tavistock Publications.
Bauman, Z. (1998). *Work, Consumerism and the New Poor*. Cambridge: Polity.
Bryman, A. (2012). *Social Research Methods* (Fourth edition). Oxford: Oxford University Press.
Casey, C. (1995). *Work, Self and Society: After Industrialism*. London: Routledge.
Cruz, K., Limkin, J., Del Castillo, N., Chua, K., Van Den Brink, R., & Galang, R. (2016). *Philippine Economic Update: Moving Full Speed ahead – Accelerating Reforms to Create more and Better Jobs*. Philippine economic update. Washington, DC: World Bank Group.
Dawson, J. (2005). A History of Vocation: Tracing a Keyword of Work, Meaning, and Moral Purpose. *Adult Education Quarterly*, 55(3): 220–231.
Dik, B. J., & Duffy, R. D. (2009). Calling and Vocation at Work Definitions and Prospects for Research and Practice. *Counseling Psychologist*, 37(3): 424–450.
DSWD. (2009). *Sama-Samang Pagtawid Tungo sa Kaunlaran: 2009 Annual Report*. Quezon City: Department of Social Welfare and Development.
DSWD. (2011). *DSWD Holds Meeting on Kalahi-CIDSS Urban Community-Driven Development (CDD) Project*. Retrieved from http://www.dswd.gov.ph/. (Accessed 11 October 2011).
Erickson, M. (2002). Science as a Vocation in the 21st Century: An Empirical Study of Science Researchers. *Max Weber Studies*, 3(1): 29–52.
Landa Jocano, F. (1980). *Social Work in the Philippines: A Historical Overview*. Quezon City: New Day Publishers.
Lassman, P., & Velody, I. (ed.) (1989). *Max Weber's 'Science as a Vocation'*. London and Boston: Unwin Hyman.
Lee-Mendoza, T. (2008). *Social Welfare and Social Work* (Third edition). Quezon City: Central Books.
Nietzsche, F. W. (1969). *On the Genealogy of Morals*, translated by Walter Kaufmann and R. J. Hollingdale. New York: Random House.
Noon, M., & Blyton, P. (2007). *The Realities of Work* (Third edition). Basingstoke: Palgrave Macmillan.
Price, J. (2014). The Philippines. In C. Aspalter (Ed.), *Social Work in East Asia* (pp. 139–156). Farnham: Ashgate.
Price, J., & Artaraz, K. (2013). Professional 'Imperialism' and Resistance: Social Work in the Philippines. *Trabajo Social Global*, 3(5): 28–53.
Raquiza, M. (2010). On Poverty, Hunger and Employment: Off-Track But Not Without Hope. *Social Welfare and Development Journal*, 4(3): 10–21.
Robson, C. (2011) *Real World Research* (Third edition). Oxford: Blackwell.
Sayer, A. (2005). Class, Moral Worth and Recognition. *Sociology*, December 39(5): 947–963.
Stark, D. (2011). *The Sense of Dissonance: Accounts of Worth in Economic Life*. Princeton: Princeton University Press.
Viloria, E., & Martinez, J. (1987). Growth and Development of Humanitarian Services in the Philippines. In C. Veneracion (Ed.), *Social Work in the Philippines: Tradition and Profession* (pp. 19–28). Manila: PASWI.
Weber, M. (1948a). Politics as a Vocation. In H. H. Gerth & C. W. Mills (Eds.), *From Max Weber: Essays in Sociology* (pp. 77–128). London: Routledge & Kegan Paul.
Weber, M. (1948b). Science as a Vocation. In H. H. Gerth & C. W. Mills (Eds.), *From Max Weber: Essays in Sociology* (pp. 129–156). London: Routledge & Kegan Paul.

Weber, M. (1958). *The Protestant Ethic and the Spirit of Capitalism.* New York: Charles Scribner's Sons.

Weber, M. (1989). Science as a Vocation. In P. Lassman & I. Velody (Eds.), *Max Weber's 'Science as a Vocation'* (pp. 3–31). London: Unwin Hyman.

Willis, P. E. (1977). *Learning to Labour How Working Class Kids Get Working Class Jobs.* Farnborough, HP: Saxon House.

Yu, N. (2006). Ideological Roots of Philippine Social Welfare. *International Social Work,* 49(5): 559–570.

7

RISK WORK IN THE FORMATION OF THE 'PROFESSIONAL' IN CHILD PROTECTION SOCIAL WORK

Emily Keddell and Tony Stanley

Introduction

The domain of child protection is a special context that shapes the professional identities of social workers who work within it. Immersed in a battle over contested content knowledge (such as what 'counts' as child abuse) and performing an ambiguous role (to support struggling families or investigate instances of child abuse), the professional identities of child protection social workers are complex. Shaped by contexts of new public management and the ubiquitous neo-liberal project, ablaze with notions of individualized risk and responsibility, the role of the child protection social worker is negotiated between demands for client surveillance and control, and value-based assertions of the profession. This paradox has led some commentators to ask if child protection work is even social work (Hyslop, 2016; Nicolas, 2015). Emergent child abuse categories like 'radicalization risk' add to this complicated picture and further undermine professional identities of social workers who work in child protection (Haslam, 2016; McKendrick and Finch, 2016; Stanley and Guru, 2015).

What has caused this widening schism between the demands of child protection work and social work as a profession? This chapter explores this growing dichotomy, and the effects on professional identities. We argue that the traditional value base of the profession is required more than ever to ensure social justice and human rights ideals remain interwoven with, and supportive of, professional identities and practice. However, this is not straightforward. An increasing faith in big data, nudge science, and information flow to improve practice and increase child safety reinforces an individualized (thus auditable) view of social problems and solutions. An increasingly harsh and punitive State agenda based on popular understandings of the nature and causes of child abuse also influences professional identities and practice options (Hennum, 2014; Keddell, 2016; Munro, 2004; Parton, 2014). This is an important juncture for the social work project as we struggle to endorse a professional identity based on social justice and human rights ideals.

The PREVENT counterterrorism policy in England, and elements of the child protection reforms in Aotearoa – New Zealand (ANZ) highlight how policy and practice responses to defining and responding to risk categories appear to be narrowing notions of rights and justice, and this affects the purpose, function and identity of social workers. Yet this narrowing of rights is not evenly spread across populations. Waquant (2014) views the differential impact of rights restrictions as evidence of the 'centaur State': increasingly 'free' for those at the top, but for the poor, increasingly restricted forms of life are possible as universal social and economic protections are removed. This contributes to worsening social conditions and a range of emerging social problems relating to those conditions, including child abuse (Waquant, 2014). Further, child protection social workers are encouraged to see themselves as agents of social control increasingly positioned within a widening securitizing State project (Stanley and Guru, 2015; Waterhouse and McGhee, 2016).

In these fraught contexts, how should social workers respond? What is the impact on child protection social work identities operating at this interface? In this chapter we explore the changes afoot in child protection social work, link these to professional identities and show how resistance to 'risk thinking' in narrow and punitive ways may offer an antidote of sorts, to help promote the shared values required for professional identities to be re-imagined into a coherent form of the 'professional' (Beddoe, 2013; Stanford, 2011). Practice leaders play an important role, as they can maintain and promote a relational and humane concept of risk management that is potentially more reflective of the profession's internationally espoused value base.

The contested environment of child protection

Professional identities are developed within a particular social milieu that relies on the development and maintenance of social capital (Bourdieu, 1986). The development of this capital requires a number of different components to be present. Beddoe (2010) describes these as:

> The key attributes of professional capital of any given profession within its social milieu include: being trusted by users of professional services, key stakeholders and other professions; having congruent values within the profession; having mutually rewarding relationships with other professional groups . . . holding a sense of collective identity and 'self-esteem'; a clear and understood knowledge-claim for practice . . . and finally, visibility in the public discourse for its distinctive contribution to social well-being.
>
> *(105–106)*

Many of these attributes are contested and complex for child protection social workers. Suspiciously viewed by service users if they have not proven themselves trustworthy and genuine (Spratt and Callan, 2004), they often see themselves as inferior to other professionals, while working in a context where media attention to child deaths constantly vilifies them or holds them publically, and personally, responsible (Beddoe and Harington, 2015). Social workers can experience dissonance between the values of the profession and the actual control roles they must perform. Their knowledge claims for practice, based on contested definitions of child abuse, notions of family functioning, child development, 'good-enough parenting' and effective solutions, all challenge the development of a clear consensus on their knowledge base (Cradock, 2014; Wattam, 1999). Due to this contested territory, child protection social workers may lack the attributes required for a strong sense of professional identity, instead leaving them vulnerable to an ambivalent sense of identity (Beddoe, 2013).

Risk, policy orientations and the 'neo-liberal child client'

The broader political environment impacts on the identities of child protection social workers. The pervasive individualization of social problems common in neo-liberal contexts affects practitioners and clients alike (Keddell, 2016; Waquant, 2014). Practitioners are expected to accept individual responsibility for the behaviour not only of themselves, but also of their clients, despite extensive scholarship on the uncertainties of predicting future harm to children and the need for systems, not individual practitioners, to be structured in ways that support good decision making (Munro, 2011; Munro, Taylor, and Bradbury-Jones, 2014; Parton, 1998). The continued expansion of the 'risk society' – one concerned with mitigating and responding to perceived risk – encourages a greater surveillance of professions charged with managing 'risky' populations, particularly those in the child welfare domain (Beddoe, 2010). Clients themselves are also 'responsibilized' to accept the construction of being a good citizen as one who accepts responsibility for oneself in all domains of life (Wilson, 2011). To resist this, or fail within it, is to be perceived as deviant and irresponsible (Rose, 2000). Help seeking or requiring support are pathologized within this broad policy dogma, despite various social work practice models promoting both as normal aspects of family life (Sanders and Munford, 2010).

One result of defining risk in individualistic ways is the magnification of the child as an individual rights holder, to the exclusion of all other considerations. This downplays the influence of social structural conditions on the life chances of children, the realities of their enmeshment and reliance on their social relationships, and diminishes the rights of parents (Bywaters, Brady, Sparks, and Bos, 2014). Their role is perceived as purely instrumental, that is, to perform as 'good parent'. There is no 'legitimate dependence' for them (Featherstone, White, and Morris, 2014; Peacock, Bissell, and Owen, 2014). The recent 'social investment' paradigm' of both the UK and ANZ further exacerbates this tendency. Drawing on neo-liberal 'price theory economics' of Gary Becker, who viewed the family as a "marriage market" (1974), children are viewed as worthy of State investment due to their future economic usefulness (Expert Panel, 2015a). Thus, risks are viewed as the immediate risk of harm, in addition to the long-term risk of lack of productivity, and both are perceived within the realm and control of direct parental responsibility. Instead of conceptualizing risk as the risk of unmet family needs or structural conditions such as poverty, thinking of risk as abusive acts from parent to child – and the cause of that being simply poor parental choices and behaviour – limits the scope of practice responses to investigatory and punitive responses (Bywaters et al., 2014).

In turn, a focus on the child in individual terms fundamentally affects the relationship of the State to the family. By focusing on specific acts towards the child, or long-term poor outcomes, the family becomes circumnavigated as a legitimate recipient of State support for either their own needs to be met, or rights upheld. Parents are viewed instead as sources of risk to children, and the child's needs are dichotomized with those of their parents (Featherstone et al., 2014). The shrinking of State responsibility in favour of individual responsibility has occurred for all but the child. Only the innocent child, full of future potential that must be protected, is worthy of State protection. In this way, neo-liberal contexts form the basis of a 'neo-liberal child-client' in need of ongoing State focus and attention, divided from the needs or interests of the family (Featherstone et al., 2014).

An emerging child-focused orientation, couched in terms of children's long-term well-being, often coalesces with a social investment policy logic. Gilbert et al. (2011) also note that the emerging child-focused orientation takes different forms in different countries. When implemented within a broadly neo-liberal macro-political context, one that construes the proper role of the State to concern itself with economic productivity rather than the welfare of citizens across their lifespan, then the convergence of a focus on the child and social investment contributes to an uneasy separation in regards to the 'deservingness' of parents and children. Children are construed as worthy of protection from ineffectual or abusive parents, and in light of their potential cost to the State over their lifespan if they are exposed to a range of risk factors, they are deemed deserving of State investment. Thus, the child protection project has legitimacy to intervene in service of social investment outcomes.

Such a separation of the worthiness of parents and children creates problems in practice, as it influences how risk comes to be seen, and this, in turn, influences how professional identities are seen and experienced. The problem for social workers is that professional communication about risk, within the child-focused–social investment context, tends to be couched in rather narrow thinking about available options for the neo-liberal child-client. The problem for families is that the child becomes the site of activity and professional gaze, resulting in responses and decision making aimed narrowly at the child. This happens, for example, in professionals' meetings that relegate parents and caregivers as problems to be resolved, rather than rights holders or bearers of needs, capacities and capabilities in their own right (Gupta, Featherstone, and White, 2016). Understanding this dynamic invites a closer examination of the institutional context wherein professional cultures and power relationships play out, and where recorded case records contribute to what we understand to be the professional social work task.

Institutional ethnography

According to Smith (2005), texts, reports, policy documents and guidance notes found in everyday work settings offer ways for us to understand how everyday work is arranged, organized and carried out. Political, professional and personal relations interact in complex ways, so understanding how this affects and shapes everyday work practice is important. The aim of institutional ethnography (IE) is to move beyond descriptions of everyday life to expose the ways in which people come to understand everyday tasks of work that are often imbued within organizational and professional power relations (McGibbon, Peter, and Gallop, 2010). IE begins by looking at the day-to-day operations of work carried out in institutions. Next, the antecedents of these work-based activities are explored – including organizational texts, guidelines, procedure manuals and polices. This offers empirical evidence that links social workers, families, managers, administrators, case records and other artefacts to the task of social work. This way we can see how work practices are connected to wider agendas that serve to set up the social work experience. An IE exploration helps us to understand why some children receive particular responses while others get a different response, by examining the documents and framing practices used to construct their problems and the procedures associated with given solutions.

The PREVENT policy and professional practice

Understanding the institutional context helps us to examine the ways that political tropes play out via institutional mechanisms to produce risk constructs in child protection contexts. By considering the neo-liberal child client, influenced by child protection and child-focused 'social investment' concepts, in the context of institutional machinations, we can trace the impact of risk discourses on practice. These concepts will now be discussed in relation to specific policy developments.

In England, the PREVENT policy and guidance, first developed by the Home Office in 2003, is aimed at targeting those at risk of being radicalized or becoming terrorists. This explicit focus on individuals encourages particular ways of thinking about risk and service users, and it promotes a narrow range of theoretical lenses through which to view both. A psychologizing effect has emerged in which the person deemed at risk of radicalization is offered an individual programme of help (mostly this involves psychological interventions to help de-radicalize). This is problematic for social workers because we consider people in context and regard family, friends and networks as possible sites of support, resources or help. Instead, the current policy and practice approaches linked to PREVENT are based solely and firmly at the individual level: thus the site of risk and the site of intervention to 'fix' rests at the individual child client. As Heath-Kelly (2013) notes, PREVENT is unstable in simultaneously presenting 'vulnerability indicators' for radicalization as threats to the wider collective; these conducts are framed as both 'at risk' and 'risky', both vulnerable and dangerous (394). This response also contains uneasy tensions around the balance between religious freedom and State punishment or control of criminal behaviour. Considering radical religious views as evidence of psychopathology that must be 'fixed' in the absence of committed actions or crime is now being constructed as a child protection issue, and with that, an expectation that child protection social workers will identify and provide a solution to the risk of radicalization or extremism (Stanley and Guru, 2015).

Data sharing is an essential and legitimized part of counterterrorist work. Mostly this means police seek information about particular families from social workers. An IE approach to this area of work illuminates how the guidance and data sharing serves State intelligence-gathering purposes to further maintain surveillance over particular families. Social workers provide police collegial information in the name of 'helping' while ignoring the rights of families in terms of the information being shared. The guidance sets up a path to work collaboratively inter-professionally and the practice follows. This constructs the professional identities of social workers as more closely aligned with the role of the security state to search out and punish those deemed deviant, sorely challenging the historical alliance of social work with social activism, social justice and radical traditions. Further, the issues concerned with privacy and confidentiality are brushed aside as the unassailable evocation of counterterrorism and child rescue are used to offer powerful legitimation of these processes without debate regarding possible negative effects or limits.

A brief practice illustration highlights this point. At a local authority in London, a senior social worker took it upon herself to search for and 'hunt down' a family suspected of travelling to Syria, and she tried to identify wider family networks from limited police intelligence and social media sites. The role and identity of the professional social worker has changed because new legitimate activities are now promoted to interrupt radicalization. Human rights and social justice ideals are overridden and ignored – no longer considered part of the social work task. An ethic of care is absent. What about the rights of family members being flagrantly ignored in the name of helping? The worker argued with one of the chapter's authors that 'protecting the children', irrespective of the rights of family members, legitimized her belief in her investigative role as the 'professional' social worker. She amassed a file on the father and his family and passed this to counterterrorism police. In the name of helping, the 'good professional' can very easily disregard professional ethics. In fact, in these cases there is active encouragement from other state agencies to do just that. The firm interface that made social work complementary but different to policing and the security services is now porous and leaky.

Child protection reforms in ANZ

The second example of changes in the ways risk is conceptualized is embedded in some aspects of the ANZ child protection reforms of 2011–2016. Reforms include the white paper on vulnerable children, the Vulnerable Children's Act 2014, the Children's Action Plan, and the recent Child Youth and Family review (Government, NZ, 2012; Expert Panel, 2015a, 2015b; Ministry of Social Development,

2012; NZ Government, 2015; Vulnerable Children's Act, 2014). Together, these incorporate an immense range of changes touching every aspect of the child welfare system, from restructuring the main child protection agency to provide a 'single point of accountability' across preventive and intervention services; to greater provisions for children in care both before and after exiting care; and to increased emphasis on the concepts of trauma and attachment (of the child) as guiding theoretical underpinnings (Expert Panel, 2015a). There is also increased attention to the safety checking of individuals employed to work with children at every level, attempts to universalize a set of knowledges or 'core competencies' required for all who work with children, and the creation of inter-professional children's teams to engage with families who are high-need but do not meet the threshold for statutory intervention. Also featuring strongly is an emphasis on increasing information sharing, database building and data developments such as predictive risk modelling, with the reasoning being that in child death cases, the lack of information sharing was a key aspect of the downfall of services to prevent the death. Little discussion of the impacts on privacy of these reforms outside of government has taken place (Keddell, 2015b; Mclean, 2015).

Across these developments, the focus on the child – using the language of 'the vulnerable child', or the need to be 'child-focused' – dominates, and despite the mention of parents feeling marginalized in the final Child Youth and Family (CYF) review report (2016), it showed minimal inclusion of parents either in the reconstruction of advocacy or the actual provision of services (Blumhardt, 2016). While there may be some increase in preventive family services available, the Children's Teams, for example, have no extra resources for direct work with families; rather, their effect is assumed to be in the sharing of information and working collaboratively. Likewise, no mention of the impact of poverty and inequalities are mentioned, effectively severing this known influence on the development of child abuse and other types of harm from the public or policy narrative regarding the causes and consequences of child abuse (Bywaters et al., 2016). Instead, methods of surveillance and information sharing have been foregrounded. For example, the need for practitioners to meet extensive new 'safety checking' requirements, and organizations to have child protection policies in place, take up the bulk of the Vulnerable Children's Act 2014, despite much of the basics such as police checking, identity verification and child protection reporting policies already being in place for most agencies and professions working with children. The use of integrated data sets across the health, justice and social sectors increasingly generate extensive knowledge about the combinations of risk factors that lead to poor social and economic outcomes, with some efforts made to apply this down to the level of individuals (Crichton, Templeton, and Tumen, 2015; Wilson, Tumen, Ota, and Simmers, 2015). English described this as a 'data highway' and suggests that 'government workers' can get "access to it, even on their smartphones, so they can draw information on people from multiple sources before making decisions that affect them" (English, 2016).

Creation of a vulnerable child's information system, for information sharing about those deemed vulnerable, is also under way. This database will allow a range of professionals to electronically record and share data about the same family. Importantly, access to this database will be for a wider range of practitioners beyond the statutory services, and comes with a lowered legal threshold (Ministry of Social Development, 2014). The threshold for sharing this information has been reduced from the legislated one of harm or risk of harm to the promotion of 'safety and well-being' (Ministry of Social Development, 2014). The types of information allowed to be shared in pursuit of the latter includes information such as families' financial circumstances, parental mental illness, parental substance abuse, parental history of domestic violence and information about a child's 'current and previous well-being' (New Zealand Government, 2015, s.7[1]). Both types of data sharing – integrated data sets relating to the whole population, and specific databases relating to those deemed vulnerable – have significant implications for how privacy, rights, justice and risk are understood and applied in professional practice, and with it, the construction of the 'good professional'.

Information flow and the seduction of 'big data'

In Western systems of child welfare, the increasing use of big data to define and develop child protection policy has been going on for some time, enabled by the integration of many types of administrative data into integrated data sets that can be used for multiple purposes. However, the use of big data sets as an aid to decision making in the child protection context has considerable drawbacks. In such a context, risk quantifiers – such as the 'risk scores' proposed in predictive risk modelling – can become reified as an accurate way of determining risk. Practitioners in high-stress work contexts tend to rely on these seemingly objective numerical quantifiers. This can occur despite the reproduction of biases and the variability of substantiation decisions that are recorded in child protection data used to develop predictive models. Predictive models also have limited accuracy, producing large amounts of both false positives and false negatives (Keddell, 2015a). For example, in the ANZ model, in the top 10% of risk, the predictive model proposed has 25% predictive accuracy; that is, 25% of those predicted in the top 10% of risk were substantiated in the child protection system within 5 years, while 75% were not (Wilson et al., 2015).

Within the broader neo-liberal social work environments governed by logics of accountability, new public managerialism and audit following these numeric quantifiers easily becomes equated with 'good practice; in turn, the use of them may become essential to the professional subjectivities rewarded in that context. McQuillan (2015) notes that the identification of particular individuals or populations via algorithms is increasingly used to guide policies or other forms of governance. When used to inform policy, these risk scores or deciles can create differential categories of people, and with them, differential levels of rights: "That is, the ordinary rules guaranteeing universal protections, for example the right to privacy, can be considered not so applicable to those individuals or groups" (2015: 4). The exception of such groups and individuals from normal legal protections is deemed acceptable, with implications for issues such as ethical practice and State intrusion on family life. McQuillan refers to this as an 'algocracy'. Notions of rights, justice and humane practice in social work are highly contested; a certain type of professional is encouraged; and the identity of the 'securitizing' social worker has emerged.

Risk work and identity work

How does all this impact on professional identities? It is widely accepted that those who do risk work (Horlick-Jones, 2005), such as social workers, can construct those who become associated with risk as calculable, governable and controllable. In both the examples given, this impetus is driving the logics of risk work in practice. The construction of risk as a calculable object enables and legitimates the identification of risks in a manner that offers legitimacy to statutory interventions, and with it, the powerful child protection social worker. Attempts to get things right and avoid a tragedy can drive the ways that 'risky' behaviour is defined in practice, and those methods that promise surety (however erroneous) can be used to ward off the anxiety provoked by fears of getting it wrong in an environment where individual blame is commonplace. When a child is killed at the hands of the family that is supposed to love him or her, it is social work that is condemned, and this in turn produces a precautionary and defensive approach to professional risk work (Alaszewski and Burgess, 2007). Pollack (2010) points out that "The impact of risk in health and social policy promotes a greater emphasis on the defensibility of decisions rather than making good decisions" (1274).

With the narrowing of risk and increasing emphasis on surveillance in the two examples of London and New Zealand described earlier comes continuing threats to the maintenance of coherent identity capital for child protection social workers based on the values of the profession. In many jurisdictions, well-intentioned reforms continually fail to offer wholesale change that could maximize the possibility for coherent professional identities for child protection social workers. Serious case reviews are now published in full in England; this will undoubtedly shape practice messages for staff about doing things right rather than doing the right thing. Practice recommendations emerging from one type of case can become the custom for every case. The implications for not following procedures is always significant when a tragedy happens, and while it is incredibly rare that parents or carers kill or seriously harm their children, social workers understand that not following rules and procedural dictates will invite blame if something goes wrong. Understandably, then, social workers are likely to err on the side of caution and develop risk-averse ways. According to Dartington (2010), the emphasis on targets and audit has made humane practice more difficult to deliver and maintain. Professional identities are easily colonized by an attitude to risk that is anathema to the relational, egalitarian values of the profession (Keddell, 2015b; Keddell and Stanley, 2015).

In the policy developments in England and New Zealand, the explicit focus on surveillance, the individualization of children and the responsibilization of practitioners and parental clients alike operates to narrow the focus and aim of intervention. It seems these developments embody what Parton has called the "surveillance investment state" (Parton, 2010), or what Featherstone et al. (2014) have called the movement from "screen to intervene". The role of social workers and their professional identities are increasingly fraught as the child protection worker role, always historically conflicted, becomes increasingly caught up with State identification, investigation and sanction.

Practice leadership – resistance to the drive for certainty

Practice leadership offers the potential to challenge risk-aversive, securitizing and narrowing practice identities. While practice leaders should not be valorized to the point of the unrealistic expectations of a "moral hero" (Marston and McDonald, 2012), nevertheless they are important actors within organizational hierarchies who can shape the parameters and tone of organizational cultures, including how an organization manages risk. One author of this chapter is the Chief Social Worker for Birmingham City – and the public face of social work for the organization. Principal social workers are located inside most English local authorities, with Chief Social Work officers in Scottish local authorities (Stanley and Russell, 2014). Promoting professional identity is a key function of the role. His agency is paying explicit attention to the ways that risk work affects and shapes identity. Helping managers understand how practice is influenced by contextual and discursive messaging is a key part of his work. Being aware of the wider contextual and cultural influences that are shaping risk-averse decision making helps to open up our thinking about risk, and the contribution that practice leaders need to make. This is important for management practice, because managers often rely on written reports about casework. Risk work then is based on paper records and verbal presentations by the social workers, who themselves may be drifting toward a more securitized understanding of the role. Defaulting to risk scores by risk factor counting happens. This tendency to view risk as definable and then manageable tends to be uncritically encouraged and promoted, often presented back to families with their acceptance required. The practice of challenging how risk work is undertaken requires engagement by managers in the intellectual *and* moral tasks of social work. An understanding of risk as existing within relational and spatial contexts within a complex human environment, like a workplace, encourages thinking that is less linear, less one-dimensional.

> Risky situations arise as the results of interplay within a non-linear complex adaptive system and not through a simple cause and effect process. Yet most risk assessment technologies are predicated on the flawed assumption that crises arise from linear cause and effect.
>
> *(Stevens and Hassett, 2012: 504)*

Practice leaders need to be research minded, and IE provides a sound foundation for understanding the complexity of workplace contexts. Promoting notions of humane, just and rights-based practice needs an understanding of how risk work happens. The promotion of practice judgments as socially mediated and positioned activities that incorporate a range of knowledges helps to open up our thinking. Promoting professional practice and creating the best workplaces where professional identities can flourish is a key role for practice leaders.

Concluding discussion

The context of child protection shapes professional identities in social work. Within neo-liberal environments that separate the child from the family, child protection policy orientations are laden with the logic of social investment in heavily bureaucratized workplaces. The uses of technical approaches to risk production appear as logical tools for the tracking and monitoring of client and professional behaviour. If the professional has not behaved in ways felt to align with objective 'facts' about an individual client, then that person can be sanctioned and his or her professional identity can be challenged. As Latour (2005) notes, "matters of fact" quickly become "matters of concern". For social workers in child protection, this shapes professional identities towards preferred 'credible performances' as 'one who can perform and adhere to risk scores' or other technical or highly selective 'risk' knowledge about a family, rather than one who can draw on that knowledge as one aspect of a wide range of types of knowledge that inform a professional judgement (see Chapter 14 in this book). Individualized, narrow and technical ways of defining risk are particularly appealing within new public management and neo-liberal contexts. Given the unstable position of social work as a legitimate profession, this ability to produce oneself as holding particular technical and scientific knowledge may be especially appealing as a way to shore up a strong professional identity claim.

Algocracy is increasingly influencing our professional identities, with little debate so far. This is accepted in the name of efficiency savings so that scarce resources can be better targeted to identify and help families. But information flow through predictive risk modelling machinery holds little safeguards for the human rights of people under discussion or suspicion (Keddell, 2015a). The PREVENT policy legitimates information sharing between social services and police services, and the role of social work in this explicit forensic investigatory function is accepted. These developments should alarm us and cause a rethinking of the role and profession of social work in these times. We need a social work system in which social and family networks are invited in and social risk methods of help are drawn on to drive our work. The family group conference is a good example. Social and non-linear models of risk are emerging (Featherstone et al., 2014) in which the widening of risk understandings related to material contexts and inequalities open up new understandings of what it means to do and be a relational social worker (Stevens and Hassett, 2012). Safety-oriented models that begin from accepting the premise of 'most families keep their children safe most of the time' also show promise (Turnell,

2008). The professional identity of social workers will continue to be contested. However, it's clear that we should encourage the reclaiming of an identity related to relational practice, human rights and critical analysis of the broader social conditions. The most vulnerable in society deserve nothing less.

References

Alaszewski, A., & Burgess, A. (2007). Risk, Time and Reason. *Health, Risk & Society*, 9(4): 349–358.

Becker, G. (1974). A Theory of Marriage. In T. W. Schulz (Ed.), *Economics of the Family: Marriage, Children, and Human Capital* (pp. 299–351). Chicago: University of Chicago Press.

Beddoe, L. (2010). Surveillance or Reflection: Professional Supervision in 'the Risk Society'. *British Journal of Social Work*, 40(4): 1279–1296. doi: 10.1093/bjsw/bcq018.

Beddoe, L. (2013). Health Social Work: Professional Identity and Knowledge. *Qualitative Social Work*, 12(1): 24–40. doi: 10.1177/1473325011415455.

Beddoe, L., & Harington, P. (2015). Social Work Aotearoa New Zealand: Social Policy, Risk and Professionalisation. In G. Palattiyil, D. Sidhva & M. Chakrabarti (Eds.), *Social Work in a Global Context: Issues and Challenges* (pp. 27–38). London: Routledge.

Blumhardt, H. (2016, May 6). How Could Parents Be Supported to Have a Voice in Cyf's Processes? Retrieved from http://www.reimaginingsocialwork.nz/.

Bourdieu, P. (1986). The Forms of Capital. In J. Richardson (Ed.), *Handbook of Theory and Research for the Sociology of Education* (pp. 241–258), translated by R. Nice. New York: Greenwood Press.

Bywaters, P., Brady, G., Sparks, T., & Bos, E. (2014). Child Welfare Inequalities: New Evidence, Further Questions. *Child & Family Social Work*, 21(3). doi: 10.1111/cfs.12154.

Bywaters, P., Bunting, L., Davidson, G., Hanratty, J., Mason, W., McCartan, C., & Steils, N. (2016). *The Relationship between Poverty, Child Abuse and Neglect: An Evidence Review*. Coventry: Joseph Rountree Foundation.

Cradock, G. (2014). Who Owns Child Abuse? *Social Sciences*, 3(4): 854–870. doi: 10.3390/socsci3040854.

Crichton, S., Templeton, R., & Tumen, S. (2015). *Using Integrated Administrative Data to Understand Children at Risk of Poor Outcomes as Young Adults* (Vol. Analytical Paper 15/01). Wellington: New Zealand Treasury.

English, B. (2016) Government Data Highway Could Change Vulnerable Kiwis Lives. *Stuff*. Retrieved from http://www.stuff.co.nz/national/politics/79078930/government-data-highway-could-change-vulnerable-kiwis-lives--bill-english.

Expert Panel. (2015a). *Expert Panel Final Report: Investing in New Zealand's Children and Their Families*. Wellington: Ministry of Social Development.

Expert Panel. (2015b). *Modernising Child Youth and Family Expert Panel Interim Report*. Wellington: Ministry of Social Development.

Featherstone, B., White, S., & Morris, K. (2014). *Re-imagining Child Protection: Towards Humane Social Work with Families*. Bristol, UK: Policy Press.

Gilbert, N., Parton, N., & Skivenes, M. (2011). *Child Protection Systems: International Trends and Orientations*. Oxford: Oxford University Press.

Government, N. Z. (2012). *Children's Action Plan: Identifying, Supporting and Protecting Vulnerable Children*. Wellington, NZ: NZ Government.

Gupta, A., Featherstone, B., & White, S. (2016). Reclaiming Humanity: From Capacities to Capabilities in Understanding Parenting in Adversity. *British Journal of Social Work*, 46(2): 339–354. doi: 10.1093/bjsw/bcu137.

Haslam, N. (2016). Concept Creep: Psychology's Expanding Concepts of Harm and Pathology. *Psychological Inquiry*, 27(1): 1–17. doi: 10.1080/1047840X.2016.1082418.

Heath-Kelly, C. (2013). Counter-Terrorism and the Counterfactual: Producing the 'Radicalisation' Discourse and the UK PREVENT Strategy. *The British Journal of Politics and International Relations*, 15(3): 394–415.

Hennum, N. (2014). Developing Child-Centered Social Policies: When Professionalism Takes Over. *Social Sciences*, 3(3): 441–459.

Horlick-Jones,T. (2005). On Risk Work: Professional Discourse and Everyday Action. *Health Risk and Society*, 7(3): 293–307.

Hyslop, I. (2016). Social Work and Social Justice:A Relationship at a Cross-Roads? 7 March. Retrieved from http://www.reimaginingsocialwork.nz/2016/03/social-work-and-social justice-a-relationship-at-a-cross-roads/.

Keddell, E. (2015a). The Ethics of Predictive Risk Modelling in the Aotearoa/New Zealand Child Welfare Context: Child Abuse Prevention or Neo-Liberal Tool? *Critical Social Policy*, 35(1): 69–88.

Keddell, E. (2015b, June 4). Predictive Risk Modelling: On Data, Rights and Politics. Retrieved from http://www.reimaginingsocialwork.nz/2015/06/predictive-risk-modelling-on rights-data-and-politics/.

Keddell, E., & Stanley, T. (2015). Moving from Risk to Safety: Work with Children and Families in Child Welfare Contexts. In K. van Heugten & A. Gibbs (Eds.), *Social Work for Sociologists: Theory and Practice* (pp. 67–84). New York, NY: Palgrave Macmillan.

Keddell, E. (2016). Child Protection Reform and Welfare Reform in Aotearoa New Zealand: Two Sides of the Same Coin? In J. Maidment & E. Beddoe (Eds.), *Social Policy for Social Work and Human Services in Aotearoa New Zealand: Diverse Perspectives* (pp. 27–36). Christchurch: Canterbury University Press.

Latour, B. (2005). *Reassembling the Social: An Introduction to Social Life*. Oxford: Oxford University Press.

Marston, G., & McDonald, C. (2012). Getting beyond 'Heroic Agency' in Conceptualising Social Workers as Policy Actors in the Twenty-First Century. *British Journal of Social Work*, 42(6), 1022–1038. doi: 10.1093/bjsw/bcs062.

McGibbon, E., Peter, E., & Gallop, R.(2010).An Institutional Ethnography of Nurses' Stress. *Qualitative Health Research*, 20(10): 1353–1378. doi: 10.1177/1049732310375435.

McKendrick, D., & Finch, J. (2016). 'Under Heavy Manners?': Social Work, Radicalisation, Troubled Families and Non-Linear War. *British Journal of Social Work*. doi: 10.1093/bjsw/bcv141.

McLean, E. (2015, January 7). Transparent Public Service Remains a Rarity, *Otago Daily Times*.

McQuillan, D. (2015). Algorithmic States of Exception. *European Journal of Cultural Studies*, 18(4–5): 564–576.

Ministry of Social Development. (2012). *The White Paper for Vulnerable Children: Children's Action Plan: Identifying, Supporting and Protecting Vulnerable Children* (Vol. 1). Wellington: NZ Government.

Ministry of Social Development. (2014). *Consultation Paper: Children's Action Plan Approved Information Sharing Agreement.*Wellington: Minsitry of Social Development.

Munro, E. (2004).The Impact of Audit on Social Work Practice. *British Journal of Social Work*, 34(8): 1075–1095. doi: 10.1093/bjsw/bch130.

Munro, E. (2011). *The Munro Review of Child Protection: Final Report, a Child-Centred System*. England:The Stationary Office Limited.

Munro, E.,Taylor, J. S., & Bradbury-Jones, C. (2014). Understanding the Causal Pathways to Child Maltreatment: Implications for Health and Social Care Policy and Practice. *Child Abuse Review*, 23(1): 61–74. doi: 10.1002/car.2266.

New Zealand Government. (2015) Information Sharing Agreement for Improving Public Services for Vulnerable Children. Retrieved from http://www.legislation.govt.nz/regulation/public/2015/0162/latest/DLM6512774.html.

Nicolas, J. (2015). Why Pretend Social Work Is about Social Justice? It's not, *Guardian*. October, 20th. https://www.theguardian.com/social-care-network/2015/oct/20/why-pretend-social-work-is-about-social-justice-its-not

Parton, N. (1998). Risk, Advanced Liberalism and Child Welfare: The Need to Rediscover Uncertainty and Ambiguity. *British Journal of Social Work*, 28(1): 5–27.

Parton, N. (2010). 'From Dangerousness to Risk': The Growing Importance of Screening and Surveillance Systems for Safeguarding and Promoting the Well-being of Children in England. *Health, Risk & Society*, 12(1): 51–64. doi: 10.1080/13698570903508697.

Parton, N. (2014). Social Work, Child Protection and Politics: Some Critical and Constructive Reflections. *British Journal of Social Work*, 44(7): 2042–2056. doi: 10.1093/bjsw/bcu091.

Peacock, M., Bissell, P., & Owen, J. (2014). Dependency Denied: Health Inequalities in the Neo-Liberal Era. *Social Science & Medicine*, 118: 173–180. doi: http://dx.doi.org/10.1016/j.socscimed.2014.08.006.

Pollack, S. (2010). Labelling Clients 'Risky': Social Work and the Neo-liberal Welfare State *British Journal of Social Work*, 40(4): 1263–1278.

Rose, N. (2000). Government and Control. *British Journal of Criminology*, 40(2): 321–339.

Sanders, J., & Munford, R. (2010). *Working with Families: Strengths-Based Approaches.* Wellington: Dunmore Publishing.

Smith, D. E. (2005). *Institutional Ethnography: A Sociology for People.* Lanham: Alta-Mira Press.

Spratt, T., & Callan, J. (2004). Parents' Views on Social Work Interventions in Child Welfare Cases. *British Journal of Social Work*, 34(2): 199–224. doi: 10.1093/bjsw/bch022.

Stanford, S. (2011). Constructing Moral Responses to Risk: A Framework for Hopeful Social Work Practice. *British Journal of Social Work*, 41(8): 1514–1531.

Stanley, T. & Russell, M. (2014). The Principal Child and Family Social Worker: A Munro Recommendation in Practice. *Practice Social Work in Action,* 26(2): 81–96.

Stanley, T., & Guru, S. (2015). Childhood Radicalisation Risk: An Emerging Practice Issue. *Practice*, 27(5): 353–366. doi: 10.1080/09503153.2015.1053858.

Stevens, I., & Hassett, P. (2012). Non-Linear Perspectives of Risk in Social Care: Using Complexity Theory and Social Geography to Move the Focus from Individual Pathology to the Complex Human Environment. *European Journal of Social Work*, 15(4): 503–513. doi: 10.1080/13691457.2012.702309.

Turnell, A. (2008). *Adoption of Signs of Safety as the Department for Child Protection's Child Protection Practice Framework.* Perth: Government of Western Australia.

Vulnerable Children's Act. (2014). New Zealand Government, Ministry of Social Development and the Ministry of Education.

Waquant, L. J. D. (2014). Marginality, Ethnicity and Penality in the Neo-liberal City: An Analytic Cartography. *Ethnic and Racial Studies*, 37(10): 1686–1686. doi: 10.1080/01419870.2014.931996.

Waterhouse, L., & McGhee, J. (2016). Agamben and the Political Positioning of Child Welfare-Involved Mothers in Child Protective Services. *Families, Relationships and Societies*, 5(1): 97–108.

Wattam, C. (1999). The Prevention of Child Abuse. *Children & Society*, 13(4): 317–329. doi: 10.1002/CHI568.

Wilson, M. L., Tumen, S., Ota, R., & Simmers, A. G. (2015). Predictive Modeling: Potential Application in Prevention Services. *American Journal of Preventive Medicine*, 48(5): 509–519. doi: http://dx.doi.org/10.1016/j.amepre.2014.12.003.

Wilson, T. (2011). Embodied Liability: The Usefulness of 'At-Risk Youth'. *Canadian Social Work Review*, 28(1): 49–59.

8

IDENTITY FORMATION, SCIENTIFIC RATIONALITY AND EMBODIED KNOWLEDGE IN CHILD WELFARE

Melissa Hardesty

Introduction

"Ugh! I got another random sample," Liz exclaimed as she took a break from her once-a-week niche role in post-adoption work to check her voicemail. It was late on a Monday afternoon, and workers were trying to wrap up at least some of the never-ending series of tasks that comprised their jobs in child welfare before heading home. Liz was one of five people on the adoption team at Kids First, a private, state-contracted social service agency in the Midwestern United States. "Random samples," as workers called them, were part of a state Department of Child Welfare (DCW) research project to determine how their foster care workers, a dispersed but highly regulated legion of service providers, were spending their time. Within this restrictive context, workers were expected to respond to random sample phone calls immediately upon receipt and report what they were doing at the exact time of the contact.

Random samples were a minor but irksome task for the hurried practitioner sorting through her voicemail while dropping into the office between home visits and court appointments. When workers missed the phone call, as they often did, they usually received a follow-up e-mail, adding to the urgency of the original demand. In a context where workers were always on the go and unlikely to spend a lot of time at their desks, the random sample sought details that were difficult to recall and categorize. This was especially true for Liz on this particular day. The adoption team at Kids First was explicitly and proudly a team of professional social workers, meaning that all workers had to have a Master of Social Work degree, and they managed a much broader range of tasks than most front-line foster care workers. This is why Liz was digging through archived adoption files from the 1950s and 1960s to write reports for late-middle-aged adoptees looking for information about their birth parents. It also explains the difficulty she had communicating with the random sample researcher. That day's tasks were unusual in a job field marked by increasing standardization and audit-friendly accountability measures. In my field notes for the day, I transcribed the phone call:"These are clients who have closed files," Liz explained. "My job includes a post-adopt component . . . some of them were in foster care, but I don't know if this case was one or not," she continued. The short call was punctuated by starts and interruptions, subtly marking the process through which the random sample researcher codified a situated social interaction as a legible and measurable category of activity.

The research methodology guiding DCW's project – its random nature and its aim to categorize caseworker activities and make generalizable knowledge claims from afar – offers a window into the exacting, scientific models increasingly used to generate knowledge about and shape the provision of child welfare services under the umbrella of approaches such as evidence-based practice and continuous quality improvement (Collins-Camargo, Ensign, and Flaherty, 2008; Gambrill, 1999; Gambrill and Shlonsky, 2001; Webb, 2001). Indeed, the social work profession has increasingly begun to rally around "science" as the most effective and morally defensible mode of achieving social change (Brekke, 1986, 2012; Gambrill, 1999). A quote from a video created by the American Academy of Social Work and Social Welfare as part of The Grand Challenges for Social Work initiative is illustrative: "To achieve a just and cohesive society, we must create social change that can be measured, scaled, and sustained: social progress powered by science" (AASWSW, 2016). The Grand Challenges for Social Work dubs itself a "groundbreaking initiative," though appeals to science as the linchpin of social work legitimacy and effectiveness date at least as far back as Mary Richmond's 1917 publication, *Social Diagnosis*. None of this is surprising. Scientific rationality may well be the most dominant logic underlying accepted modes of thinking, reasoning, and claims to authority in modern culture (Daston and Galison, 2007; Feldman, 2004) – and science has much to offer. It promises unmediated access to the real world, information untainted by subjectivity, bias, and politics, information that is more likely to be taken seriously because it is thought to exist independently of the social location and motives of those who produced it. Scientific knowledge is abstracted, frequently quantified, and generalizable (see Bruno Latour's 2004 discussion of the shifting relation between "matters of fact" and "matters of concern"). But in social work, calls to embrace science occur alongside contradictory professional logics that value nuanced, contextually rich, and embodied knowledge about our clients and the social world. Many would argue that it is values, not a fixed cache of specialized knowledge, that coheres social work and shapes the professional identity of practitioners. Yet the theoretical and conceptual incompatibility of science and many of social work's other guiding logics are rarely labelled, much less interrogated in social work.

In this chapter, which comes from a larger fifteen-month ethnographic study that explores the nature of professional identity formation in child welfare, I describe two conflicting epistemological imperatives wired into the caseworker job: one that asks workers to understand clients from a disembodied or so-called objective standpoint and another that asks workers to stand in the client's shoes and understand them from an embodied standpoint. Indeed, workers were literally taught to and expected to gather information about clients from an embodied perspective; but within an institutional and cultural milieu that privileges scientific rationality, they were simultaneously asked to render all information they had about clients in the discourse of objectivity. Workers accomplished this through what I call *techniques of objectification*. These techniques, described briefly here, highlight the power and politics of institutional rules and procedures to reveal that objectivity, as it operates in this site, is not in fact a harbinger of detachment and neutrality. Instead, it conceals institutionally legitimated norms and values by aligning DCW's procedures and goals with reality and equating dissenting norms and values with bias and error. Analysis of the US child welfare system and its imperatives suggests that scientific objectivity is a practical impossibility in front-line casework and that it actually gets in the way of child welfare's aims, which are irreducibly value centred, political, and dynamic (see Latour, 1987).

Objectivity and embodied knowledge

Caseworkers at Kids First frequently struggled to square the knowledge they acquired from situated, intensive interactions with clients with DCW and family court rules about what constitutes legitimate evidence. Workers, it seemed, knew things about clients that they could not voice within the constraints of the child welfare system, and this often led to long meetings and ethical quandaries. When a worker faced these ethical dilemmas, or even value conflicts with the agency or DCW, managers and fellow workers would often advise, "You just need to be objective." In this context, objectivity was understood as a principle that, if enacted, would offer a way out of moral and ethical quagmires. It would result in the correct recommendation or right course of action.

Yet objectivity is itself a contentious term and is frequently invoked in debates about the value and merit of scientific endeavours and the legitimacy of professionals and their decisions (Hacking, 2015). At Kids First, being objective meant detaching what one sees in a client from one's own embodied perspective, values, and emotions. This definition of objectivity is consistent with logical positivist science and has been referred to as "aperspectival objectivity" (Feldman, 2004) and "vision from nowhere" (Haraway, 1988). This use of objectivity is consistent with the culturally dominant logic of scientific rationality in which knowledge and values, and knowledge producers and objects of scientific investigation, are supposed to be kept separate. Importantly, to be kept separate, they must be separable. Whereas aperspectival objectivity denotes a form of knowledge production that can be abstracted from its historical, cultural, and political context and from the norms and values of the person that created the knowledge, situated knowledge is grounded in an incompatible epistemology. Situated knowledge obtains that the social location of the knowledge producer is "epistemologically salient" (Alcoff, 1991). That is, any knowledge claim is inextricable from the context in which it was generated (Latour, 1987). Therefore, no knowledge can be understood as aperspectivally objective, neutral, or apolitical. I argue that simultaneous calls for objective and situated knowledge are wired into the institutional fabric of DCW, and perhaps even into the social work profession.[1] Yet, as I show here, objectivity is the institutionally and culturally dominant mode of knowledge production and professional claims-making.

Standing in the client's shoes . . . objectively

Conflicts between a situated, embodied mode of understanding and responding to clients and objectivity can be seen in family engagement[2] training, a daylong module that was developed as part of DCW's efforts to develop staff in accordance with evidence-based practices and the department's so-called family centred, trauma-informed, and strengths-based approach, which was officially adopted by the department in 2007 and continues today. Throughout the training, workers were repeatedly reminded that the work of interpreting clients' feelings and viewing the world from their embodied perspectives is a critical "step in the [family] engagement process" (DCW Family Engagement Training Materials) and is consonant with good casework. The "invisible suitcase" exercise is a good example.

In the training slides, the invisible suitcase concept is depicted in a sketch of a person whose back is hunched under the strain of a large backpack emblazoned with the word "WORRY" and a suitcase in each hand, labelled "FEAR" and "GUILT" respectively. The backpack and invisible suitcases are a diagrammatic version of what is colloquially known in popular psychology as emotional baggage, which is most often understood as negative psychological feelings about the past that prevent a person from behaving in a desirable or healthy way in the present. In addition to conceptualizing client problems from an individualist (rather than a broader structuralist) standpoint, the invisible suitcase exercise is meant to help trainees visualize emotions as baggage and understand the risks of not properly deciphering and tending to client parents' emotions.

Facilitators are instructed to incite workers' own emotions about attending a mandated DCW training session and to draw parallels between their feelings about having to "drop everything (pressing casework activities, for example) and come here" and the feelings of the mandated birth client. Notes to the facilitator are illustrative: "We are welcoming an open expression of feelings to help them get into the shoes of families: mandated, overwhelmed, voiceless, stressed, angry, inconvenienced." Notice that the worker's own emotions are harnessed in the service of understanding. By drawing a parallel between their own feelings about mandated training and the alleged feelings of the mandated client, the facilitator hopes to incite empathy (for analysis of the darker side of empathy as deception and violence, see Bubandt and Willerslev, 2015). Feelings and empathy, not detached or objective understanding, are used to illustrate the importance of "unpacking" with the client. In fact, one may argue that the ends of the exercise (getting the worker to invest in and practice behaviours consistent with family engagement) and the means (eliciting emotions and empathy) are driven by norms and values, not objective knowledge or evidence.

The value-laden nature of the training is brought into sharp relief when the facilitator addresses hypothetical attendees who may not share DCW's enthusiasm for opening themselves up to clients' negative emotions.

> "Now," the facilitator says to the trainees, "one of the thoughts some of you may be having is, 'I don't really care what is in the suitcase of a person who has treated their child so poorly.' You might remember the conversation we had during our last [training] about biases. Might it be easier to care about the content of their suitcase if we remember that most parents are trying to do their best and ultimately want to teach their children how to survive."[3]

Dropped into the middle of a training session that teaches workers to take another person's perspective, the word *bias* provides a window into DCW's logic and the process through which the complex emotional labour of seeing, receiving, and unpacking the invisible suitcase – which at first appears to rely upon situated and embodied knowledge generation – is also imagined as a wholly detached and technical exercise done in the pursuit of politically neutral goals. Both within this specific training module and DCW trainings more generally, words such as *bias, evidence, reliable, valid,* and *objective* – key terms in logical positivist science – pepper instructions on how workers should engage families, document their work, and adjudicate between competing claims about what constitutes a child's best interest. While simultaneous calls for embodied and objective knowledge are an epistemological impossibility, a careful analysis of the word *bias* as it is used in this training and other DCW materials shows that correcting so-called worker bias is not about replacing a skewed, subjective interpretation with an accurate and neutral rendering of the client. Rather, it is about replacing the ostensibly biased interpretation with a preferred but nevertheless inherently value-laden interpretation.

In this training, the warning about bias appears to be directed at workers who are biased against birth parents, but the facilitator's suggestion to "remember that most parents are trying to do their best" is not actually about correcting a bias; it is about creating a different perspective, one that is consonant with DCW's family engagement ethic. This use of the word *bias* to denote the "wrong" perspective, suggests several things. First, that the work of caring about the parent who abused her child is unbiased (a detached or value-free action with no ethical or political consequences for the client or the worker). Second, that DCW's value is superior to the value held by the dissenting worker, not because it is unequivocally more just or humane, but because it is construed as value-free.

The word *bias* operates similarly in a host of DCW documents. In a different family engagement presentation, the concept of bias was introduced via a slide labelled "Initial Impressions: The Effects of Personal Bias." In the accompanying picture, a house cat gazes into a mirror and sees the image of a lion reflected back.[4] The slide asserts that personal bias is a misperception of an otherwise knowable world. In the image, the house cat represents an incontestable reality, and the lion is a perceptual error enabled by personal bias (Sunny Skyz, 2014). The slide appears to be directed at workers who have a grandiose perception of themselves; the analogy is consistent with social work trainings that urge workers to recognize and reflect upon their positions of power relative to their clients.

The reflective work of recognizing one's position of power and interrogating one's own perceptions is widely espoused in social work training as an integral component of ethically sound work. But in this case workers who see themselves as big and powerful are construed not only as unethical; they are also depicted as seeing themselves inaccurately. Their perception is wrong.[5] While many would agree that the perspectival work of reining in one's sense of power or importance in social service work is critical to good service delivery, the tendency of DCW's ideological discourse to define matters of perspective as matters of fact can marginalize workers.[6] After all, workers are commonly asked to perceive and interpret concepts that are not concretely knowable to the senses. If dissenting opinions are construed as bias, and bias is a perceptual error, then DCW's family engagement policy becomes an accurate and therefore incontestably ethical stance.[7] By placing its own values on the side of the real, DCW renders something that can most accurately be called a difference in values or politics as a difference between fact and opinion (Latour, 2004). Those who disagree with DCW because they subscribe to a different value lose traction not because their values are out of sync with societal values or other registers of morality, but because they are construed as wrong. In effect, those workers are discredited, the political dimensions of DCW are obscured, and its institutionalized perspectives are insulated from critique.

Identifying and objectifying emotions

In addition to muddying embodied knowledge generation with the language of objectivity, DCW also construes emotions as simultaneously rooted in situated perspectives and knowable from a disembodied, objective perspective. A situated understanding of casework suggests a terrain in which emotions inform perspectives, and where workers must continually reflect upon their own emotions in order to take stock of clients' emotions and perspectives. Objective constructions of casework ask workers to bracket their personal feelings in order to generate facts. In muddying these incompatible stances, DCW construes the effective practitioner as a feeling and reflexive thinker whose emotions, nonetheless, obscure objective reality and pose a threat to competent service delivery. In fact, the idea that emotions can impede effective service is not without precedent in social work and mental health practice literatures. Smith (2014) describes a similar logic in Therapeutic Crisis Intervention (TCI), a patented and widely used crisis prevention and intervention programme for residential child-care organizations. In TCI, trainees are cautioned that angry emotions can easily derail the systematic, lucid, and rational decision-making process that, according to TCI's creators, ought to guide practitioner behaviour during real-time crisis situations.

Likewise, the definition of objectivity provided in DCW's child welfare licensing study guide states, "Objectivity means treating or dealing with facts without distortion by personal feelings or prejudices." The definition suggests that child welfare workers regularly work with facts that are concrete and knowable, and that these facts can be distorted or made inaccurate by personal feelings or prejudices. There is also the subtle introduction of a hierarchy in which facts are privileged over personal feelings.

The tension between facts and emotions, and the notion that facts can be abstracted from emotions, are also evident in the foster parent handbook, which warns its readers in boldface type: "Being able to separate your emotions and remain objective isn't easy, but it's necessary to fairly represent the best interests of any foster child." Whereas the process of learning how to engage families requires workers to reflect upon their own emotions and then draw parallels between their emotions and those of their clients ("to get into the clients' shoes"), this text states that separating emotions is necessary for fair (read, unbiased) representation. In other words, the same emotions that prompt workers to better understand their clients, cultivate empathy, and deliver ethical services are simultaneously considered a barrier to fair representation.

DCW's endorsement of objectivity tacitly offers a way out of the feelings/objective reality conundrum by bringing emotions into the universe of factually knowable things. The objectification of emotions is precisely what the invisible suitcase exercise accomplishes by the end of the first family engagement training module. According to DCW, the invisible suitcase is not just a metaphor for engaging clients, but it also helps workers to see and recognize the previously unseeable. "Much of what we are talking about can't be seen by those around you at first glance," says the trainer, implying that emotional baggage is a concrete fact of social reality that workers can be trained to recognize and decipher. Note that in making concrete entities that are invisible and interpretive, family engagement training objectifies and reifies the very emotions that it, only a few moments prior, discussed from an embodied and interpretive epistemological standpoint.

In medical literature, Jodi Halpern describes how norms of detachment and objectivity have led to narrow, cognitively based definitions of clinical empathy (2003). Not surprisingly, DCW also defines empathy as a disembodied, cognitive practice, thereby allowing the department to construe the interpretive and value-laden work of unpacking the invisible suitcase as objective and technical. Empathy, according to DCW, is "a core condition of the helping relationship" that entails "tuning into a person's emotions and communicating understanding without losing objectivity" (DCW Foster Care Worker Training Materials).

The realization of this definition of empathy in practice requires workers to objectify their own emotions and those of their clients. It also begs several interesting questions, the first of which is how a worker can communicate understanding from an objective standpoint. Is communicating understanding a matter of verbalizing to the client that one has correctly identified the client's emotional state, or does expressing understanding also require the workers to draw upon and express their own emotions? If the latter, this suggests that workers should be able to enact objectified emotions, as sincerely felt emotions would threaten the workers' objectivity unless they are able to simultaneously feel and bracket emotions. Workers, it seems, are supposed to care about their clients and understand them from their own embodied perspectives, in part through managing their own affects and responding appropriately to their clients, but they are also supposed to bracket their emotions in the service encounter. Therefore, we must also ask how objectivity can be practiced in a context that asks practitioners to think and feel in the same instant. Objectivity's temporal dimensions are anything but instantaneous. Whereas objectification freezes emotional moments in time and abstracts them from context, offering the practitioner the chance to draw causal links between situations, emotions, and their outcomes, emotional displays are elicited and enacted continuously by clients and practitioners in real-time service encounters. Workers cannot pause the service encounter to identify and categorize emotions and behaviours.[8]

In addition to objectivity's practical limitations for the thinking, feeling practitioner, it also poses important ethical questions. While the DCW suggests that being personal introduces bias, one might alternatively argue that the guise of objectivity risks perpetuating discrimination because the observers of objective facts are never called upon to interrogate their own relationship to that which is being observed – in this case, the client, over whom they have relative power (Haraway, 1988).

Techniques of objectification

Given irreconcilable demands to generate embodied and objective knowledge about clients, and a social service context in which agencies are frequently mandated to account for their work using quantitative and ostensibly objective outcome measurements, child welfare workers are repeatedly called upon to translate their actions and evaluations of clients into objective language. I identified four techniques through which workers made child welfare work objective: documentation, collectivization, institutionalization, and audit. I will describe these techniques – what motivates them and their consequences – before discussing the implications of conflicting epistemologies and the institutional dominance of scientific objectivity for identity formation in social work.

Documentation: According to Stephenson-Valcourt, whose 8-Frame Window Model for child welfare caseworker documentation is included as one of many resources DCW distributes to workers, "Documentation remains the one priority that if not done in a timely manner, negates all the other priorities or tasks undertaken by a caseworker" (2009–10: 163). Stephenson-Valcourt's quote invokes the sentiment of an oft-repeated admonition in hospital and social service settings: if it wasn't documented, it wasn't done. This aphorism reveals a paradox at the heart of documentation in that the very mechanism that is supposed to render professionals transparent and accountable is considered more valuable than reality itself. The window metaphor is also telling. Windows are transparent; they are also a distinct if largely invisible barrier between the observer and the observed. But there is unacknowledged tension between the window's promise of a clear, unimpeded, and complete picture of a family and the 8-Frame Model's categorical and methodical simplification of information through the use of frames. In fact, while the act of creating an accurate and complete description of an event might conceivably entail documenting the minutiae of social interactions in all of their mundane detail – without deciding a priori what is important and what is not – the genre of the case note is predetermined; it exists independent of the individual case and the specific interaction it aims to capture. Workers are instructed to document concisely and effectively, and to exclude superfluous details. For front-line workers, whose knowledge and opinions about clients is derived from situated and intensive interactions that unfold over time, the case note genre could actually prevent them from documenting evidence to support their recommendations and opinions. The case note does not neutrally reflect an external social reality; it is an artefact whose attributes are defined by the social and cultural context of child welfare. The practice of gathering such documentation over time begins to produce the impression that it is possible, bit by bit, to distinguish types of incompatible veridications.

Collectivization: Gaps between situated knowledge garnered in day-to-day interactions with clients and the type of evidence that makes its way onto paper, or even into the courtroom, proved to be a continual source of frustration for caseworkers at Kids First. This happened both because case notes were structured and abbreviated stand-ins for reality and because the family court judges who made decisions about cases did not read case notes. Instead, workers gave summary reports to the court in which they reported the exact dates of services and notable events, and the number of parent-child visits and treatment sessions clients attended. Often, these were poor substitutes for the detailed situated knowledge workers had about the parents and children on their caseloads. However, expert opinions were considered objective and were admissible as evidence to the family court. This meant that workers could attempt to objectify their own opinions by sharing information and notes with recognized experts, and by selectively calling on experts to objectify opinions that the workers, themselves, had already formed. I refer to this technique as *collectivization* because the expert, and allegedly objective, opinion that results is arrived at via collective social interactions. In one instance, agency staff spent twenty minutes weighing the pros and cons of getting a "bonding assessment" for a parent, whom they were already convinced was not appropriately bonded with her daughter. The danger lay in the potential of the expert assessor – who, notably, would spend only a limited amount of time with the parent – to arrive at a contrary opinion.

Institutionalization: Given that caseworkers' decisions and opinions are not considered legitimate and the fact that they have to form opinions and make decisions in the day-to-day, workers had to rely on yet another technique of objectification in order to give their opinions traction: de-voicing personal opinions by attaching them to institutional authority (Carr, 2010). For example, Val, who was known among adoption team staff for her shrewd court testimony skills, said that attorneys frequently try to expose and exploit the uncertainty surrounding case recommendations by asking caseworkers about their "personal" opinions. Val imitated her response to a hypothetical attorney by insisting, repeatedly, that she "does not have a personal opinion," only a "professional opinion" and that that opinion is "the opinion of the agency." In reiterating and standing by the professional or agency opinion, and denying a personal opinion, the service recommendation is detached from the situated or embodied perspective of the, often multiple, people who weighed in on the opinion and the uncertainty that led to the singular, disembodied, and seemingly objective opinion.

Audit: In light of these pressures to determine with accuracy which children are and are not in danger of being harmed by their parents, risk assessment protocols and tools are increasingly lauded for the ability to cut through the dense thicket of information gathered by professionals on the ground and to produce clear and unbiased evidence for decision making (Coohey et al., 2013; Shlonsky and Wagner, 2005). Audit techniques, including risk assessments and quantitatively measured goals and outcomes, have become some of the most widely implemented and researched techniques of objectification used in child welfare today. Indeed, some such instruments are designed, explicitly, to replace "clinical judgment," "intuitive judgment," and the "professional experience of the worker" (Shlonsky and Wagner, 2005: 410).

Risk assessments bring the certainty of measurement to otherwise subjective verifications; outcome measurements indicate a culture of accountability and improvement (Webb, 2006). Both kinds of measurement tools present the image of a transparent and fair system (Strathern, 2000) in which mistakes can be minimized and interventions demonstrably improved. Buried in the calculating discourse of objectivity and numbers is the promise that child maltreatment can be subject to prediction and control. At the same time, the notion that human behaviour can be predicted and controlled has its downside for workers. It also means that blame can be assigned when something goes wrong (Parton, 1998). Part of the problem for workers is that auditing and risk assessment suggest a level of control that is impossible to achieve, and therefore a level of accountability that is out of proportion with the efficacy of child welfare interventions (Munro, 1999). On the one hand, most of the risk factors that workers are supposed to assess are abstract concepts with no obvious physical manifestations. Workers cannot see, feel, hear, or otherwise sense these risk factors (Parton, 1998). On the other hand, these risk factors are treated precisely as if they are concrete and knowable. Moreover, when risk assessments pare down case knowledge to dichotomous checklists and exclude situated knowledge, and when workers' professional opinions are mistrusted, workers can be and frequently are put in the position of managing child placements with which they feel uncomfortable. Such is the case when the worker's opinion derives from information that does not rise to the level of evidence.

Concluding discussion

With a set of core values that privilege human relationships (National Association of Social Workers, 2008), perspectival and ethical labours have remained an important, if poorly theorized, component of professional identity for social workers who are engaged in direct service provision. This study shows how incommensurate demands upon workers to be simultaneously perspectival, empathic, and producers of disembodied objective knowledge compel workers to legitimate their identity through techniques of objectification. As part of this process of justification they cut away the nuances and value judgments that inform the many evaluations they make while doing front-line practice (see Boltanski and Thévenot, 1991). Therefore, objectivity obscures, even while it is lauded as the harbinger of unbiased and transparent practice.

It is important to point out that DCW, the broader child welfare field, and social work at large are not solely, or even primarily, responsible for creating and perpetuating discourses implicated in the devaluation of child welfare workers or the many women employed in its ranks. Science and objectivity are valorized in American culture, as are dichotomies between subjects and objects, and rationality and emotion. To the extent that society privileges rational thinking, science, and objectivity over ethics, social work's many attempts to improve its status and demonstrate its efficacy through scientific knowledge are understandable. Likewise, the impetus to demonstrate accountability and fairness appears easily justifiable when one considers the disproportionate effect of child welfare on poor and minority families and the level of intrusion that child welfare presents in the United States, where individual freedom and family privacy are idealized. At the same time, the discourse of objectivity that accompanies the operationalization of child welfare tends to subsume equally important aspects of the work that cannot be measured, namely its personal, moral, and political components.

In pointing to the many dilemmas that arise when calls for objectivity are inserted alongside calls for perspectival, embodied work in child welfare practice, I do not intend to suggest that the tools of science should not be used in child welfare. Instead, I want to draw attention to the context in which particular scientific rationalities are deployed, in part to reveal their inherent limitations vis-à-vis value-laden human interactions, and to expose the moral and ethical dimensions of casework that cannot be accounted for through disembodied scientific objectivity, in particular. These ethical dimensions are critically important for enacting socially just services and for identifying and retaining the high-quality workers whose efforts to provide individually attuned and equitable services should accord their work greater value. The complex, reflexive, and ethical work called upon so often in front-line child welfare is easily marginalized in a system that is evaluated primarily through objectified evidence. Likewise, the attempt to make objective those aspects of social work that rely on perspectival evaluations is problematic for clients and workers. For the former, objectivity can mean that case decisions are made based upon a subset of the evidence available to workers and that these decisions are sometimes at odds with what skilled workers view as the best decisions.

Given objectivity's incompatibility with the perspectival and morally fraught decision making that punctuates all social service work, child welfare ought to interrogate more critically imbrications between knowledge and values and adopt a more rigorous and inclusive definition of evidence. Such a definition does not mean that risk assessment tools and other quantitatively based quality improvement techniques ought to be discarded or backgrounded. Rather, the notion that these tools can be objective – that they can exist independent of the cultural and political contexts in which they are mobilized and the perspectives of those who administer them – must be challenged. One approach may include reading risk assessments alongside workers' contextually informed and nuanced interpretations of their clients. On a more macro level, child welfare systems and workers should continually revisit the terms of risk assessments and the political work they do, not excepting the tendency of risk assessments to be understood as scientific techniques capable of reducing or eliminating opinions and values. After all, as Eileen Munro (1999) argues, no form of technology, no matter how accurate, can define child abuse or determine the threshold for intervention.

Finally, social work's efforts to reclaim the professional terrain of child welfare should not shy away from emotional and perspectival work and value-laden modes of expertise when staking claims to legitimacy. As countless other practitioners and scholars have noted, social work's cohesiveness and professional identity stem from its historical and political underpinnings, not from exclusive claims over a defined cache of social and psychological knowledge and techniques. In fact, the dilemmas described here might be best resolved not by substantively changing the specific interventions and tools commonly used in child welfare today, but by rejecting the premise that disembodied objectivity is an epistemic virtue and recognizing that people, context, and values underlie all forms of evaluation.[9]

Notes

1 I frame this dilemma as an epistemological and ethical dilemma. However, these conflicting epistemologies can also be interrogated from the institutional logics perspective (see Thornton, Ocasio, and Lounsbury, 2012) according to which objectivity and situated knowledge are conflicting institutional logics.

2 Family engagement was a ubiquitously articulated service ethic in DCW training materials and is broadly consistent with workers' perceptions that the culture of DCW is now strongly in favour of reuniting children with their birth parents rather than pursuing alternative living arrangements such as permanent guardianship or adoption.

3 This statement is rhetorical and is written with a period, rather than a question mark, in slide notes to the facilitator.

4 Though I first encountered this image in DCW training, a Google search for "lion cat mirror" results in more than 3 million hits for this image, which can be found via the following link: http://www.sunnyskyz.com/happy-pictures/248/Cat-sees-lion-in-mirror. Most often, the image appears as part of a meme, with various phrases superimposed on the picture.

5 As an Internet meme, the picture takes on different meanings depending upon what phrase is superimposed.

6 In fact, Ferguson, drawing heavily upon Anthony Giddens, outlines a historical process whereby late-modern reflexive citizens and reflexive systems increasingly observe themselves in order to manage self-generated errors and risks (1997).

7 A host of child welfare scholars have interrogated the issue of birth parent engagement and have come to very different conclusions. Elizabeth Bartholet (1999) argues against the

family preservation ethic and that some children labelled "at risk for removal" should be defined as "in need of liberation" (1999, 53). Bartholet's position, while controversial, is no more biased than DCW's stance; rather, it represents a different value stance.

8 In contrast to objective constructions of empathy, Carl Rogers (1975), the originator of person-centred therapy, asserts that empathy requires the therapist to sincerely care about the client. "It is impossible accurately to sense the perceptual world of another person unless you value that person and his world – unless you in some sense care" (Rogers, 1975: 6).

9 A version of this chapter was published in *Social Service Review*. See: Hardesty, M. (2015). Epistemological Binds and Ethical Dilemmas in Frontline Child Welfare Practice. *Social Service Review*, 89(3): 455–498.

References

Alcoff, L. (1991). The Problem of Speaking for Others. *Cultural Critique*, Winter, 20: 5–32.

American Academy of Social Work and Social Welfare. (2016). The Grand Challenges for Social Work. Retrieved from https://www.youtube.com/watch?v=oKbj3y-LUbw.

Bartholet, E. (1999). *Nobody's Children: Abuse and Neglect, Foster Drift, and the Adoption Alternative*. Boston, MA: Beacon Press.

Boltanski, L., & Thévenot, L. (1991). *On Justification: The Economies of Worth*. Princeton: Princeton University Press.

Brekke, J. S. (1986). Scientific Imperatives in Social Work Research: Pluralism Is not Skepticism. *Social Service Review*, 60(4): 538–554.

Brekke, J. S. (2012). Shaping a Science of Social Work. *Research on Social Work Practice*, 22(5): 455–464.

Bubandt, N., & Willerslev, R. (2015). The Dark Side of Empathy: Mimesis, Deception, and the Magic of Alterity. *Comparative Studies in Society and History*, 57(1): 5–34.

Carr, E. S. (2010). *Scripting Addiction: The Politics of Therapeutic Talk and American Sobriety*. Princeton, NJ: Princeton University Press.

Collins-Camargo, C., Ensign, K., & Flaherty, C. (2008). The National Quality Improvement Center on the Privatization of Child Welfare Services: A Program Description. *Research on Social Work Practice*, 18(1): 72–81.

Coohey, C., Johnson, K., Renner, L. M., & Easton, S. D. (2013). Actuarial Risk Assessment in Child Protective Services: Construction Methodology and Performance Criteria. *Children and Youth Services Review*, 35(1): 151–161.

Daston, Lorraine, & Galison, P. (2007). *Objectivity*. Brooklyn: Zone Books.

Feldman, S. P. (2004). The Culture of Objectivity: Quantification, Uncertainty, and the Evaluation of Risk at NASA. *Human Relations*, 57: 691–717. doi: 10.1177/0018726704044952.

Ferguson, H. (1997). Protecting Children in New Times: Child Protection and the Risk Society. *Child and Family Social Work*, 2(4): 221–234.

Gambrill, E. (1999). Evidence-based Practice: An Alternative to Authority-based Practice. *Families in Society: The Journal of Contemporary Social Services*, 80(4): 341–350.

Gambrill, E., & Shlonsky, A. (2001). The Need for Comprehensive Risk Management Systems in Child Welfare. *Children and Youth Services Review*, 23(1): 79–107.

Hacking, I. (2015). Let's not Talk about Objectivity. In F. Padovani, A. Richardson & J. Y. Tsou (Eds.), *Objectivity in Science: New Perspectives from Science and Technology Studies* (pp. 19–33). Switzerland: Springer International Publishing.

Halpern, J. (2003). What Is Clinical Empathy? *Journal of General Internal Medicine*, 18(8): 670–674.

Haraway, D. (1988). Situated Knowledges: The Science Question in Feminism and the Privilege of Partial Perspective. *Feminist Studies*, 14(3): 575–599.

Latour, B. (1987). *Science in Action: How to Follow Scientists and Engineers' through Society*. Harvard: Harvard University Press.

Latour, B. (2004). Why Has Critique Run Out of Steam? From Matter of Fact to Matters of Concern. *Critical Inquiry*, Winter, 30(2): 225–248.

Munro, E. M. (1999). Protecting Children in an Anxious Society. *Health, Risk, & Society*, 1(1): 117–127.

National Association of Social Workers. (2008). Code of Ethics of the National Association of Social Workers. Retrieved from https://www.socialworkers.org/pubs/code/code.asp.

Parton, N. (1998). Risk, Advanced Liberalism and Child Welfare: The Need to Rediscover Uncertainty and Ambiguity. *British Journal of Social Work*, 28(1): 5–27.

Richmond, M. (1917). *Social Diagnosis*. Philadelphia: Russell Sage Foundation.

Rogers, C. R. (1975). Empathic: An Unappreciated Way of Being. *The Counseling Psychologist*, 5(2): 2–10.

Shlonsky, A., & Wagner, D. (2005). The Next Step: Integrating Actuarial Risk Assessment and Clinical Judgment into an Evidence-based Practice Framework in CPS Case Management. *Children and Youth Services Review*, 27(4): 409–427.

Smith, Y. (2014). Rethinking Decision Making: An Ethnographic Study of Worker Agency in Crisis Intervention. *Social Service Review*, 88(3): 407–442.

Stephenson-Valcourt, D. (2009–2010). Documenting Case Notes in Child Welfare: The 8-Frame Window Model. From the Practitioners Desk. *Illinois Child Welfare*, 5(1): 162–168.

Strathern, M. (2000). The Tyranny of Transparency. *British Educational Research Journal*, 26(3): 309–321.

Sunny Skyz. (2014). Cat Sees Lion in Mirror. Retrieved from http://www.sunnyskyz.com/happypictures/248/Cat-sees-lion-in- mirror.

Thornton, P. H., Ocasio, W., & Lounsbury, M. (2012). *The Institutional Logics Perspective: A New Approach to Culture, Structure and Process*. Oxford: Oxford University Press.

Webb, S. A. (2001). Some Considerations on the Validity of Evidence-based Practice in Social Work. *British Journal of Social Work*, 31(1): 57–79.

Webb, S. A. (2006). *Social Work in a Risk Society*. London: Palgrave.

9

FIELD, CAPITAL AND PROFESSIONAL IDENTITY

Social work in health care

Liz Beddoe

This chapter will explore social work identity in health care settings, a significant field of practice in many parts of the world, including North America and Australasia. The influence of the French sociologist Pierre Bourdieu's philosophical framework is explored in a consideration of professional identity. His concepts of 'field' and 'capital' are used to analyse the influence of power relations, utilising an additional concept of 'professional capital'. Social work may be perceived as successful in health contexts as it is not as subject to media and critical public scrutiny as children's social work is, but health social workers still often express feelings of marginalisation (Beddoe, 2013a). In Bourdieu's terms, social work may be viewed as a collective of 'agents' occupying a field, playing out their roles in a "structured social space, a field of forces" (Bourdieu, 1998: 40). In such fields there may be palpable competition between actors for the accumulation of different kinds of capital, and it is here perhaps that social work identity is less secure.

Introduction

Historical accounts of social work in health care place the earliest developments in the USA with the work of Ida Cannon in the first decades of the 20th century (Bartlett, 1975). Cannon is reputed to have described social work in hospitals as being practice in a "host setting". This notion of social work being a 'guest' in a host setting is highly significant in an analysis of the development and nature of social work identity in health. Richard Cabot, a doctor and early supporter of social work, with whom Cannon worked, published a series of essays on the relationship between an emerging social work occupation and the medical profession (Cabot, 1919). These early conceptions of social work in health care implied a social practice dependent upon the sponsorship of doctors and, to a lesser extent, the will-ingness of nurses to allow social workers access. Bartlett writes:

> Her [Cannon's] approach was to proceed quietly, using gentle pressure and watching for opportunities to move the idea ahead. She always kept the central focus on the patient's needs and the doctor's concern for giving good care. She was careful not to go too fast and showed extraordinary patience in waiting over the years for the readiness of the physicians on the various services to come to her and request the assignment of a social worker.
>
> *(1975: 214)*

In a similar vein, the story is told of the career of Anne Cummins, "at first sight so self-effacing and submissive", and yet it is noted that,

> far from restricting her role to the support of doctors in their individual treatment of patients she instituted a preventive ante-natal care system in the district, with what we would now call self-help groups, was responsible for establishing the first maternity ward in a general hospital, and organized a widespread 'community care' scheme for tuberculosis patients.
>
> *(Bell, 1961, cited in Bywaters, 1986: 663)*

Despite the sense of heroism invoked, these early texts are nonetheless imbued with notions of patronage and of women pioneers playing a highly gendered role in order to insert social work into the hallowed spaces of medicine. Much later, Bywaters (1986) wrote of health social workers: "they are exhorted in the literature of social work to act as partners, when many experience their position as being barely tolerated visitors" (665).

In New Zealand, where health social work emerged in the 1930s, the profession lacked a clear demarcation between social workers and nurses or midwives. Nurses learned "the tenets of social service" within their nursing practice (Beddoe and Deeney, 2012: 44). Nonetheless, social work in health care in New Zealand, from its inception, added a holistic dimension to health care, as indicated in Spensley's simple description: "It is difficult to enumerate a daily routine of her duties as they vary from day to day, but *by uniting the medical and social needs of the individual she seeks to help the person as a whole*" (Spensley, 1953: 177, emphasis added). Regardless of the challenges faced, social work developed rapidly in the early decades of the last century, with educational opportunities in the social sciences leading to qualified social workers appearing in greater numbers. In the same year that Cabot's book was published (1919), Todd, a sociologist, advised social workers to adopt a scientific approach in their practice, arguing: "the scientific spirit is necessary to social work whether it is a *real profession* or only a *go-between craft*" (Todd, 1919: 66, emphasis added). Todd's sociological viewpoint and appeal to science suggests the potential for social work to carve a more discrete role in the health field, with less focus on the body and illness and more on social factors. This laid the groundwork for social work in contemporary health care to be underpinned by an understanding of the profound impact of sociocultural inequalities evident in health disparities. Both Todd and Cabot recognise social work as intrinsically preoccupied with the alleviation of suffering at individual, family and community levels, while acknowledging that social change is needed to reduce health inequalities. Where Todd and Cabot "differ significantly is in their understanding of social work's striving for a distinctive space and a knowledge base so as to develop into more than a 'go-between craft'" (Beddoe, 2013a: 25, also see Abbott, 1995 on social work as working across boundaries. Here social work is a complex defended turf in a complex system of professions).

The history of social work in health care is one of growth and adaptation, and yet the literature also articulates a struggle to be defined within a complex health system inhabited by many powerful players in the 'field of forces' alluded to earlier (Bourdieu, 1998). Bywaters (1986: 663) describes another history, "viable but less articulated, a history of inter-professional conflict, of the widespread emasculation of social work in hospitals". The unequal power relationships and differential statuses of health professionals reflect very old but still powerful dynamics. Power, gender and managerialism exert an influence in the contemporary environment, defining and restricting social work identity. Bourdieu's (1984) concept of "distinctive space" proves useful in exploring the enduring struggle for recognition and respect for social work in health care to be discussed further in this chapter (Beddoe, 2010, 2013a).

Social work in health care: an overview

As social work has been introduced into health care provision at primary, secondary and tertiary levels, it has tended to define itself by its focus on the relationship (at the macro level) between the social, cultural and economic determinants of health and the impact of illness on personal and family coping. In addition, social work has advocated for social and emotional support for those with health needs and stressed the importance of multi-professional collaboration to address individual and community health problems. In its 11 decades of social work in health care, the profession has clearly nailed its colours to the mast of a holistic concept of health, often referred to as the 'biopsychosocial model'. Auslander's Delphi study identified that social work's greatest contribution to health care has been its "influence on mainstream health care to adopt a broader conception of health and illness" (Auslander, 2001: 210).

In the UK in the 1980s a social model of health was proposed by Bywaters (1986: 670–674). Such a model would incorporate clear principles: health was conceptualised as a human right with an understanding that social and environmental factors created direct impacts on health and illness; 'patients' were to be recast as citizens and consumers rather than merely the subjects of an expert-dominated system. The mandate for social work was to value social care as well as treatment;

to advocate for support as a right; for social work activity to be unrestricted by gatekeepers; and to develop and support self-help groups and assistance for health services users and carers to find and disseminate alternative sources of information (Bywaters, 1986). This aspirational view suggests a more confident profession. It envisages social work standing its ground in its fight on two fronts, between those they wanted to help (who may be deeply demoralised) and the "administrations and bureaucrats divided and enclosed in separate universes" (Bourdieu, 1999:190).

There is a significant body of literature exploring the development of social work in health care through a lens of power and influence and, in particular, its status within the professions. From a US perspective, McCoyd et al. (2016) describe social work in health care as going through a pre-professional phase in the face of a struggle to establish its foothold. They comment, "while social workers lived their values and did not assert professional privilege" (33), the habits of deferring to others and being associated with people of low status paradoxically interfered with progress towards recognition of social work as a health profession. They note that this resulted in social workers being seen "as helpers rather than professionals in their own right. This paradox continues to influence health social work today" (33) and whether social work is a profession or a 'semi-profession' is still debated.

Etzioni (1969) coined the term "semi-profession" to describe teaching, nursing and social work, inferring they had not developed the degree of monopoly power and public esteem associated with medicine and law. The semi-professions drew on theory and knowledge, promoted membership and participation, and adopted codes of ethics, but they did not seek to position themselves above the communities they worked in and for. Freidson has suggested that the professions represent the organisation of particular kinds of (codified) knowledge and skill into 'disciplines' in the Foucauldian sense, the constructed notion of:

> Institutions *set apart from everyday life*. Special groups of intellectual workers embody the authority of those disciplines, their work being to create, pre- serve, transmit, debate and revise disciplinary content. The formal knowledge of particular disciplines is taught to those aspiring to enter specialized occu- pations with professional standing.
>
> *(2001: 29; emphasis added)*

Instead nurses, teachers and social workers preferred to keep close to the pupils, patients and service users – the people they worked alongside. Another defining feature for Etzioni (1969) was that these 'semi'-professionals were employed within large bureaucratic institutions; this is significant for social work in health care, given the prevailing depiction of social workers as guests in a host setting.

One additional salient aspect is gender. Bywaters (1986: 665) talks about medi- cal social work being perceived as "a soft option" in the 1970s and 1980s as the influence and prominence of statutory social work grew. Statutory social work may have been seen as more attractive to men, given Bywaters' comment that health social work was "caricatured by sexist and ageist stereotypes" (Ibid.). In health care the association of social work with nursing led to its positioning as an occupation *invited into* hospitals and clinics and thus under the patronage of men. The gendered nature of social work has always been a salient issue in considering the journey to professional status. The seminal work of Ann Witz is useful here. In *Professions and Patriarchy* Witz examines the gendering of professionalisation projects: "indeed, gender was integral to the very definition of a 'semi-profession' which, according to Etzioni (1969), has a second defining feature. It is one in which women predominate" (Witz, 1992: 57).

The somewhat presumptuous, patriarchal interpretation of this predominance was that women preferred to work in close proximity to the families and caregivers who may also have an interest in a service user's welfare. Witz, however (1992: 88–93), challenged this suggestion of 'preference' in relation to nursing and midwifery, suggesting that the history of medicine included deliberate attempts to exclude women from medical school. As evidence of a continuing androcentric approach to the study of professions, she cites Rueschemeyer's remark (1986: 137) that the "high devotion/low power syndrome" of the social service professions "articulates well with women's traditional roles" (Witz, 1992: 58). This notion of devotion echoes Bourdieu's idea of social work as "a profession of faith" emerging (like teaching and nursing) during a period where the middle classes sought new occupations. Jenkins (1992: 144–145) noted that Bourdieu included such employment as a solution for those whose access to higher education in the 1960s had "created a disjuncture between their subjective expectations and their objective probabilities".

In Witz's feminist analysis, professions are constructed as integral features of patriarchal societies. The gendered activities of caring and support, originally intra-familial roles, which developed last century into paid occupations in health and social care, still underpin the nature of the helping professions. Witz's case study of midwifery (1992: 104), for example, demonstrates the processes by which midwives battled with the new medical specialisation of obstetrics for autonomy within the highly contestable territory of childbirth. The struggle over midwives' roles and professional autonomy remains a potent example of "turf-conflict" many years later (Abbott and Meerabeau, 1998).

Despite the contested nature of its status, social work persists as a player in health care; it remains a substantial field of practice, especially in North America and Australasia. The field makes well-established contributions to patient care in both physical and mental health. In many countries, health social workers are highly educated and increasingly participate in health research and service development. Joubert (2006) writes of the establishment of academic-practice partnerships leading to active collaboration between universities and major hospitals in Melbourne, Australia. Health social work has a strong literature base, with journals focussing on many aspects of social work such as mental health, primary and public health. It is assertive in the development of practitioner research and the development of leadership in a highly articulate professional sub-sector, not simply utilising research in practice but producing it. An excellent example of this development is found in

New York's Mt Sinai Medical Center exchange programme, which promotes visits of practitioners and academics to Victoria and New South Wales in Australia and, more recently, other countries (Fouché, 2015; Rehr and Rosenberg, 2006).

So what are the contemporary challenges and opportunities for social work in health care? What is reported in the contemporary literature? The growth of a health research culture as an indication of professional confidence suggests gains have been made (Joubert, 2006); however, calls continue for further development of social work contributions to research (Brough, Wagner, and Farrell, 2013; McNeill and Nicholas, 2012). Despite these gains, social workers arguably remain in positions of low visibility (Morriss, 2016) and potential disempowerment in host settings, despite decades of significant contribution to health care. Whether this is a consequence of medical dominance in health care organisations or a feature of the natural ecosystem of health organisations may be contested as a matter of perspective. What is clear is the impact of wider social change on the political economy and the management of health services.

Contemporary perspectives

Recent literature about social work in health care addresses two recurring themes: first, the role of social workers in changing health system contexts; and second (and connected to the former), the reconciliation of social work's espoused commitment to social justice and human rights with the kinds of practice occurring in systems often dominated by managerialist and even commercial concerns. In the USA, Spitzer, Silverman, and Allen (2015) recognise the long-standing challenges for social work in health contexts but see great potential for social work under the Patient Protection and Affordable Care Act 2010, which positions social work as integral to integrated care. They extol a highly pragmatic position, urging social work to "reconcile the gap between professional competence and ideology" (Spitzer et al., 2015: 197). Health social workers, in their view, "reside in an ecosystem that does not naturally support social work life" (198).

Advocating for an organisational competency approach, Spitzer et al. assert that the profession should "lead with social work competency rather than ideology" (2015: 199). Success and the prospect of an "expanded marketplace" for social work services will come to those who are strategic and can "adeptly align their competencies with organisational goals" (199). Essentially this position urges social workers to resist the urge to challenge managerial systems head-on, but rather to adopt the patient and tactful strategies of Ida Cannon. The health social work virtues of patience, tact and non-confrontation have a long shelf life.

So what about the experiences of social workers themselves in contemporary health care? Haultain writes about the range of challenges impacting on health social work in New Zealand:

> These challenges include the ever-increasing global prominence of market-driven, cost-containment strategies . . . reduced length of hospital stay and

pressure for rapid discharge . . . demographic changes such as the aging population . . . growing numbers of patients with multiple, chronic health problems . . . health inequalities . . . and the impact on the profession of a constantly changing health environment.

(2015: 40)

These features are not isolated (see for example, Cleak and Turczynski, 2014; Judd and Sheffield, 2010; Mizrahi and Berger, 2005). Several texts are useful here in illuminating the lived experience of social workers practising in these constrained and stressful environments. Wilder Craig (2007), writing about the nature of the social work role in the restructured health care environment, underscores the importance of the profession telling its own 'stories' of practice. She cites Weick (2000), who wrote of the submerged "first voice" of social work which, in the midst of the neo-liberal regime of market-driven health care, is a voice "framed by logic, rationality and rules, where right and might are more important than care and comfort and where winning eclipses warmth and worry" (Weick, 2000: 398). The domination of this "second voice" has rendered "mute the profession's collective wisdom and power" (Weick, 2000: 396). Wilder Craig writes:

Most of us have become experts in using this voice as it is the voice of the larger corporate culture that is so much part of our world. However, it is a voice that is not up to the task of either describing adequately what we do or of differentiating social work from the work of other helping professions. Weick suggests that the voice that is capable of doing this is what she calls our 'first voice' – the voice of storytelling.

(2007: 436)

Thus, research that captures the lived experiences of social workers can help us to understand contemporary roles. Craig and Muskat (2013) interviewed 65 health social workers in a large Canadian city. Their study focused on the self-described roles, contributions and professional functioning of social workers. Their thematic analysis identified seven roles: "bouncer, janitor, glue, broker, firefighter, juggler and challenger" (2013: 10). These data produce a picture of a complex set of functions and roles with a central unifying focus on using highly developed relationship skills to sort out 'messes' and to meet immediate needs, whether these are providing pants for a person being discharged from an emergency department or providing emotional support for colleagues in the multidisciplinary team. This suggests a professional tendency to being indispensable in messy, complex situations, echoing Wilder Craig's description of a day in her life as she responds to a mix of the practical, the emotional, the crisis, the long-haul planning and the sometimes bizarre 'referrals' that typify a health social worker's daily experience (Wilder Craig, 2007). This breadth of focus can be critiqued as being a weakness; one of the authors' own research participants commented, "social work is such a broad kind of profession that you come out like a jack of all trades but master of none" (Beddoe, 2013a: 35).

But it could also be seen as where our strength lies: having strong values which mean social workers meet needs with skill rather than insisting on rigid roles. Morriss (2016) interviewed social workers who were isolated in mental health services in England and describes their depiction of social work visibility/invisibility; she cites participants reporting that social workers had freedom but that "this freedom comes partially from being 'the people who mop up the stuff [others] don't want to do'. Thus, social work's 'space' is again depicted as liminal; operating in the gaps left by other professions" (2106: 5). Social work identity can be forged in in-between spaces, performing actions that may be unappealing to others, or that may fall between their understood roles.

Such research hints at a world of practice where social workers, in part at least, construct their identities in interaction with others. Their relationships with other professionals, in multidisciplinary teams for example, may lead to perceived weakening of professional identity, as noted by students (Wiles, 2013 and Chapter 3 in this volume) and among members of mental health teams (Barnes, Carpenter, and Dickinson, 2000). As Leigh (2014: 642) has observed in her study of child protection social workers, a "different meaning of profession" may emerge when researchers talk directly with professionals who deal with "certain cultural scripts". If identity develops as a result of "interactions with others", then Leigh argues, "narratives show how these social workers have constructed their own, in part, through the discourses that have been made available" (642). While Leigh's participants were constructing identity in the face of unrelentingly negative narratives about social work, Craig and Muskat's participants were building theirs through interactions with other professionals in the spaces created in health care settings for their 'useful' work.

Health social work: professional capital in health settings – the utility of Bourdieu's concepts

What emerges from these narratives is a need to focus our attention briefly on the power relations between professions and how these might position social work. In health care, I argue, the system of power is expressed in symbolic acts and material practices. Clothing and equipment may, for example, signify hierarchies and differential positioning. Social work may have a significant role in the hospital but lack the accoutrements indicating special (or specialised) contributions – no stethoscope around the neck, no uniform (Beddoe, 2010; Scholar, 2016) – and limited control of the spaces in which health care happens. It is rarely enacted *on* the body, but the body is central to health care for almost all other health professionals (Cameron and McDermott, 2007). Social workers feel that their work is often a site of struggle, over patients and their rights, acting as active agents in the broad and expansive field of health and welfare (Beddoe, 2013a).

Gartman (2007: 391) writes: "Bourdieu conceives of society not as one big unified struggle for a few common resources, but as a conglomeration of relatively independent struggles for a variety of resources". Modern societies include 'fields' such as economics, religion, science, academic institutions, health and justice systems and large 'welfare' bureaucracies within the state apparatus, where professionals perform distinct roles, often in situations demanding clear demarcation. This demarcation (and the status and expertise which accompanies it) can be a site of struggle. Bourdieu rejected a conceptualisation of the state as one large body manipulated by the ruling class; and Garrett (2009: 345) argues that the neo-liberal state comprises "multiple identities and multiple boundaries". Furthermore, Garrett suggests "the state may be less a 'battlefield' site and more an expansive terrain on which occurs a series of seemingly discrete and unconnected skirmishes" (345). While undeniably the immediacy of patient needs may often place clinical leadership in physicians' hands, this does not explain the extension of medical dominance over all aspects of health care. Bywaters (1986) warned of the risks of "unconditional collaboration", urging the adoption of a set of principles for social work in health, noting that "power will not be relinquished lightly by the medical profession and its allies, either to other workers or to lay people" (1986: 674). But Bywaters could not have foreseen the huge changes to power and control that would later be visited upon the health care sector by managerialism.

More recently it has been asserted that medical dominance has waned and, in large part, this is held to be a consequence of new forms of management and governance in health care. Willis (2006) and Coburn (2006) have argued that, with the advent of new models of public management, technologies of control such as evidence-based practice (EBP) and clinical governance (Webb, 2001), bureaucracies assert greater control of professions – and with these changes even the dominance of medicine has been weakened. Professions had been criticised over the last four decades for their use of power, based on their disciplinary control of knowledge and expertise (Evetts, 2006). Coburn suggests that the growth of 'managed' environments means that the claim of specialist knowledge is no longer sufficient to guarantee autonomy. Epistemological changes, the influence of mass media and the vast access to information offered by the Internet have altered some aspects of the previously "unbreakable tie between knowledge/expertise and power" (Coburn, 2006: 438).

Neo-liberalism also brought into play the idea of EBP as a solution to burgeoning health budgets. EBP challenges the potency of an exclusive knowledge claim for any profession, and this is one of the essential components of professional status (see Webb, 2001). Accordingly, while EBP might symbolise the power of medical expertise, some deconstruction of this idea suggests it represents a *weakening* of power. EBP aims to evaluate practices against other practices, using the so-called gold-standard method of random controlled trials. The results of these projects create codified knowledge packaged as 'best practice'. Coburn (2006: 439) points out that, while medical scientists contribute to the production of this knowledge, the codification process is under bureaucratic control which shifts the intellectual activity further away from clinicians. In the neo-liberal regime, of course, EBP does what it is intended to do: empower bureaucratic agents to apply 'science' to rationing. Thus, social work is exhorted to ensure its survival in this climate by contributing to the production of knowledge and to defend its contribution with evidence of its effectiveness (see, for example, Sheldon and Macdonald, 1999). Health care social workers participating in a study of continuing education were notably concerned to keep up with other professionals in research in the 'battlefield' of the multidisciplinary field (Beddoe, 2013a).

Research became a highly desirable social work practice (Fouché, 2015; Joubert, 2006) and is often linked to status and power differentials with other professions: see for example Björkenheim, whose participants in focus group interviews

> felt it would be good to do some research themselves, because it would give them a higher status in the university hospital, where research is highly valued. They wanted to do research in order to get 'hard facts' that they could present to their colleagues of other professions.
>
> *(2007: 273)*

However, they also identified a problem in health care:

> doing social work research in a multiprofessional setting [makes it] hard to distinguish the social work part from the work of other professionals. When doing research within a multiprofessional team, there is also a risk that other professions take the lead.
>
> *(Ibid.)*

While the uncritical adoption of EBP has been challenged by many scholars (van Luitgaarden, 2009; Webb, 2001), this imperative has put research on the agenda, and the adoption of research-mindedness and skill is a well-embedded and important aspect of social work education and professional development (Fouché, 2015).

It is clear that knowledge is a major facet of professional identity for social workers. In health care in particular, this is linked to codified knowledge and the power that accompanies it. Elsewhere I have conceptualised this as "professional capital" (Beddoe, 2010, 2013b). The professional capital construct is an extension of cultural and social capital (Bourdieu, 1984; Bourdieu and Passeron, 1977), and is a form of symbolic capital, "where prestige, status and influence in institutional life . . . are significant to social workers, because they perceive themselves as lacking" (Beddoe, 2013b: 53–54). Professional capital is relatively undeveloped conceptually, although there is considerable literature concerned with Bourdieusian constructs of social and cultural capital as applied to professional *practices* and social work identity (Garrett, 2007a, 2007b; Houston, 2002), and education (Bourdieu and Passeron, 1977). References to professional capital are found mainly in discussion of the challenges faced by contemporary professions, including those of multidisciplinary teams. Chau (2005: 671) similarly uses the term "professional capital" in a summary of an unpublished conference paper on knowledge in nursing, stating that she uses it "to inscribe a profession's value, as being recognised and appreciated, by other professions" (also see Leigh, Chapter 14 in this volume). Chau offers "a preliminary definition of 'professional capital' as the value of recognition and understanding of the contributions of a profession to include trust, appreciation, reciprocation, and the allowance of growth through change within the context of related professions" (2005: 671). Developed via a qualitative study of social workers' engagement in continuing education (Beddoe, 2010), professional capital can be defined as the aggregated value of several attributes: the holding of mandated educational qualifications; the occupation of social 'distinction' based in the territory we call health and social care/services; and finally, the achievement of the economic value of occupational closure, a key artefact of professional status (Witz, 1992; also see Abbott, 1988).

Concluding discussion

Social work practice in health care has many strengths. Craig and Muskat (2013) and Wilder Craig (2007) evoke imagery of a professional role rich with multiple identities. Paradoxically, this diversity and multiplicity can be framed as a strength, expressed in the pervasive idea that carrying out psychosocial support tasks that other professions prefer not to do is still a territory of sorts. More than a century after its inception, health social work can be usefully conceived as positioned within a field of forces (Bourdieu, 1998) holding ground in spite of medical dominance, EBP and managerialist institutional regimes. The fields of health and social care are populated by active agents taking ideological standpoints on many aspects of social care or health: social justice; challenges to privilege; seeing humans as productive or unproductive, deserving or undeserving; favouring universalism or targeting in meeting health and social needs; and so forth. This field is a site of competing discourses about inequalities and how to address them, and it remains a place of struggle and contestation over power and resources. This complex, contested space is a valid place for social work to stand. Social workers employed in the health sector remain deeply engaged in the enduring goal of holistic, socially focused health care, while seeking simultaneously to improve their own status and influence. That social workers articulate their concerns using the language of competition, even the military metaphors of the battlefield (Beckett, 2003; Beddoe, 2013a), suggests an enduring struggle to achieve professional capital. They remain optimistic and future focused. They are up for the fight.

References

Abbott, A. (1988). *The System of Professions: An Essay on the Division of Expert Labor*. Chicago: University of Chicago Press.

Abbott, A. (1995). Boundaries of Social Work or Social Work of Boundaries? *Social Service Review*, 69(4): 545–562.

Abbott, P., & Meerabeau, L. (1998). *The Sociology of the Caring Professions*. London: University College Press.

Auslander, G. (2001). Social Work in Health Care: What Have We Achieved? *Journal of Social Work*, 1(2): 201–222.

Barnes, D., Carpenter, J., & Dickinson, C. (2000). Inter-professional Education for Community Mental Health: Attitudes to Community Care and Professional Stereotypes. *Social Work Education*, 19(6): 565–583.

Bartlett, H. M. (1975). Ida M. Cannon: Pioneer in Medical Social Work. *Social Service Review*, 49(2): 208–229.

Beckett, C. (2003). The Language of Siege: Military Metaphors in the Spoken Language of Social Work. *British Journal of Social Work*, 33(5): 625–639.

Beddoe, L. (2010). *Building Professional Capital: New Zealand Social Workers and Continuing Education*. (Unpublished PhD dissertation). School of Health and Social Development, Deakin. Victoria, Australia.

Beddoe, L. (2013a). Health Social Work: Professional Identity and Knowledge. *Qualitative Social Work*, 12(1): 24–40.

Beddoe, L. (2013b). A 'Profession of Faith' or a Profession: Social Work, Knowledge and Professional Capital. *New Zealand Sociology*, 28(2): 44–63.

Beddoe, L., & Deeney, C. (2012). Discovering Health Social Work in New Zealand in its Published Work: Implications for the Profession. *Aotearoa New Zealand Social Work*, 24(1): 41–55.

Björkenheim, J. (2007). Knowledge and Social Work in Health Care: The Case of Finland. *Social Work in Health Care*, 44(3): 261–278.

Bourdieu, P. (1984). *Distinction: A Social Critique of the Judgement of Taste*, translated by R. Nice. London: Routledge & Kegan Paul.

Bourdieu, P. (1998). *On Television and Journalism*, translated by P. P. Ferguson. London: Pluto Press.

Bourdieu, P. (1999). An Impossible Mission. In A. Aracardo, P. Bourdieu & P. P. Ferguson (Eds.), *The Weight of the World: Social Suffering in Contemporary Society* (pp. 189–202). Palo Alto, CA: Stanford University Press.

Bourdieu, P., & Passeron, J.-C. (1977). *Reproduction in Education, Society and Culture*, translated by R. Nice. London: Sage.

Brough, M., Wagner, I., & Farrell, L. (2013). Review of Australian Health Related Social Work Research 1990–2009. *Australian Social Work*, 66(4): 528–539.

Bywaters, P. (1986). Social Work and the Medical Profession: Arguments against Unconditional Collaboration. *British Journal of Social Work*, 16(6): 661–667.

Cabot, R. C. (1919). *Social Work: Essays on the Meeting-Ground of Doctor and Social Worker*. Boston, New York: Houghton Mifflin Company.

Cameron, N., & McDermott, F. (2007). *Social Work and the Body*. Basingstoke: Palgrave Macmillan.

Chau, C. (2005). *Professional Capital: An Informational Approach to Nursing*. Paper presented at the Knowledge management: Nurturing culture, innovation and technology conference, North Carolina USA. Retrieved from http://www.worldscientific.com/world scibooks/10.1142/5971.

Cleak, H. M., & Turczynski, M. (2014). Hospital Social Work in Australia: Emerging Trends or More of the Same? *Social Work in Health Care*, 53(3): 199–213.

Coburn, D. (2006). Medical Dominance then and Now: A Critical Reflection. *Health Sociology Review*, 15(5): 452–443.

Craig, S. L., & Muskat, B. (2013). Bouncers, Brokers, and Glue: The Self-Described Roles of Social Workers in Urban Hospitals. *Health & Social Work*, 38(1): 7–16.

Etzioni, A. (ed.) (1969). *The Semi-Professions and Their Organizations: Teachers, Nurses and Social Workers*. New York: Free Press.

Evetts, J. (2006). Introduction: Trust and Professionalism, Challenges and Occupational Changes. *Current Sociology*, 54(4): 515–531.

Fouché, C. B. (2015). *Practice Research Partnerships in Social Work: Making a Difference*. Bristol: Policy Press.

Freidson, E. (2001). *Professionalism: The Third Logic*. Cambridge: Polity.

Garrett, P. M. (2007a). Making Social Work More Bourdieusian: Why the Social Professions Should Critically Engage with the Work of Pierre Bourdieu. *European Journal of Social Work*, 10(2): 225–243.

Garrett, P. M. (2007b). The Relevance of Bourdieu for Social Work: A Reflection on Obstacles and Omissions. *Journal of Social Work*, 7(3): 355–379.

Garrett, P. M. (2009). Examining the 'Conservative Revolution': Neo-liberalism and Social Work Education. *Social Work Education*, 29(4): 340–355.

Gartman, D. (2007). The Strength of Weak Programs in Cultural Sociology: A Critique of Alexander's Critique of Bourdieu. *Theory and Society*, 36(5): 381–413.

Haultain, L. (2015). Facing the Challenges Together: A Future Vision for Health Social Work. In L. Beddoe & J. Maidment (Eds.), *Social Work Practice for Promoting Health and Well-being: Critical Issues* (pp. 39–50). London: Routledge.

Houston, S. (2002). Reflecting on Habitus, Field and Capital: Towards a Culturally Sensitive Social Work. *Journal of Social Work*, 2(2): 149–167.

Jenkins, R. (1992). *Pierre Bourdieu: Key Sociologists*. London: Routledge.

Joubert, L. (2006). Academic-Practice Partnerships in Practice Research: A Cultural Shift for Health Social Workers. *Social Work in Health Care*, 43(2/3): 151–162.

Judd, R. G., & Sheffield, S. (2010). Hospital Social Work: Contemporary Roles and Professional Activities. *Social Work in Health Care*, 49(9): 856–871.

Leigh, J. T. (2014). The Process of Professionalisation: Exploring the Identities of Child Protection Social Workers. *Journal of Social Work*, 14(6): 625–644.

McCoyd, J. L. M., Kerson, T. S., & Associates. (2016). Primer on Micro Practice in Social Work in Health Care. In J. L. M. McCoyd & T. S. Kerson (Eds.), *Social Work in Health Settings: Practice in Context* (Fourth edition, pp. 25–35). Oxon, UK: Routledge.

McNeill, T., & Nicholas, D. B. (2012). Strategies for Research Development in Hospital Social Work: A Case Study. *Research on Social Work Practice*, 22(6): 672–679.

Mizrahi, T., & Berger, C. (2005). A Longitudinal Look at Social Work Leadership in Hospitals: The Impact of a Changing Health Care System. *Health and Social Work*, 30(2): 155–163.

Morriss, L. (2016). Being Seconded to a Mental Health Trust: The (In)visibility of Mental Health Social Work. *British Journal of Social Work*. doi: 10.1093/bjsw/bcw022.

Rehr, H., & Rosenberg, G. (2006). *The Social Work-Medicine Relationship: 100 Years at Mount Sinai*. New York: Haworth Press.

Rueschemeyer, D. (1986). *Power and the Division of Labor*. Stanford, CA: Stanford University Press.

Scholar, H. (2016). The Neglected Paraphernalia of Practice? Objects and Artefacts in Social Work Identity Practice and Research. *Qualitative Social Work*. doi: 10.1177/1473325016637911.

Sheldon, B., & Macdonald, G. M. (1999). *Research and Practice in Social Care: Mind the Gap*. Exeter, UK: Centre for Evidence-Based Social Services, University of Exeter.

Spensley, R. G. (1953). The Nurse as a Medical Social Worker. *New Zealand Nursing Journal*, 46(6): 177.

Spitzer, W., Silverman, E., & Allen, K. (2015). From Organizational Awareness to Organizational Competency in Health Care Social Work: The Importance of Formulating a 'Profession-in-Environment' Fit. *Social Work in Health Care*, 54(3): 193–211.

Todd, A. J. (1919). *The Scientific Spirit and Social Work*. New York: Macmillan.

van de Luitgaarden, G. M. J. (2009). Evidence-based Practice in Social Work: Lessons from Judgment and Decision-Making Theory. *British Journal of Social Work*, 39(2): 243–260.

Webb, S.A. (2001). Some Considerations on the Validity of Evidence-based Practice in Social Work. *British Journal of Social Work*, 31(1): 57–79.

Weick, A. (2000). Hidden Voices. *Social Work*, 45(5): 395–402.

Wilder Craig, R. (2007). A Day in the Life of a Hospital Social Worker: Presenting Our Role through the Personal Narrative. *Qualitative Social Work*, 6(4): 431–446.

Wiles, F. (2013). 'Not Easily Put into a Box': Constructing Professional Identity. *Social Work Education*, 32(7): 854–866.

Willis, E. (2006). Introduction: Taking Stock of Medical Dominance. *Health Sociology Review*, 15(5): 421–431.

Witz, A. (1992). *Professions and Patriarchy*. London: Routledge.

10

INTER-PROFESSIONAL COLLABORATION

Strengthening or weakening social work identity?

Julia Emprechtinger and Peter Voll

Introduction

Across Europe an effective inter-professional workforce is now acknowledged by policymakers and strategists as critical for the health, social care and welfare of future generations (e.g. Byrne, 2004; SAMW, 2014). However, as has been noted in social work research and elsewhere, inter-professional partnerships are "hard work", (Wildridge et al., 2004: 4) may be conflictive, are dependent on the development of a common terminology (Machura, 2016), rely heavily on interpersonal relationships and groupwork (Pullen-Sansfaçon and Ward, 2014) and may decisively shift the power balance between the professions involved (Salhani and Coulter, 2009; also see Chapter 2, in this volume).

This chapter examines how the increasing push towards inter-professional collaboration might impact on professional identity in social work, using the recently created interdisciplinary Swiss child and adult protection authorities or courts[1] as an example and field of observation.

In legal commentary and political debate in Switzerland, social work was appointed as one of the key professions alongside law in this context. Social workers thus met new opportunities in terms of new positions in the child and adult protection system, particularly that of a member of the decision-making board. At the same time, they were confronted with new challenges (or recurring residual ones), namely that of situating their knowledge and experience against that of other professionals in the newly created inter-professional boards, involving mainly lawyers, but also psychologists and educationalists. With and against them, they had to develop new ways of affirming their professional identity, i.e. of negotiating their disciplinary profile, signature skill set and competences.

The new authorities thus can be seen as a new arena of inter-professional competition and, as a corollary, of identity formation. Observing this field in the making is all the more intriguing, as Switzerland's high degree of federalism allows for much variation in organizational structure and thus for studying the interplay of organizational context, professional status and individual identification processes.[2]

This chapter presents some preliminary reflections on this relationship: the first section discusses basic theoretical concepts which have currency in the literature on professional identity and allow for identifying the dimensions of empirical observation. In the second section, a brief description of the child and adult protection field in Switzerland is given in order to enable readers to adequately grasp the practitioners' situation. The third section, based on several small-scale studies conducted since 2013, attempts to trace the evolution of the professional field and roles and functions played by social workers.

Theoretical context

Boundaries of professions and inter-professional collaboration

Traditionally, theories of professionalization focus on the client-professional dyad from which they propose structural requirements of professions and professionalism, as, most notably, specific and systematized knowledge, techniques of diagnoses and intervention, and ethical norms as well as control over education and access to the field (Parsons, 1951). Power and conflict theories, in contrast, see professions as groups trying to advance individual status through collective action (Sarfatti Larson, 1977), essentially by limiting access to prestigious and economically attractive occupational fields (Collins, 1990). In this endeavour, the ability to define the framework in which professional action is carried out is a central element in a triple process: (i) the defining power to frame the theoretical knowledge that gives plausibility to professional practice, (ii) the defining power to set standards of legitimate professional practice and (iii) the power to control access to such fields of practice. According to this approach, professionalization is conceptualized as a continually ongoing process dependent on the working environment. Therefore inter-professional collaboration has to be seen as a territorial arena where rivalling professions sharpen their profile and try to prove the competitive advantage of their specific concepts, diagnoses and interventions (Abbott, 1988). Professionalization, understood as the formation of a profession, is a prominent instance of boundary making, i.e. of the formation of groups by demarcation from other groups (Lamont and Molnár, 2002).

In recent years, inter-professional collaboration has increasingly attracted attention, especially in the field of health and social care. Complex needs of clients on the one hand, and the division of labour and corresponding specialization on the other, enforce collaboration between specialists from different professions (Pullen-Sansfaçon and Ward, 2014). In this sense, the positive effect of cooperation – of unifying different competences and knowledge to offer the best intervention – is put forward. In much the same way and with reference to the work of Susanne Leigh Star (Leigh and Griesemer, 1989), Lamont and Molnár (2002: 180–181) point out the connecting, bridging and inclusionary potential of boundaries, i.e. of the boundary as a prerequisite of collaboration. This is undeniable, but the aspect of competition between different professions that collaborate is irrefutable when it comes to question like: who has the sovereignty of interpretation concerning diagnosis, intervention and inference? Or: how is the definition of a possible common profile negotiated? Furthermore, using the concept of separating *and* connecting boundaries allows for conceiving of inter-professional collaboration in different variants, from an interdisciplinary approach where disciplinary boundaries are maintained to a transdisciplinary approach where disciplinary boundaries are dissolved and a new common knowledge base is generated.

Framing professionalization in terms of boundaries and boundary making also allows for a further question in specific terms about the relation between profession and professional knowledge: if one distinguishes, as Lamont and Molnár (2002) suggest, between symbolic and social boundaries, then one may ask questions about how symbolic boundaries or conceptual distinctions are affected by social boundaries and vice versa or how symbolic boundaries can be crossed without crossing social boundaries (or the other way round in the case of interdisciplinary cooperation). One can also ask who has the power to establish or cross boundaries and identify which mechanisms permit this. Thus, with regard to social mobility (upwards as well as downwards within scales of professional prestige) the permeability of group boundaries, and hence the properties of boundaries and the social and symbolic crossing strategies available, becomes a key element of justification (Boen and Vanbeselaere, 2001).

The individual and the collective processes of identification

Professionalization and boundary work have been situated, so far, as collective processes of a profession's development. However, collective mobility strategies must not be seen in isolation from individual positioning strategies and individual professional identity construction. Both levels mutually condition each other. To concur with Jenkins (2000), individual identity does not make sense without collective membership, and the collective does not exist without individuals producing and reproducing it in practice.

In this sense, it is instructive to look briefly at processes of professional identity development. On the individual level, Cohen-Scali (2003) distinguishes between *socialization for work* (through education) and *socialization by work* (through work experience). The latter is essential at the beginning of a career, but remains important for the development of professional identity during professional activity, above all in case of career transitions. Ibarra (1999) shows the importance of role models in the workplace for selecting and learning a new professional role: individuals learn from peers who convey a certain interpretation of the job. This interpretation, however, is held to be a collective one too – whether or not it be in line with the model proposed by *collective professionals*, i.e. by members of the professional community working, at some distance to "ordinary practice", for the development of the profession at different levels, notably education, research and policymaking (Scott, 2005).

Drawing boundaries or boundary work is a key component of identity work, and both are done in collaboration by individual practitioners and collective professionals. In the production of collective sense to which practitioners refer to, two elements are decisive: (i) the self-description of the group and (ii) the categorization from outside the group (Jenkins, 2004). This dialectical understanding of identity construction assumes identity as something procedural, negotiable and flexible. For identity, as for other professional boundaries, the question is one of the power relations between in- and out-groups: who has the power and sovereignty to impose basic categories and standards, and thus set boundaries against those of others. With regard to inter-professional collaboration within the same team, several collectivities (own profession, organization or a newly created transdisciplinary network or universe of discourse) might be at disposal as reference for an individual practitioner. Thus one may further ask how such "offers for identification" are prioritized and selected. What are the consequences for the individual practitioner and the profession's collective identity?

Social work as source of identification in inter-professional relations

As the focus is on professional identity in social work, it might be useful to take a glance at social work as a collective identity and its usefulness for practitioners for the positioning in inter-professional collaboration. Current literature on social work in inter-professional collaboration offers a wide range of views, but is, in general, not very optimistic with regard to the social worker's ability to develop a sharply contoured as well as recognized role profile. Their signature skill set contribution and hence their function often seem far less than obvious. The absence of a solid knowledge base has led some scholars to focus on the integrative, transdisciplinary identity of social work (Büchner, 2012). Thus, Oliver (2013) stresses the "boundary spanning" role of social workers, and others underline their interpersonal and processual competences and their values (Korazim-Körösy et al., 2014) or their expertise in group dynamics to foster successful collaboration (Pullen-Sansfaçon and Ward, 2014). For Maddock (2014) it is the inter-professional communication and role negotiation skills regarding their own expertise and competence that social workers lack in inter-professional teamwork. Dewees (2005) sees another crucial point for social workers' success or failure in collaboration with other professions: they find themselves caught between the values of client advocacy and of a team consensus about an adequate distributive intervention strategy.

To state the problem with reference to one of Abbott's central concepts, one might say that social work claims a comprehensive and thus diffuse jurisdiction (Scherr, 2002). Being the process manager able to address the client to specialized services supposes a broad (as opposed to deep) knowledge of neighbouring disciplines. One could thus argue: if modern society is characterized by an advanced division of labour (and thus specificity, as Parsons, 1951, would have had it), social work is characterized by the opposite of conveying a general (over)view. If comprehensiveness and, as a corollary, diffuseness are cornerstones of social work's collective identity, the question inevitably arises of how the profession as a whole and individual social workers manage to communicate their identity and profile within their own group. Together, social workers manage to defend their environmental turf, especially against neighbouring, and potentially competing professions.

Significance of the organizational context

Like other professionals, social workers rarely work independently, but are most often embedded in organizations. As a consequence, they are not only committed to their profession's principles, but also to the organization's values, norms, classifications and procedures. According to Bommes and Scherr (2012: 192ff), we may distinguish three types of organization that frame social workers' professional action: public welfare administration, social work organizations and organizations belonging to specialized subsystems dominated by other professionals (like courts or hospitals). Each type produces different constraints and thus gives different leeway for collective and individual professional discretion and strategies of preserving professional autonomy (e.g. Lipsky, 1980; Sosin, 2010).

Concerning social work, child and adult protection authorities may be counted among the organizations of the third type. Even though most of them are administrative authorities, their overall identity is framed by the administration of justice. They are, thus, typically headed by non-social work professionals, mostly legal, leaving social workers in a position of professional "heteronomy" (Abbott, 1988; Scott, 1969, 1992). This normally implies working under the supervision of somebody applying professional standards other than their own, based on other professional classifications and thus elementary symbolic boundaries.

Whatever the dominant profession (if any), organizations impose classifications and hierarchies of their own, in line with their stated goals, with their history and with the vested interest of their members; among these classifications, those defining conditions and status of membership are of particular importance (Jenkins, 2004). In this way, organizations form arenas of inter-professional competition, defining the rules and resources (not least in terms of symbolic power) that weaken or strengthen individuals and groups in their intra-organizational competition (Abbott, 1988). The organizational frame is thus expected to be important if not decisive for the outcome of jurisdictional competition.

If organization is a variable structuring inter-professional competition, it can also be seen as a source of institutional logics and as such a reference for individual identity construction (Barbour and Lammers, 2015). We might, in consequence, differentiate between *professional* and *organizational* dimensions of a practitioner's work identity. Within the organization, group boundaries might then (individually) be drawn along different criteria, e.g. according to organizational or managerial choices as well as individual identification preferences. With respect to social work, the study of the Swiss child and adult protection authorities might contribute to an understanding of how organizational "identification offers" are received by social workers and how this might be related to collective identification support within the profession.

The social context: child and adult protection authorities in Switzerland

Switzerland has a strong tradition of citizens' voluntary participation at all political levels (including decision making in social welfare or education). In line with this tradition, before 2013, child and adult protection authorities (so-called tutelary authorities) were composed of laypersons on the local level (Häfeli and Voll, 2007; Voll, 2006). Exceptions were to be found in some French-speaking cantons, which had already organized the former child and adult protection authorities in courts, and in some bigger cities where the responsibilities had already been professionalized (albeit not necessarily around social work). The revision of the Swiss Civil Code in 2013 thus not only brought about a fundamental shift in the law from a control to a protection perspective, but a comprehensive reorganization of the competencies for decision making.[3] Unsurprisingly, the revision, the status and the composition of the new Child and Adult Protection Authorities (CAPAs) were among the most controversial issues in the reform procedure (Häfeli, 2013a). The compromise finally adopted was centred on the notion of a "specialist authority" composed of at least three members of different disciplines (art. 440 CC).

The formal professional qualifications of these members is subject to debate. Commentators (e.g. Hausheer, Aebi-Müller, and Geiser, 2010) agree on the requirement of having at least one lawyer and having also members qualified in other relevant disciplines, notably psychology and/or medicine/psychiatry and social work. Besides these minimal exigencies, the cantons are free to design the authority's organization according to their needs and traditions. Accordingly, across the cantons we find a panoply of CAPA structures (in the narrow sense of the decision-making board), surrounded by an equally impressive diversity of auxiliary services (CAPAs in the wider sense), in which lawyers, social workers, psychologists and other professionals may play quite different roles. Three of the most important dimensions of variation concerning the organization of these authorities are (for a general overview, see Häfeli, 2013b) the following.

- *Legal status*: in some cantons, the CAPA is part of the court system; in others, it has administrative status.
- *Eligibility criteria* for board members and presidency: some cantons explicitly require social work professionals being members of the board, while others state eligibility criteria in terms of degree only but not of discipline; some reserve the presidency to members of the legal profession, while others do not.
- *Permanent vs. temporary/associate membership*: in several cantons, non-legal professionals have the status of associate members ("assesseurs") which are associated on a case-by-case base, according to competencies assumed to be necessary. Most CAPAs, however, are composed of permanent members.

Other differences, such as size, structure, composition and function of the auxiliary services, or the wider context of local/cantonal social assistance organization, have to be considered important as well. Equally, the continuity or discontinuity of former structures and players in the new system should not be ignored (Emprechtinger et al., 2016). Especially in municipalities where the social services had a decisive role for preparing decisions of the lay authorities, the creation of a professional authority exercising its role as decision-making and supervisory authority had a major impact on the relationships with these social services.

The nationwide compulsory transformation from lay to professional interdisciplinary authorities changed, and potentially boosted, the role of social work in the field of child and adult protection. As comprising a professional group with comprehensive experience in the implementation of protection measures as guardians or deputies to child and adults and, in a great number of municipalities, in preparing the decisions that the lay authorities then formally adopted, social work was appointed as one of the key professions next to law. Such appointments opened new opportunities in terms of new strategic positions in the child and adult protection system – that of members of the decision-making board.

Interplay of organization, profession and individual identification

As outlined earlier, the CAPAs are an interesting field for observing dynamics and processes of inter-professional negotiation of jurisdiction roles and signature competences. Twenty-six different cantonal legislations offer as many different organizational frames that have an important impact on collaboration and identity construction of the involved individuals as well as professional groups. The following reflections emerged from several different empirical research and evaluation projects in the context of the CAPAs since their start in 2013. Empirical material consists of interviews, focus groups and documents as well as observations of media discourse, conferences and discussions with key persons. Data were not collected in order to treat the question asked in this chapter, but to allow valuable insights into the interaction of inter-professional collaboration and professional identity with special regard to the impact of the organizational context.

Boundary work in a "fuzzy transdisciplinary field"

Understanding the significance of inter-professional collaboration as an arena for sharpening professional profile by boundary work (Abbott, 1988), the organizational context as structuring this arena should not be overlooked. The wide variations of organizational models around the same federal core elements described earlier allow for a rich comparative perspective. As noted, an organization may offer an open frame for jurisdictional competition or, on the contrary, narrowly determine professional boundaries so that jurisdictional competition is excluded. The CAPA system examined here showed models of both permitting and excluding jurisdictional competition. Two of them will be described hereafter for illustration before going into detail of professional boundary making in what we've described as the "fuzzy field".

With this first model of jurisdictional operations, the CAPAs have the legal status of a court. Professional judges are permanent members of each CAPA. To fulfil the exigency of interdisciplinarity, further professionals are assigned on a case-by-case basis as assessors to the decision-making boards. In practice, for all casework undertaken two professionals with different backgrounds (e.g. social work and psychiatry) are attached for the hearing of the case and subsequent decision making in the board. All the preparatory work, from the initial decision to process a case, to social enquiry and mandating external expertise, to preparing the hearing and finally drawing up the decision, is done by the permanent member of the court and its internal support service, all professionals with legal backgrounds. Interdisciplinarity comes into play at a point where pre-decisions have already been taken by one profession. The board that was studied in this context[4] demonstrated a strict division of labour between the involved professions. The professional judge clearly leads in the case and is responsible for the procedurally and materially correct interpretation of the law. As for the social worker in the board, the judge appreciates the expert knowledge concerning social institutions, the social security system and possible alternatives to a protection measure. The social worker, in turn, benefits from the recognition of their expertise and positively evaluates the prospect of bringing their perspective to bear during the hearing and the decision-making process. The court as organizational context defines very clearly the position that practitioners with non-legal background can assume. Boundaries tend thus to be very clear; and in this case they appear to be accepted by the practitioners involved.

In contrast to the example discussed earlier, wherein the assessors are clearly subordinated to the judge (even if their votes have equal weight), the second CAPA exemplifies a different model based on a transdisciplinary interpretation of the collaboration within the decision-making board. This authority is an administrative one wherein all of the board members are permanent employees and have the same status and autonomy for leading proceedings. That means that every board member – regardless of their professional background – has to fulfil the same work during a proceeding they are responsible for, from the receipt of a "notification of danger" (signalling a child or adult potentially in danger and need of assistance) to the decision. In consequence, social workers are expected to perfectly carry out the legal elements in a proceeding and, vice versa, lawyers are expected to integrate "the social" in their work (to just mention these two professions in the board). A president of a CAPA that follows this second model illustrates this understanding when he says that good board members are social workers with legal competences and lawyers with social work competences. Interdisciplinary dialogue takes place in team meetings where certain cases are discussed in the presence of all disciplines, or, informally, in bilateral peer counselling. The hearing normally is conducted by one member only; the decision, then, is taken by the board of three persons. The degree of discussion, however, can vary significantly according to the complexity of a case and the individual decision of the responsible board member.

In the first example, social workers have a weaker position in status due to different membership statuses of the board members, but have – in turn and due to a clear division of labour– a very clear profile that is recognized by colleagues in the legal profession. Social work identity may be stated as rather strong with distinct boundaries of competences. In the second example, the transdisciplinary CAPA, the status of social workers is procedurally equal to that of lawyers and other professionals; it can thus be said to be higher than in the first CAPA described. But what happens to social work identity if a transdisciplinary understanding of collaboration renders boundaries along professional profiles more diffuse?

Of course, professional boundaries continue to exist in a transdisciplinary model as well, as a CAPA has to meet the formal requirement of different disciplines in the decision-making board. It might also be assumed that board members preserve basic elements of their professional origins in their new identification: they have to adapt to a new common (transdisciplinary) profile, but they do so on the bases of their original categories and distinctions. Observations of CAPAs that pursue such a transdisciplinary model did not reveal the way the transdisciplinary common profile is created and necessary skills are negotiated. Nonetheless, the observations allow for some interpretations regarding the ways of boundary making and jurisdictional claims of social workers in these negotiation processes.

The organizational context as quasi-judicial administrative authority emphasizes the importance of legal correctness of the proceeding. A transdisciplinary profile of a board member is thus based on the knowledge and skills to lead correct legal proceedings. This knowledge, as described in law and books, is comparatively well defined and thus easy to communicate to non-lawyers. Social work knowledge, on the contrary, was much more fluidly addressed in the interviews. Lawyers vaguely named it "the social" or "the way they talk to people". Social workers' statements lacked clear definitions of what particular knowledge other professions should adopt from social work. This might be because the question was not asked specifically. The data suggest, however, that this is, indeed, less clear and thus more difficult to communicate. As social workers in the first CAPA model often refer to their professional experiences in the former system of child and adult protection, this expertise is less useful for collectivization as social work knowledge and skills.

Therefore, in this case of a new and still "fuzzy transdisciplinary field" where professionals collaborate, it might be suggested that social work identity is not sharpened but rather individualized and thus blurred. If there is no common social work knowledge body – as knowledge is often labelled as individual experience – and, in return, another profession's knowledge base offers useful elements, professional boundaries of social work tend to be dissolved from inside and outside the profession.

Collective identification support for boundary-making processes

If the organizational context is promoting the dissolution of professional boundaries and thus leading to a "fuzzy" field of transdisciplinary professionalism, professionals are individually challenged to position themselves in the board. As outlined earlier, individual professional experience is often put forward to legitimate the individual exclusive position in the board. The position as a board member in the CAPA is new for social work and so is, more generally, the position as a judge (or quasi-judge in the administrative authorities). Therefore, social workers in this position initially did not have any role models offering possible identities to experiment with. In the absence of such models – the importance of which has been demonstrated in Ibarra's (1999) study on identity construction after career transitions – the question of alternative sources of board members' new professional identities has to be addressed. Basically, one may distinguish two such sources or references of identity: (i) the organization, as already addressed as structuring element in the previous section and (ii) the profession of social work as collective professional identity.

Social workers in the CAPA system are not merely situated in relation to their profession, but importantly, as members of the organization. As such they are, quite naturally, developing an identity as board members with their colleagues in their respective authority. In the transdisciplinary model, the identification processes seem to happen, at least in part, collectively across professional boundaries because each member finds themselves in a new position. However, the selection criteria for social workers and lawyers as board members seem to differ between disciplines. As the interview data suggest, social workers often were selected not so much for their formal qualification, but for their work experience in the field of child and adult protection or relevant neighbouring fields. In contrast, lawyers did not generally have experience in child and adult protection, and their formal law qualification was the necessary and sufficient criterion for the membership in the CAPA. Thus, the experiential casework referred to as significant experience of social workers is counterpoised to an education-based collective identity of law, the latter being more prominent in the organization's identity. If it was clear what social workers had to learn from lawyers in order to correctly function as board members (the CAPA is applying the law, thus social workers have to know how to do this correctly, as several interviewees said), it was much less clear what lawyers could learn of social workers besides accumulating their experiences.

Support for the identity construction of social workers in CAPA decision-making boards is expected to come from social work as a profession. Support includes fellow social workers in other CAPAs, the Swiss association of social workers, and the collective identity of social work as profession and discipline. In addition, support for the fulfilling of this distinctive role could be expected from those groups that carried out lobbying activities to push social workers into the formally high positions in the decision-making boards. Surprisingly, little networking activity is currently deployed to develop a collective social work identity as board members. Special conferences on social work in child and adult protection or special issues of the professional journal only partly focus on the special role of social workers as board members. Mainly, they address social workers in the system of child and adult protection in general. Once again, a comparison with the lawyers in the CAPA system is informative: several legal commentaries on the new law on adult protection were published before and after 2013. What is a usual claim of jurisdiction in this sector (as in every sector of new legislation) has also been seen as strong collective support from the legal discipline for their members in the legal discipline for their members in the CAPA system in general. Social workers heavily rely on these support mechanisms as well, at least where they have to manage the procedural dimension of child and adult protection. Interviews with social workers who practise as assessors suggest that, as experts for "the social", they are less inclined towards legal matters than their social work counterparts in transdisciplinary boards. Instead, they are more focused on their specific aspects of professional intervention and knowledge. Identification support from collective professionals is thus mainly occurring whether emphasis is placed on the organizational boundaries (e.g. postgraduate qualification for the field designed for all professionals) or on the professional background (e.g. social work in the child and adult protection system), none of them especially focussing on the specific role of social work in the decision-making board. Consequences for the standing of social work in the CAPAs and the usefulness of the obtained knowledge for jurisdictional competition in the inter-professional collaboration in the decision-making boards are still to be observed.

Boundary-making processes within social work and consequences for professional identity

As the creation of the interdisciplinary CAPAs opened up a new profile for social work in the field of child and adult protection, it triggered a necessary differentiation between social workers as members of decision-making boards and social workers executing the decisions that were taken in decision-making boards in the function as a guardian or deputy. One might say that an internal stratification of social work is occurring: there are now social workers in decision-making boards who are hierarchically above their fellow social workers in the social services.

In this perspective, it is not only the intra-organizational collaboration in CAPAs that challenge social workers to sharpen their profile, but there is – in most of the CAPAs – also an inter-organizational collaboration with fellow social workers that has an impact on professional identity. As mentioned earlier, social workers were often recruited into CAPAs for their professional experience as guardians or deputies or as secretaries of the former lay decision boards (and sometimes both). Some interviews revealed that lacking profound experience in the field was seen as a disqualification for the position, above all from fellow social workers outside the CAPA. In their new role as board members, social workers still can make use of their experience, but this experience can no longer be the basic object of their identification.

Where the presence of social workers in the CAPA system is seen as an element of a largely functional differentiation within the field of social work, this perception is accompanied by expressions of relief to have a representative of one's own professional group ("one of our own professional kind") in the CAPA. This relief is based on expectations that these co-professionals assume a bridging function between front-line social workers (deputies or guardians) and the world of the lawyers. If the perception of stratification and hierarchy between CAPAs and deputies or guardians predominates, the latter often deny that CAPA social workers are still doing social work. As the function no longer comprises direct work with clients, it is doubted to be "real" social work. In addition, CAPA social workers are devaluated as arguing only with paragraphs, just as do lawyers. The differentiation of worksites of the two groups of social workers underlines the different positions in status hierarchy. Due to the common worksite, social workers in the CAPA system are, logically, in closer interaction with the other board members than with their professional peers in the social services. To ensure the bridging function to the social workers in the front-line services that cooperate with the CAPAs and, thus, being successful in (exclusively) occupying this competence within the CAPAs, social workers have to make sure that they continue being perceived as representatives of social work. It is difficult to imagine how this could be done without a common abstract knowledge base, and it is equally difficult to imagine how such knowledge could be created as long as the focus is on personal social work experience.

Concluding discussion

The reform of the Swiss child and adult protection system brought professions of unequal status and types of knowledge together in one and the same authority under the rubric of interdisciplinarity. The diverse existing organizational models provide compelling insights into the nature of professional identity in social work. Where this interdisciplinarity is understood as trans-disciplinarity, it is accompanied by a blurred professional identity, as far as it requires negotiation and creation of a common profile. Therefore, the result might not be a combination of the different professions and their disciplinary knowledge, but the outcome of rather vague or even hinted jurisdictional claims as well as of individual positioning strategies. Whether social work identity is strengthened or weakened in inter-professional collaboration depends in large part on processes of negotiation and the individual practitioner's negotiating skills. If we want to transcend the latter, collective professional identification support is needed; otherwise, the generally weak collective professional identity in social work, combined with the blurry profile of social work in agencies like the CAPAs, will lead to individualistic strategies of status gain. Such individual strategies might strengthen individual professional identity as social workers (with different collective references), but undermine the positioning of social work as a knowledge-based profession and, thus, the ability to make successful collective jurisdictional claims.

Notes

1 As explained further on, depending on cantonal law, child and adult protection authorities may have different legal status (court vs. administrative) without consequences for their formal function and competences.

2 The authors are currently funded by the Swiss National Research Foundation ("Professionalisation by Interdisciplinary Cooperation? Strategies of Social Workers in the

Context of the Swiss Child & Adult Protection Authorities"). The present chapter reports results from preliminary studies done in collaboration with Favre, Gaspoz, Jurisch Praz, Köppel, Marti, Claudia Peter and Mélanie Peter and with two groups of students during their research course. The authors are grateful for those collaborations as well as for the permission to use the material for the present purpose.

3 The revision of the Civil Code of 2013 referred to in this chapter materially concerns the law on adult protection only. The child protection section was revised earlier, in 1976/1978, but because the adult protection authority also "carries out the tasks of the child protection authority" (art. 440 al. 3 CC), the organizational and procedural changes apply to the child protection system as well.

4 The organizational model we studied consists of several different but structurally similar units.

References

Abbott, A. (1988). *The System of Professions: An Essay on the Division of Expert Labor.* Chicago: University of Chicago Press.

Barbour, J. B., & Lammers, J. C. (2015). Measuring Professional Identity: A Review of the Literature and a Multilevel Confirmatory Factor Analysis of Professional Identity Constructs. *Journal of Professions and Organization,* 2(1): 38–60. doi: 10.1093/jpo/jou009.

Boen, F., & Vanbeselaere, N. (2001). Individual versus Collective Responses to Membership in a Low-Status Group: The Effects of Stability and Individual Ability. *The Journal of Social Psychology,* 141(6): 765–783.

Bommes, M., & Scherr, A. (2012). *Soziologie der Sozialen Arbeit: eine Einführung in Formen und Funktionen organisierter Hilfe0* (Second edition). Weinheim/München: Juventa Verlag.

Büchner, S. (2012). *Soziale Arbeit als transdisziplinäre Wissenschaft: Zwischen Verknüpfung und Integration.* Wiesbaden: VS. Verlag für Sozialwissenschaften.

Byrne, D. (2004). *Enabling Good Health for All: A Reflection Process for a New EU Health Strategy.* European Commission. Retrieved from http://ec.europa.eu/health/ph_overview/Documents/pub_good_health_en.pdf.

Cohen-Scali, V. (2003). The Influence of Family, Social, and Work Socialization on the Construction of the Professional Identity of Young Adults. *Journal of Career Development,* 29(4): 237–249.

Collins, R. (1990). Market Closure and the Conflict Theory of the Professions. In M. Burrage & R. Torstendahl (Eds.), *Professions in Theory and History: Rethinking the Study of the Professions* (pp. 24–43). London: Sage.

Dewees, M. (2005). Postmodern Social Work in Interdisciplinary Contexts. *Social Work in Health Care,* 39(3–4): 343–360.

Emprechtinger, J., Favre Bourban, E., Gaspoz, V., Jurisch Praz, S., Peter, M., & Voll, P. (2016). Les autorités de protection en Suisse romande – premières expériences comparées. *Zeitschrift für Kindes- und Erwachsenenschutz/Revue de la protection des mineurs et des adultes,* 71(1): 26–45.

Häfeli, C. (2013a). Die Entstehung des Gesetzes. In A. Büchler, C. Häfeli, A. Leuba & M. Stettler (Eds.), *Famkomm Erwachsenenschutz* (pp. 3–29). Bern: Stämpfli.

Häfeli, C. (2013b). *Grundriss zum Erwachsenenschutzrecht.* Bern: Stämpfli.

Häfeli, C., & Voll, P. (2007). Die Behördenorganisation im Kindes- und Erwachsenenschutz aus rechtlicher und sozialwissenschaftlicher Sicht. *Zeitschrift für Vormundschaftswesen,* 62: 51–64.

Hausheer, H., Aebi-Müller, R. E., & Geiser, T. (2010). *Das neue Erwachsenenschutzrecht.* Bern: Stämpfli.

Ibarra, H. (1999). Provisional Selves: Experimenting with Image and Identity in Professional Adaptation. *Administrative Science Quarterly*, 44(4): 764–791.

Jenkins, R. (2000). Categorization: Identity, Social Process and Epistemology. *Current Sociology*, 48(3): 7–25. doi: 10.1177/0011392100048003003.

Jenkins, R. (2004). *Social Identity* (Second edition). London: Routledge.

Korazim-Körösy, Y., Mizrahi, T., Bayne-Smith, M., & Garcia, M. L. (2014). Professional Determinants in Community Collaborations: Interdisciplinary Comparative Perspectives on Roles and Experiences among Six Disciplines. *Journal of Community Practice*, 22(1–2): 229 255.

Lamont, M., & Molnár, V. (2002). The Study of Boundaries in the Social Sciences. *Annual Review of Sociology*, 28(1): 167–195. doi: 10.1146/annurev.soc.28.110601.141107.

Leigh, S. S., & Griesemer, J. R. (1989). Institutional Ecology, 'Translations' and Boundary Objects: Amateurs and Professionals in Berkeley's Museum of Vertebrate Zoology, 1907–1939. *Social Studies of Science*, 19(3): 387–420.

Lipsky, M. (1980). *Street Level Bureaucracy: Dilemmas of the Individual in Public Services*. New York: Russell Sage Foundation.

Machura, S. (2016). Inter- and Intra-Agency Co-Operation in Safeguarding Children: A Staff Survey. *British Journal of Social Work*, 46(3): 652–668. doi: 10.1093/bjsw/bcu101.

Maddock, A. (2014). Consensus or Contention: An Exploration of Multidisciplinary Team Functioning in an Irish Mental Health Context. *European Journal of Social Work*, 18(2): 246–261.

Oliver, C. (2013). Social Workers as Boundary Spanners: Reframing Our Professional Identity for Inter-professional Practice. *Social Work Education: The International Journal*, 32(6): 773–784.

Parsons, T. (1951). *The Social System*. London: Routledge & Kegan Paul.

Pullen-Sansfaçon, A., & Ward, D. (2014). Making Inter-professional Working Work: Introducing a Groupwork Perspective. *British Journal of Social Work*, 44(5): 1284–1300. doi: 10.1093/bjsw/bcs194.

Salhani, D., & Coulter, I. (2009). The Politics of Inter-professional Working and the Struggle for Professional Autonomy in Nursing. *Social Science & Medicine*, 68(7): 1221–1228. doi: http://dx.doi.org/10.1016/j.socscimed.2009.01.041.

SAMW. (2014). *Charta Zusammenarbeit de Fachleute im Schweizerischen Gesundheitswesen*. Basel: Schweizerische Akademie der Medizinischen Wissenschaften.

Sarfatti Larson, M. (1977). *The Rise of Professionalism: A Sociological Analysis*. Berkeley, Los Angeles, London: University of California Press.

Scherr, A. (2002). Das Studium der Sozialen Arbeit als biographisch artikulierte Aneignung eines diffusen Wissensangebots. In M. Kraul, W. Marotzki & C. Schweppe (Eds.), *Biographie und Profession* (pp. 225–250). Bad Heilbrunn: Klinkhardt.

Scott, W. R. (1969). Professional Employees in a Bureaucratic Structure: Social Work. In A. Etzioni (Ed.), *The Semi-Professions and Their Organization: Teachers, Nurses, Social Workers* (pp. 82–140). New York: Macmillan.

Scott, W. R. (1992). *Organizations: Rational, Natural and Open Systems* (Third edition). London: Prentice-Hall International.

Scott, W. R. (2005). Evolving Professions: An Institutional Field Approach. In T. Klatetzki & V. Tacke (Eds.), *Organisation und Profession* (pp. 119–141). Wiesbaden: VS. Verlag für Sozialwissenschaften.

Sosin, M. (2010). Discretion in Human Service Organizations: Traditional and Institutional Perspectives. In Y. Hasenfeld (Ed.), *Human Services as Complex Organizations* (pp. 381 403). Thousand Oaks, CA: Sage.

Voll, P. (2006). Vormundschaftsbehörden und Sozialdienste: Eine Untersuchung zur institutionellen Kooperation im Kindesschutz. *Fampra.ch*, 6(2): 262–285.

Wildridge, V., Childs, S., Cawthra, L., & Madge, B. (2004). How to Create Successful Partnerships – a Review of the Literature. *Health Information & Libraries Journal*, 21: 3–19. doi: 10.1111/j.1740–3324.2004.00497.x.

11

COMMITMENT IN THE MAKING OF PROFESSIONAL IDENTITY

Stewart Collins

Introduction

The term 'commitment', which has its origins in existential philosophy, means involving oneself actively, deeply and tenaciously in what one is doing, with the activity perceived as meaningful and important. The term has been prominent in sociology and organisational behaviour literature. It has been defined as "a force that binds an individual to a course of action" (Meyer and Herscovitch, 2001: 301), involving psychological attachment and as "a specific psychological bond" between a person and their targets characterised by dedication, caring, a willingness to give of oneself and responsibility (Klein et al., 2012: 137). The targets can be stand-alone elements or be multidimensional, for example, one of, or a combination of, a profession, an organisation, a supervisor/team leader, a team, colleagues and service users (Clements et al., 2014). The targets can both complement or conflict with each other and involve the self-concept and professional identities of practitioners.

Meyer et al. (2006) distinguished 'identity' from commitment. They suggest that, in essence, identity is the emphasis on a more passive psychological self in relation to collectives, groups and organisations, while commitment involves more active focus on behaviours, social exchange and strategies. Identity is seen as a precursor to commitment but differs in meaning and mindset. In addition, distinctions between motivation, job satisfaction and commitment are important. Motivation is linked to shorter term, energising forces and more specific task performances (Meyer et al., 2004). Commitment is more stable. It involves persistence and consistency over longer periods of time than motivation and job satisfaction, the latter being linked to feelings of liking or disliking one's job (Freund et al., 2012).

Meyer and Allen (2014) identify three components of commitment: (i) affective, (ii) continuance and (iii) normative. Affective commitment emphasises wanting to stay, a desire to belong, individual value congruence and "positive feelings of identification with, attachment to, and involvement in the work" (Meyer and

Allen, 1984: 375). Employees remain because they care and want to do so; they are more likely to exercise initiative and take positive actions. Affective commitment has been well-researched and is positively associated with job satisfaction, job performance and well-being (Neininger et al., 2010). It is enhanced by worker/organisational culture 'fit', collegiality, perceived support, leadership and active engagement. Those with low affective commitment are seen to be more liable to difficult behaviour at work, absences and higher turnover rates (Freund et al., 2012). Continuance commitment is seen as the instrumental exchange of involvement in work for personal rewards, is less self-determined and involves more externally based compliance, a necessity with few attractive employment alternatives, i.e. commitment "by virtue of the costs [employees] feel is associated with leaving as a result of accumulated investment" (Meyer and Allen, 1984: 375). They remain because they have to, and need to, do so. Clearly these two elements, continuance and affective commitment, can operate in combination, but "affective commitment has been seen as more important [as it has] the strongest and most consistent relationship with work outcomes" (Collins, 2015: 162). Meyer and Allen (2014) included a third element – normative commitment – entailing a worker doing their 'duty', what they feel they 'should' or 'ought' to do, but this concept has less support from empirical research, in particular, regarding the distinction from affective commitment (Clements et al., 2014).

The commitment concept has been criticised. Criticisms include perceived differences in definitions, the scales used to measure the concept, a lack of attention to cultural differences, the preoccupation with individualised attitudes, and a blurring with other concepts such as identification, involvement and engagement. Klein et al. (2012) suggest that dedication would be a more suitable concept to explore.

Professional commitment and social work

Commitment in social work is important because of its association with motivation, values, recruitment, job satisfaction, job retention, job turnover and work performance (Westbrook et al., 2006). Social workers who are committed to their jobs are more likely to ensure good-quality, committed service to their organisations and service users.

Professional commitment has been defined as "one's attitude towards one's profession or vocation" (Blau, 1985: 20). It can be seen as "a measure, or indicator, of behaviour towards one's profession and the efforts that are invested in it" (Collins, 2015: 32). Social work includes both attributes of profession and vocation. Martin (2000: 76) has contrasted the instrumental attitude of "devotion to professional standards defining professional competence" with embracing "the professional role as a vocation, as a set of activities one feels one is well suited to, strongly identifies with, sees inherent value in, and affirms with commitment, enthusiasm and caring" (also see Hardesty, Chapter 8 in this volume). The behaviours are reflected in personal autonomy, professional values and interactions with other professions (Freund et al., 2012). Practitioners with strong commitment invest resources in the professional role, persevere with continuing education and develop a strong professional identity (Giffords, 2009). Wallace (1993) and Yam (2004) highlighted elements linked to professional commitment including:

- collegiality, a distinctive sense of community characterised by a shared professional identity, signature knowledge, skills and values;
- provision of a code of ethics, conduct and registration;
- a professional career with opportunities to progress along a career ladder;
- autonomy, involving individual discretion, judgement and control over tasks;
- altruistic dedication to service to others;
- a sense of boundaries in interactions with other professionals; and
- a sense of professional identity that stems from professional roles.

However, professional commitment is a contested concept. For instance, it has been suggested that in order to maintain objectivity, professionals should maintain some interpersonal distance from clients and should not get involved emotionally. The traditional view of a profession includes the perception of individuals who are "committed to service their clients . . . placing the interests of clients . . . above their own interests" (Banks, 2012: 103). But at the same time, professional power and expert knowledge have long been heavily criticised, with strong demands for a shift in the balance of power between professionals and 'recipients' of their services. Hence, 'new' or 'democratic' professionalism is more likely to have a stronger commitment from social workers. More emphasis is placed on partnership, co-production and empowerment. This "involves a higher degree of personal identification by the professional with the situation, values, needs and aspirations of clients" (Clark, 2006: 83), more responsiveness to clients, and perceptions of them as fellow citizens, as knowledgeable 'experts,' working together in collective alliances with social workers (Beresford et al., 2008). Therefore, professionalism is "expressed . . . as dedication to . . . committed practice that is of value to others" (Freidson, 1994: 9–10), reasserting "the . . . notion of professionals as having a selfless commitment to the public good", being morally committed, trustworthy and recognising that "claims for exclusive 'scientific' expertise and . . . strong autonomy in decision making need to be modified" (Banks, 2012: 106).

Personal commitment

Personal, moral commitment is seen as an identity which comes from the individual, the person, beyond the role of social worker and is based, for instance, on caring for people and social justice, and not from externally imposed professional social work ethics, duties or guidelines. A belief-based, 'moral' commitment – a 'moral' identity, a focus on meeting human need rather than an excessive focus on outcomes – is seen as particularly important. The value base incorporates respect for the individual, possibilities for change and a sense of 'calling' or vocation (Collins, 2015; also see Erickson and Price, Chapter 6 in this volume). As Banks (2010: 2174) notes, "commitment links to identity conferring projects with which we are . . . extensively . . . identified . . . [involving] people acting from motives and interests that are most deeply their own".

A personal commitment to social work can emerge from a variety of sources. These include strengths or difficulties in family experiences; friendships; voluntary or work experiences; political or religious views; a desire to 'work with people', to care for and help individuals and families; empathy with the 'underdog' and marginalised groups; and a desire to 'make a difference', to 'do something useful', to 'make a contribution to society', to seek a fairer and more just society – and to have financial rewards, job security and a career (Freund et al., 2012). Hence, personal commitment plays a large part in committing oneself to undertake social work – and, as Fors (2016) points out, such commitment can be very strong *before* commencing social work. Adams et al. (2006) and Banks (2010) note that personal commitment becomes accommodated and assimilated into a professional identity developed during pre-course social work experiences and professional education and training. The individual becomes committed to professional values which develop during early socialisation experiences.

This process may engender tensions across personal and professional spheres. For example, there has been long-standing debate about the desirability of political commitments of social work students and social workers – the extent to which politics are either part of the professional role or separate from it. Similarly, social work students may feel a range of commitments relating to a particular class, gender, sexuality, religion, ethnicity, language or place. Adams et al. (2006) argue that while several identity commitments may naturally coexist, it is professional commitment that is often the most significant for practitioners. Therefore, if personal and professional commitments are congruent, then a high degree of the latter is likely.

Social work students and professional commitment

Commitment to social work arises, in part, because people chose social work as an alternative to other professions such as law, teaching and nursing (Beddoe, 2011). It is likely practitioners will emphasise equality, reduce power differentials and emphasise service user choice. Applicants to social work courses appear not to aspire to the perceived prestige and 'expert' status of some professions. Social work then becomes an in-group with which one identifies and feels a sense of belonging, with other professions seen as out-groups (Adams et al., 2006; Green, 2006).

There are great variations in the type and length of pre-course, voluntary or unqualified social work experiences undertaken by social work students. These can influence, for instance, their commitment to voluntary or statutory social work organisations. In turn, commitments can change and alter during social work education. Commitment to the social work *profession* is likely to remain stable, but clearly other commitments can be fluid, for example, in relation to specific roles and a career.

Social work students may have had experiences that led them to have a commitment to working with children, older people and people experiencing learning disabilities or mental health problems. Hence, prior to course commencement, students may feel the 'pull' towards working with a particular service user group. An involvement with child welfare work may be linked to both status and likely future job location. However, Wilson and McCrystal (2007) show students' commitment to work with children as a future career declined from just over half of the student group at the start of a course to just under a third in the later stages, following concerns about high workloads and potential burnout. Boehm and Cohen (2013), in relation to community practice, indicated *affective commitment* as taking precedence over cognitive commitment. For students in their study, personal, emotional experiences of positive learning placements rather than academic input or supervisory encouragement led to them feeling committed to practice with a particular service user group.

It is clear that social work students may have a commitment to job roles other than front-line practice. A significant number of students in Wilson and McCrystal's (2007) study intended to become managers in their future careers. This raises the question of 'career' commitment – an area that has been largely underexplored in the literature, especially in the UK (Freund et al., 2012). It is difficult to know the manner in which 'career commitment' interacts with other forms of commitment. Many social work students may well pursue professional commitment without thought to a career, while others may see career commitment as a natural progression and as deriving from professional commitment. Goulet and Singh (2002) raise interesting questions about the centrality of a person's career to their identity, how much thought they may have given to this and how concerned they may be – or not – to pursue a career.

More generally, social work education involves a commitment to knowledge, skills and values that bring social work students closer to a professional identity (Clements et al., 2014). "Experiences of education and professional socialisation have important implications for sustaining . . . commitment to the profession" (Wilson and McCrystal, 2007: 37). Collins (2015) found that "a significant proportion of students were committed to enhancing their potential for serving and being committed to disadvantaged groups and communities" (x164). Collins et al. (2010) suggests that despite considerable demands, persistent pressure and significant stress, commitment of students to the profession remains high during social work courses. However, Fors's (2016) Norway study found that social work students experienced *weaker* professional commitment at the end of their course compared to at the beginning. The commitment can also come at a cost: commitment to the social work profession may not sit well with the attitudes and values of some students' family or friendship networks (Clements et al., 2014; Wiles, 2013). Hence, commitment to social work education and training can lead to a re-evaluation of, and possibly alienation from, relationships with family members or friends.

It is worth noting that in the UK membership in the social work profession involves a requirement to register and to abide by standards and codes of practice and performance (for example, HCPC, 2012). Commitment to social work's standards, ethics and the values on which they are based helps unite social workers to take a collective stance (Banks, 2012). Adherence to appropriate professional conduct and willingness to be subject of disciplinary procedures forms an important part of professional commitment (Wiles, 2013). Hence the professionally qualified worker is 'set apart', with a visibly distinct identity and vocabulary, attitude and behaviours.

Social workers' professional and organisational commitment

Commitment to social work is thought to develop in the early stages of a social worker's working life, during pre-course experiences and during education and training. It is seen as 'intrinsic', while organisational commitment has been described as being 'extrinsic', with affective commitment to an organisation taking place over a period of time (Clements et al., 2014). Much has been written about organisational commitment and social workers (for example, Giffords, 2009). A social worker may develop organisational commitment working for a particular agency, and a strong belief in an organisation's goals and values. Such a social worker may exert considerable effort on behalf of the organisation (Jaskyte and Lee, 2009). Research into organisational commitment suggests that it associates with role clarity, loyalty, reduced absences, less stress, lower turnover intentions and less actual turnover (Boyas and Wind, 2010). Organisational commitment involves important behavioural traits such as productivity, willingness to take on extra tasks and provision of quality services for service users (Giffords, 2009). The organisation can bring positives. These include access to 'instrumental' benefits such as financial security, pensions and paid holidays. Opportunities to work with families, groups of service users and particular communities can involve job satisfaction. Studies have also emphasised the significant role of teams, colleagues, supervisors and line managers in maintaining organisational commitment.

Klein et al. (2012), however, have questioned the significance of organisational commitment in a transient, changing world, with short-term contracts and high-turnover internal labour market movement. Freund (2005) found that commitment is congruent with organisational opportunity. If opportunities are not available within the organisation, then the worker may well leave. Many see this as an inevitable, desirable part of organisational life, although research has expressed concerns about the 'turnover' of social workers (Boyas et al., 2013; Curtis et al., 2010; Webb and Carpenter, 2012). In the UK an increasing numbers of social work practitioners are employed as freelance 'general agency workers'. Social workers are 'hired out' on short-term bases as 'briefly situated' rather than 'deeply structured' members of that organisation. In some cities agency-based workers comprise around a quarter of the statutory social work workforce (Carey, 2013). As a consequence, Webb and

Carpenter (2012) consider long-term organisational commitment to be unrealistic. It is also interesting to note that the average 'working life' of a social worker in the UK is reckoned to be eight years (Curtis et al., 2010). Furthermore, excessive commitment to badly resourced organisations and roles can lead to stress and, in the longer term, burnout (Collins, 2015).

Tensions and contradictions may well be present in a social worker's commitment to their organisation. Workers can be encouraged to develop commitments which link to managerial objectives that operate "more or less intentionally and in/effectively . . . influence employees' self-construction in terms of coherence, distinctiveness and commitment" (Alvesson and Willmot, 2002: 619). Organisational control can be achieved by practitioners themselves becoming self-disciplined, identified with and committed to managerially driven discourses. Alternatively, social workers can commit themselves to resistance, to maintain professional commitment by challenging organisational practices. Radical and ecological approaches encourage the targeting and influencing of one's own organisation to try to change policies, procedures and guidelines. Professional values include a requirement to challenge harmful, unjust and unfair practices (BASW, 2012). Hence, the concept of critical commitment is likely to alleviate the dangers of becoming socialised into accepting organisational mandates in a repetitive and unreflective way (Collins, 2015). Researchers have pointed out workers' abilities to challenge, undermine, question and subvert organisational practices. Chieliotis (2006: 321) has described these as the "various forms of resistance whereby actors hold true to their world view . . . and commitments". This can take the form of covert actions, spoiling techniques or 'suppressed' resistance involving quiet, hidden discourses or through colleagues, unions or professional collectives such as the Social Workers Action Network (SWAN). Hence, there is still scope for professional autonomy and resistance in certain organisational contexts.

Newly qualified social workers and commitment

Various research studies have emphasised a range of opportunities to enhance the commitment of newly qualified workers. In the UK Carpenter et al. (2015) highlighted the significance of feelings of self-confidence; the provision of regular, good-quality, reflection-based supervision offering both practical and emotional support; perceived support from team members; and having manageable workloads. In the USA a longitudinal study by Faller et al. (2010) also emphasised the significance of good supervision and variety of work in maintaining and enhancing commitment to the organisation. Jaskyte and Lee (2009) found induction courses were significant, emphasising the importance of workers' strengths, capabilities and transferable skills. In the UK Carson et al. (2011) noted that an emphasis on mutual sharing of experiences and emotional support was more highly valued by many newly qualified social workers, rather than focusing on organisational procedures. Webb and Carpenter (2012) have shown that on the job, continuous professional development opportunities have a small but positive impact on organisational commitment. Westbrook et al. (2006), Giffords (2009) and Carson et al. (2011) suggest social workers *themselves* place more emphasis on informal training. Hussein at al.'s (2014) research discovered three main variables predicted enjoyment of work for newly qualified workers: the ability to put values into practice (linking to professional commitment), feeling well prepared by social work programmes and a high level of engagement with the agency's work (linking with organisational commitment). Furthermore, important studies in the USA indicated stronger organisational commitment was significantly associated with lower perceived job stress, less emotional exhaustion and fewer feelings of depersonalisation – all of which protected retention rates (Boyas et al., 2013; Boyas and Wind, 2010).

Experienced social workers

Research in Wales by Evans and Huxley (2009) revealed that almost all experienced social workers enjoyed their work with team members and service users – suggesting very high professional commitment to these aspects. Huxley et al. (2005: 1073) in a large-scale survey of mental health workers in the UK discovered affective commitment to team members and service users was an important factor in retention of staff, while "commitment to the goals and values of the profession in serving users and carers helped motivation for staying in the job". However, UK research has also demonstrated *much less commitment to social work organisations*. McLean and Andrew (2000) found that "one quarter of their respondents felt little loyalty to their organisations, only a third felt proud to be working for it, while forty per cent believed their values were different to those of their organisation" (Collins, 2015: 9). In Evans and Huxley's (2009) research less than a third of social workers were satisfied with their employers, one quarter had mixed feelings and a quarter were already seeking another post. These studies and that of Huxley et al. (2005) suggest only limited commitment from a significant number of workers to their organisation.

McLean and Andrew (2000) found length of service was significant in affective commitment to the organisation. Those with longer service identified more with the organisation and its norms than new employees. Affective commitment scores for managers were significantly higher than for social workers, thus suggesting for the latter "a lower level of involvement with the organisation and a reduced commitment to stay" (McLean and Andrew, 2000: 108–109). The most committed employees were those who were satisfied with employee relationships, enjoyed good experiences with line managers, had positive perceptions of the overall departmental management, received recognition for good-quality work, had attention paid to their suggestions for change and had good promotion opportunities. Affective commitment, involving those who really wanted to stay, was closely associated with intrinsic job satisfaction, variety of work, involvement in decision making, freedom to choose working methods and amount of responsibility. Each of these points emphasise autonomy and discretion in organisational commitment (McLean and Andrew, 2000).

There is evidence of a high degree of long-term professional commitment from experienced social workers working with children in the UK, USA and Finland (for instance, Ellett et al., 2009; Poso and Forsman, 2013; Stalker et al., 2007). In addition, Westbrook et al. (2006), Depanfilis and Zlotnik (2008) and Brannen et al. (2009) argue that for experienced social workers, work with vulnerable children was more than just a paid job: it involved an ethics of care, 'moral' commitment, a 'calling' or mission (also see Erickson and Price, Chapter 6 in this volume). This links to 'continuance commitment' among experienced social workers, which may be more important because they have invested significant time and energy in the organisation. Developing loyalty to its aims and having established relationships with co-workers may be at stake (Boyas et al., 2013). Workers may also remain because of 'instrumental' reasons such as family and geographic convenience, job, pension and financial security, and impending retirement (Ellett et al., 2009; Evans and Huxley, 2009). A social worker quoted by Carey (2014: 137) reflects this: "My commitment is nominal because this is just a job. . . . I don't really care much about providing a service. . . . This job pays my bills rather than anything – I just live for the evenings and the weekends".

The role of line managers

There has been a tendency to stereotype line managers as controlling, restrictive figures, excessively committed to new managerialism, neo-liberalism and organisational conformity (Gray and Webb, 2013). However, Blomgren and Waks (2015) helpfully note that organisations can incorporate managerialism, and market *and* democratic and professional logics, which can involve conflicts for both social workers and their managers. Aronson and Smith (2010, 2011) pointed out the divided, contradictory commitments of social services managers in Canada: they were split, torn, 'tightrope walking' between their existing professional commitment to maintaining and preserving their values – to supporting people in marginalised communities and providing progressive public services – and the prevailing conflicting, neo-liberal, audit-oriented managerial culture. Aronson and Smith (2011) note their 'oppositional' resistance as a form of leadership amongst these multiple and conflicting demands.

Evans (2011, 2013) draws attention to the professional commitment of team leaders in the UK, for instance, to rights and justice, linking in with the similar professional commitment of main-grade social workers. Team managers are often drawn from the same professional group as practitioner social workers. Evans also pointed out that while 'managerialism' within social services may have curtailed practices, the key division in social services is between upper, 'higher' management and the 'periphery' – the local teams. Team leaders from a professional background in social work with a shared professional commitment transcended the division between managers and workers at a local level with a "commitment to professional support and guidance, autonomy, discretion and the needs of service users rather than hierarchical control" (Collins, 2015: 169). Evans (2013) highlighted the differences in emphasis within two groups of managers and social workers: one group focussed on organisational commitment to rule following, impartiality and procedural fairness; another group placed more emphasis on professional commitment, professional judgment and discretion in achieving fair outcomes for the best interests of, and the complexities presented by, the needs of individual service users.

Social work as vocation: further ways to develop commitment

Commitment is clearly a significant factor in professional identity formation. Various ways of developing commitment have been noted. In what ways can the commitment of social workers be further developed? Several pieces of research evidence are available, many from the USA. One starting point is at the stage of selection for employment in social work. 'Realistic job previews' are one way of attempting to improve social work job applicants' 'fit' (Faller et al., 2009). They enable applicants to have a better sense, understanding and awareness of the expectations and challenges, which is intended to enhance employees' initial commitment. This involves provision of detailed information in various formats, including video, to increase awareness of matching potential employees to what is expected of a particular job.

Extensive research findings emphasise the need for social workers to feel respected, valued, cared for and appreciated (for instance, Ellett et al., 2009; Evans and Huxley, 2009). Equally, studies have demonstrated that good opportunities for formal and informal support from peers and team colleagues have an important part to play (for example, Freund, 2005; Giffords, 2009). Line managers have a significant role in providing positive reinforcement, recognition for good-quality work and differential supervision that recognises emotional demands, but does not become too intrusive (Boyas et al., 2013; Boyas and Wind, 2010). The provision of experienced managers or workers as mentors who do not have line management responsibilities has also proven effective in enhancing the commitment of both mentors and mentees (Cohen-Callow et al., 2009). Interestingly, the place of autonomy in commitment is subject to debate. Some have seen this as a crucial element – i.e. freedom to complete work tasks and control over individual decision making (Claiborne et al., 2011; Giffords, 2009; Hussein et al., 2014) – while others have seen it as less important (Westbrook et al., 2006). If workers feel they have been treated fairly and justly by the organisation, with equal treatment for workers all around (e.g. promotional and training opportunities and accommodation matters), then they have more commitment to their employer (Webb and Carpenter, 2012).

The opportunities for grass roots participation, to have a 'say' and a 'voice' in organisational procedures and decision making, is also seen as important in maintaining commitment. Research on 'design teams' has shown their effectiveness in reducing staff turnover and improving communication (Strolin-Golzman et al., 2009). In addition, Claiborne et al., (2011) have highlighted the importance of the organisation being seen as innovative, open to new ideas and willing to change. Research shows organisations could facilitate more time for face-to-face contact with service users, with less emphasis on computer-based case management and 'form filling' (Westbrook et al., 2012). Organisations should intervene to ensure appropriate workload allocation. This has been demonstrated to have a small but positive impact upon commitment (Faller et al., 2010; Webb and Carpenter, 2012). Excessive workloads are known as a frequent source of stress and role conflict for social workers. Surprisingly, the impact of salaries on commitment has been queried in research by Hussein et al. (2014). Equally, there has been debate about the impact of contracts and conditions of employment on commitment, involving job sharing, part-time work, home working, flexi-time and 'time out' for experienced workers, but there is evidence that provision of a range of opportunities increases commitment (Westbrook et al., 2012).

Sound administrative support and comfortable working environments are also seen to enhance commitment. The use of 'hot desking' and 'agile working' has led to criticisms that they undermine the commitment of workers who need quiet space in order to undertake tasks such as confidential telephone calls and report writing. It is also argued that these practices reduce much-needed opportunities for informal team and colleague support. However, as noted earlier, some workers may naturally wish to take up posts beyond immediate service user contact: for instance, specialist work, training, education and management roles (Evans and Huxley, 2009; Poso and Forsman, 2013).

Concluding discussion

Commitment for social workers involves strong attachments, long-term bonds, active dedication, caring, a strong sense of responsibility and the provision of reliable, committed responses to service users. There is clear evidence that commitment to social work as a profession is resilient and enduring as a major source of identity. However, there are tensions and contradictions between professional and organisational commitment, with social workers generally being less committed to organisations. Social workers tend to maintain a questioning, critical approach to organisational resources, policies and procedures.

Efforts can be made to develop opportunities for increasing worker commitment to organisations and to increase retention rates, reduce turnover and maintain high-quality provision for service users (Burns, 2011). There is the need to develop a better understanding of the commitment concept and the implications it has for the selection of social work students and social workers. Developing commitment involves recognising the needs of newly qualified and experienced social workers for respect, care and positive recognition for valuable contributions.

Maintaining and developing commitment is a complex, multi-sided phenomenon. It requires flexible responses at many levels, including social work education, continuing professional development, social work organisations, line managers, teams, colleagues, professional associations, unions and, perhaps most importantly, the policy and political context. Ultimately, the core aspects of commitment such as attachment and bonding are strongly associated with positive attitudes and an ethics of care, but these must be located within the organisational, policy and political contexts. Professional identities and commitment of social workers can be developed, but they will always remain susceptible to these wider ecological influences.

References

Adams, K., Hean, S., Sturgis, P., & Clark, J. (2006). Investigating the Factors Influencing Professional Identity of First Year Health and Social Care Students. *Learning in Health and Social Care*, 5(2): 55–68.

Alvesson, M., & Willmott, H. (2002). Identity Regulation as Organizational Control: Producing the Appropriate Individual. *Journal of Management Studies*, 39(5): 619–644.

Aronson, J., & Smith, K. (2010). Managing Restructured Social Services: Expanding the Social. *British Journal of Social Work*, 40(2): 530–547.

Aronson, J., & Smith, K. (2011). Identity Work and Critical Social Services Management: Balancing a Tightrope. *British Journal of Social Work*, 41(3): 432–448.

Banks, S. (2010). Integrity in Professional life: Issues of Conduct, Commitment and Capacity. *British Journal of Social Work*, 40(7): 2168–2184.

Banks, S. (2012). *Values and Ethics in Social Work*. Hound mills, Basingstoke: Palgrave Macmillan.

BASW. (2012). *The Code of Ethics for Social Workers: Statement of Principles*. Birmingham: BASW.

Beddoe, L. (2011). Health Social Work: Professional Identity and Knowledge. *Qualitative Social Work*, 12(1): 24–60.

Beddoe, L. (2015). Continuing Education, Registration and Professional Identity in New Zealand Social Work. *International Social Work*, 58(1): 165–174.

Beresford, P., Croft, S., & Adshead, L. (2008). We Don't See Her as a Social Worker: A Case Study of the Importance of the Social Worker's Relationship and Humanity. *British Journal of Social Work*, 38(1): 1388–1407.

Blau, G. (1985). The Measurement and Prediction of Career Commitment. *Journal of Occupational Psychology*, 58(1): 277–288.

Blomgren, M., & Waks, C. (2015). Coping with Contradictions: Hybrid Professionals Managing Institutional Complexity. *Journal of Professions and Organizations*, 2(1): 78–102.

Boehm, A., & Cohen, A. (2013). Commitment to Community Practice among Social Work Students: Contributing Factors'. *Journal of Social Work Education*, 49(2): 601–618.

Boyas, J., & Wind, L. (2010). Employment-Based Social Capital: Job Stress and Employee Burnout: A Public Child Welfare Employee Structural Model. *Children and Youth Services Review*, 32(1): 380–388.

Boyas, J., Wind, L., & Ruiz, E. (2013). Organisational Tenure amongst Child Welfare Workers, Burnout, Stress and Intention to Leave among Child Protection Workers: Does Employment-Based Social Capital Make a Difference. *Children and Youth Services Review*, 35(1): 1657–1669.

Brannen, J., Mooney, A., & Statham, J. (2009). Childhood Experiences: A Commitment to Caring and Care Work with Vulnerable Children. *Childhood*, 16(3): 377–393.

British Association of Social Workers. (2012). *The Code of Ethics for Social Work: Statement of Principles*. Birmingham: BASW.

Burns, K. (2011). Career Preference, 'Transients' and 'Converts': A Study of Social Workers' Retention in Child Protection and Welfare. *British Journal of Social Work*, 41(3): 520–538.

Carey, M. (2013). The Last Resort? Similarities and Differences between Contingency 'Agency' Employment in Social Work and Nursing. *International Social Work*, 56(2): 482–495.

Carey, M. (2014). Mind the Gaps: Understanding the Rise and Implications of Different Types of Cynicism within Statutory Social Work. *British Journal of Social Work*, 44: 127–144.

Carpenter, J., Shardlow, S., Patsios, D., & Wood, M. (2015). Developing the Confidence and Competence of Newly Qualified Child and Family Social Workers in England: Outcomes of a National Programme. *British Journal of Social Work*, 45(1): 153–174.

Carson, E., King, S., & Papatraianou, L. (2011). Resilience amongst Social Workers: The Role of Informal Learning in the Workplace. *Social Work Education*, 25(5): 267–278.

Chieliotis, L. (2006). How Iron Is the Iron Cage of the New Penology? The Role of Human Agency in the Implementation of Criminal Justice Policy. *Punishment and Society*, 8(3): 313–340.

Claiborne, N., Auerbach, C., Lawrence, C., Liu, J., McGowan, B., Fernades, G., & Magnano, J. (2011). Child Welfare Agency Climate Influence on Worker Commitment. *Children and Youth Services Review*, 33: 2096–2102.

Clark, C. (2006). Moral Character in Social Work. *British Journal of Social Work*, 36(1): 75–89.

Clements, A., Kinman, G., & Guppy, A. (2014). You Could Damage Someone's Life: Student and Lecturer Perspectives on Commitment. *Social Work Education*, 33(1): 91–104.

Cohen-Callow, A., Hopkins, K., & Kim, H. (2009). Retaining Workers Approaching Retirement: Why Child Welfare Needs to Pay Attention to the Aging Workforce. *Child Welfare*, 88(5): 209–227.

Collins, S. (2015). The Commitment of Social Workers in the UK: Committed to the Profession, the Organisation and Service Users? *Practice: Social Work in Action*, 28(3): 159–179.

Collins, S., Coffey, M., & Morris, L. (2010). Social Work Students: Stress, Support and Wellbeing. *British Journal of Social Work*, 40(3): 963–982.

Curtis, L., Moriarty, J., & Netten, A. (2010). The Expected Working Life of a Social Worker. *British Journal of Social Work*, 40(5): 1628–1643.

Depanfilis, D., & Zlotnik, J. (2008). Retention of Front Line Staff in Child Welfare: A Systematic Review of Research. *Children and Youth Services Review*, 30(9): 995–1008.

Ellett, A. J., Ellett, C. D., Ellis, J., & Lerner, B. (2009) A Research-Based Child Welfare Employee Selection Protocol: Strengthening Retention of the Workforce. *Child Welfare*, 88(5): 49–68.

Evans, S., & Huxley, P. (2009). Factors Associated with the Recruitment and Retention of Social Workers in Wales: Employer and Employee Perspectives. *Health and Social Care in the Community*, 17(3): 254–266.

Evans, T. (2011). Professionals, Managers and Discretion: Critiquing Street Level Bureaucracy. *British Journal of Social Work*, 41(2): 368–386.

Evans, T. (2013). Organizational Roles and Discretion in Adult Social Work. *British Journal of Social Work*, 43(4): 739–758.

Faller, K., Graberek, M., & Ortega, R. (2010). Commitment to Child Welfare Work: What Predicts Leaving and Staying? *Children and Youth Services Review*, 32(6): 840–646.

Faller, K., Masternak, M., Grinnel-Davis, C., Graberek, M., Sieffers, J., & Bernatovicz, P. (2009). Realistic Job Previews in Child Welfare: State of Innovation and Practice. *Child Welfare*, 88(5): 23–47.

Fors, J. (2016). Development of Professional Commitment among Students in Social Work Education. *Social Work Education*. doi: 10.1080/02615479.2016.1221065.

Freidson, E. (1994). *Professionalism Reborn: Theory, Prophecy and Policy*. Cambridge: Polity.

Freund, A. (2005). Commitment and Job Satisfaction as Predictors of Turnover among Welfare Workers. *Administration in Social Work*, 29(2): 5–21.

Freund, A., Blit-Cohen, E., Cohen, E., & Dehan, N. (2012). Professional Commitment in Novice Social Work Students: Socio Demographic Characteristics, Motives and Perceptions of the Profession. *Social Work Education*, 32(7): 239–253.

Giffords, E. (2009). An Examination of Organizational Commitment and Professional Commitment and the Relationship to Work Environment, Demographic and Organizational Factors. *Journal of Social Work*, 9(4): 386–404.

Goulet, L., & Singh, P. (2002). Career Commitment: A Examination and an Extension. *Journal of Vocational Behaviour*, 61(1): 73–91.

Gray, M., & Webb, S. A. (2013). The Speculative Left and the New Politics of Social Work. In M. Gray & S. A. Webb (Eds.), *The New Politics of Social Work* (pp. 209–224). Basingstoke: Palgrave.

Green, L. (2006). Pariah Profession, Debased Discipline? An Analysis of Social Workers' Low Academic Achievement and the Possibilities for Change. *Social Work Education*, 25(3): 245–264.

Health Care Professions Council. (2012). *Standards of Conduct, Performance and Ethics*. London: Health Care Professions Council.

Hussein, S., Moriarty, J., Stevens, M., Sharpe, E., & Manthorpe, J. (2014). Organizational Factors, Job Satisfaction and Intention to Leave among Newly Qualified Social Workers. *Social Work Education*, 38(3): 381–396.

Huxley, P., Evans, S., Gately, C., Webber, M., Mearns, M., Peaks, S., Kendall, T., Medina, J., & Katona, C. (2005). Stress and Pressure in Mental Health Social Work: The Worker Speaks. *British Journal of Social Work*, 35: 1063–1079.

Jaskyte, K., & Lee, M. (2009). Organizational Commitment of Social Workers: An Exploratory Study. *Administration in Social Work*, 33: 227–241.

Klein, H., Molloy, J., & Brinfield, C. (2012). Reconceptualising Work Place Commitment to Redress a Stretched Concept: Revisiting Assumptions and Removing Confounds. *Academy of Management Review*, 37(1): 130–151.

Martin, M. (2000). *Meaningful Work: Rethinking Professional Ethics*. New York: Oxford University Press.

McLean, J., & Andrew, T. (2000). Commitment, Satisfaction, Stress and Control among Social Service Managers and Social Workers in the UK. *Administration in Social Work*, 22(3/4): 93–117.

Meyer, J., & Allen, N. (1984). Testing the 'Side Bet' Theory of Organisational Commitment: Some Methodological Considerations. *Journal of Applied Psychology*, 69: 372–378.

Meyer, J., Becker, T., & Vanberghe, C. (2004). Employee Commitment and Motivation; A Conceptual Analysis and Integrative Model. *Journal of Applied Psychology*, 88(6): 991–1007.

Meyer, J., Becker, T., & Van Dick, R. (2006). Social Identities and Commitments at Work: Toward an Integrative Model. *Journal of Organizational Behaviour*, 27: 665–683.

Meyer, J., & Herscovitch, L. (2001). Commitment in the Workplace: Toward a General Model. *Human Resource Management Review*, 11: 299–326.

Neininger, A., Lehmann-Willenbreck, N., Kufeldt, S., & Henschel, A. (2010). Effects of Team and Organizational Commitment: A Longitudinal Study. *Journal of Vocational Behaviour*, 76: 567–579.

Poso, T., & Forsman, S. (2013). Messages to Social Work Education: What Makes Social Workers Continue and Cope in Child Welfare? *Social Work Education*, 32(5): 650–661.

Stalker, C., Mandell, D., French, K., & Harvey, C. (2007). Child Welfare Workers Who Are Exhausted Yet Satisfied with Their Jobs: How Do they Do It? *Child and Family Social Work*, 12(2): 182–191.

Strolin-Golzman, J., Lawrence, C., Auerbach, C., Caringi, J., Claiborne, N., Lawson, H., McCarthy, M., McGowan, B., Sherman, R., & Shin, M. (2009). Design Teams: A Promising Organizational Intervention for Improving Turnover Rates in the Child Welfare Workforce. *Child Welfare*, 88(5): 149.

Wallace, J. (1993). Professional and Organizational Commitment: Compatible or Incompatible? *Journal of Vocational Behaviour*, 42: 333–349.

Webb, C., & Carpenter, J. (2012). What Can Be Done to Promote the Retention of Social Workers? A Systematic Review of Interventions. *British Journal of Social Work*, 42: 1235–1255.

Westbrook, T., Ellett, A., & Asberg, A. (2012). Predicting Child Welfare Employee Intentions to Remain Employed with the Child Welfare Organization Culture Inventory. *Children and Youth Services Review*, 34: 214–222.

Westbrook, T., Ellis, J., & Ellett, A. (2006) Improving Retention among Public Child Welfare Workers: What Can We Learn from the Experience of Committed Survivors? *Administration in Social Work*, 30(4): 37–62.

Wiles, F. (2013). 'Not Easily Put into a Box', Constructing Professional Identity. *Social Work Education*, 32(7): 854–866.

Wilson, G., & McCrystal, R. (2007). Motivations and Career Aspirations of MSW Students in Northern Ireland. *Social Work Education*, 26(1): 35–52.

Yam, P. (2004). From Vocation to Profession: The Quest for Professionalization of Nursing. *British Journal of Nursing*, 13(16): 978–982.

12

PROFESSIONAL IDENTITY IN THE CARE AND UPBRINGING OF CHILDREN

Towards a praxis of residential childcare

Mark Smith

Introduction

This chapter considers the professional identity of residential childcare. From a UK perspective, this is bound up in its relationship with the wider social work profession. I consider some of the tensions that surface in seeking to conceptualize residential childcare within social work, arguing that the tasks, the sites of practice and the means through which they are enacted mask fundamental differences between what might be thought of as two players in the wider field of child welfare. These differences have intensified over time, reflecting, I argue, a wider epistemological tension in the nature of respective roles and tasks. It is perhaps only when this is opened up that residential childcare workers might begin to articulate claims towards a confident professional identity. Having made this case for aspects of a discrete professional identity, I take something of a step back and express some concerns about current plans in Scotland to introduce a separate qualification for residential childcare, concluding that questions about the professional identity of residential childcare may actually reflect wider directions of travel and consequent identity issues in social work which render it difficult to accommodate the essentially practical and relational features of care work within it.

The professionalization of social work

Social work was professionalized in the UK in the early 1970s following on from the Seebohm (1968) and Kilbrandon (1964) recommendations in England and Scotland respectively. A newly established Central Council for Education and Training in Social Work (CCETSW) assumed responsibility for setting and regulating education for the profession. In 1973, a CCETSW working party identified some of the particular requirements of residential work, including the holistic, spiritual and charismatic dimensions of practice, concluding with a somewhat equivocal assertion that residential work was social work.

Despite this claim, the relationship between residential childcare and what might be thought of as community-based social work has often been troubled. The intention that residential care workers become qualified to the same level as social workers never materialized. One consequence of this was that community social work grew to possess a greater store of intellectual and cultural capital than residential childcare and has therefore been able to speak with a greater legitimacy about what might be identified as the 'field' of children and families social work (Bourdieu, 1986, 1993). Such apparent legitimacy, however, has rarely translated to the development of an appropriate knowledge base through which to better understand or work within residential childcare. Indeed, social work knowledge, especially as it has increasingly converged around ideas of protection, might be argued to have stunted the growth of an appropriate knowledge or practice base for residential work.

Different knowledge bases

In its quest for professional identity, social work looked to the emerging social sciences and to psychology to provide its underpinning body of knowledge. Early social work education was hugely influenced by Goffman's highly influential anti-institutional tract *Asylums* (1961). Considered through such a theoretical lens, it became easy to view residential care, irrespective of its size and quality, as inherently damaging and an intervention to be avoided. Running alongside this structural critique, the growing influence of attachment theory, evident in seminal documents such as *Children Who Wait* (Rowe and Lambert, 1973), saw the family identified as the preferred model of care for children.

Pulled along on the coattails of social work's quest for identity, residential childcare similarly looked to psychology to provide the kind of 'scientific' provenance that was lacking in mere care. It thus flirted with an array of psychodynamic ideas, behaviourism, social learning theory and more recently, attachment theory (Smith, 2009). Yet, the language of psychology does not necessarily 'fit' with the kind of work that residential care practitioners do (Phelan, 2001).

The search for a knowledge base in disciplines such as sociology and psychology shifted the nature of residential childcare away from responding to the needs of the 'concrete other' child to echo broader, universalizing discursive and social policy agendas around risk, rights and protection (Steckley and Smith, 2011). What had been a largely domestic task, centring around practical and emotional considerations, became a more abstracted and ostensibly 'professional' one.

'Professionalization' saw a shift away from the live-in staff who had been at the heart of previous models of care to what Douglas and Payne (1981) called an 'industrial model' in which the personal and professional selves of carers became separated as a result of the introduction of shift systems, but also by ideas that made particular assumptions of what it was to be 'professional' (Smith, 2009). The model of the 'bureau professional' expected by local authority bureaucracies was premised on qualities of 'objectivity' and 'professional distance' (Meagher and Parton, 2004), which did not necessarily fit comfortably with caring roles.

Different epistemologies

Notions of objectivity and the separation of the personal and professional belie a dominant Enlightenment worldview which privileges reason over sentiment. They are based on 'taken for granted' assumptions "which privilege positivist ways of knowing, based on an understanding of the natural sciences that were seen to be 'value-free, mathematized and scientific' " (Holligan et al., 2014). And, as Sewpaul notes, social work is a child of modernity:

> Born within the period of modernity . . . social work began to take on the omniscient voice of science. . . . It is within this culture of cure and control that the discipline has seen its most pronounced development. . . . Given its birth during the period of modernity with its emphasis on reductionist, logical positivist rationality . . . social work took on this dominant discourse in the pursuit of status and professionalism.
>
> *(2005: 211)*

These origins have led professional social work in the direction of method and technique, its mode of consciousness largely technocratic or technical/rational. This chapter argues that residential childcare is, by its nature and in contrast to the technical rationality of much current social work, a practical moral task (Moss and Petrie, 2002). Its identity ought to converge around a task articulated in terms of care and upbringing. These are major ontological and cultural endeavours, being dispositional, relational and contextual: they cannot be subsumed to technique.

The tasks of residential childcare: care and upbringing

The tendency to look to universalizing discourses, such as rights and protection, is inappropriate or certainly insufficient in terms of understanding or practising residential childcare. I argue (Smith, 2009) that the primary tasks of the sector are those of care and upbringing, ideas that are largely unarticulated and, as Meagher and Parton (2004) claim, marginalized within social work. There is, however, an important and growing body of literature around care, drawing, largely, from a feminist perspective and more recently around child upbringing. I now go on to consider some features of these.

Care

Some of the most important work around the nature of care is contained in the expanding literature about care ethics that was initially associated with Gilligan's *In a Different Voice* (1982). Gilligan was a student of Kohlberg, who expounded what has become the standard model of human moral development. She challenged Kohlberg's model as reflecting predominantly male ways of thinking and acting on questions of morality. Men are deemed to speak and act from a 'justice' voice or orientation, where qualities of objectivity, rationality and general principle predominate, women from a 'care' orientation drawing on 'softer' attributes of intuition, connection and compassion in reaching moral decisions. Care ethics have moved beyond narrow gender binaries to encompass a growing body of work on moral theory across a range of disciplines.

Following from Gilligan's seminal work, Tronto (1993) conceptualized care as a practice or set of practices rather than a set of rules or principles. A moral person attains that status in the ways in which they respond to the injunctions to care that present themselves in everyday life. Care "involves both particular acts and a 'general habit of mind' to care that should inform all aspects of a practitioner's moral life" (1993: 126–127). Sevenhuijsen (1998) locates care within concepts of concrete responsibilities and relationships rather than abstract rules and rights. Care needs to be responsive, active and dispositional rather than instrumental and rule driven.

Another care ethicist, Nel Noddings (1984), differentiates between 'caring for' and 'caring about', a distinction which might cast some light on the difference between care workers and social workers. Residential workers 'care for' children and youth. They work at the level of the face-to-face encounter, engaging in the dirty and messy aspects of care such as intervening in the moment in issues of personal hygiene or getting involved in physical restraint. They are faced with negotiating issues of intimacy and related boundary issues (Coady, 2014). There is an inevitable rawness and unpredictability about 'caring for'.

'Caring about' puts more of a distance between the one caring and the cared for. It does not require direct care, rather more a general predisposition to see that children are cared for. However, 'caring about' isn't enough on its own. Professing to 'care about' can get workers off the hook of 'caring for'. As Noddings says, 'caring about' can involve a certain benign neglect; it is empty if it does not result in caring relations. This can be evident in some workers and students not really wanting to get involved in the dirty aspects of care, preferring to see the task as one of 'counselling'. This can, in turn, result in a tendency to criticize and blame those who do become involved in the messier and more ambiguous areas of care. Care workers themselves can find value, dignity even, in 'dirty work' (Stacey, 2005). It is rarely, however, valorized within a 'professional' context. A tangible consequence of this failure to acknowledge messiness in caring might be seen to be evident in the disproportionate numbers of residential care workers disciplined by social work's professional bodies.

Upbringing

The idea of upbringing – often mentioned in reports on childcare, but rarely articulated – augments ideas of care by bringing a cultural dimension central stage. I draw here on the work of the German social pedagogue, Mollenhauer, and his theory of upbringing advanced in *Forgotten Connections: On Culture and Upbringing* (1983). Upbringing, according to Mollenhauer, is a universal experience, and is first and foremost a matter of passing on a valued cultural heritage to prepare children to face the future (see Smith, 2013).

This idea of upbringing is afforded some conceptual purchase in the German terms *Erziehung* and *Bildung*. *Erziehung* can be translated, loosely, as 'education' or 'upbringing', blurring the boundary between school and home, personal and professional. *Bildung* can be thought of as being close in meaning to 'socialization' in that it describes the process of formation by self and others, across multiple contexts: familial, scholastic and recreational. Residential care workers in essence become 'upbringers' "on behalf of society" (Cameron and Moss, 2011: 13). The nature of their task might be understood as drawing out children's inner potential and initiating them into what is deemed to be culturally important across generations. The role is enacted through involvement in everyday life events; upbringers are "experts in everyday life" (Cameron, Reimer, and Smith, 2016). The orientation is broadly socio-educational rather than overtly therapeutic. Such a conception of upbringing contrasts with the narrow concerns with 'treatment' or safety which dominate current residential childcare policy and practice.

Implications of an orientation towards care and upbringing

Acceptance that the underpinning tasks of residential care are to support children's care and upbringing has implications for any conceptualization of professional identity. Residential child care needs workers who are engaged and embodied rather than detached and abstracted; it requires that they become involved in everyday practices of care, manifesting perhaps in joint participation in activities and in interventions that involve emotional and often bodily contact (Steckley, 2012). Care is enacted in the daily events of wake-up and bedtime routines; of shared meals, chores and recreation; in episodes of quarrelling and squabbling and the ramifications of these (Smith, Fulcher, and Doran, 2013). The messiness and contingency of such involvement cannot be accommodated within the technical rational exhortations towards the elusive 'best practice', shorn of dilemmas and mistakes, expected by managers and regulators (Whyte, 2016).

The sites and practices of residential childcare

Residential childcare practitioners "take as the theatre of their work the actual living situations as shared and experienced by the child" (Ainsworth, 1981: 234). This is a life-space orientation (Trieschman et al., 1969) whereby workers seek to use everyday life events to promote children's care and upbringing. In working in such a way, a carer's glance or countenance may be of more import than the latest programmed intervention (Smith, 2013). Life-space is, Steckley (2013) suggests, a threshold concept which is prerequisite for understanding and practising in residential childcare and which differentiates it from other types of social work.

A further feature differentiating group care from other areas of social work is the group element, where understanding ideas of teamwork and group dynamics are essential. Indeed, social work (and much current residential childcare) has come to see groups as problematic rather than sources of strength and support (Emond, 2003).

Care and upbringing in a neo-liberal world

While there are some fundamental practical and underlying epistemological differences between residential care and other areas of social work, any tensions were perhaps manageable so long as community social work maintained a focus on direct and relational work with children and families as it had done in the period following its professionalization. However, underlying differences have been brought into sharp relief as a result of social work's direction of travel in recent decades. That direction was set by the neo-liberal political and economic paradigms that came to dominate after the election of Margaret Thatcher as Prime Minister in 1979. Neo-liberalism is described by Harvey as a "theory of political economic practices that proposes that human well-being can best be advanced by liberating individual entrepreneurial freedoms" (2005: 2). Such a perspective was conceived to encompass even intimate relations; Gary Becker (1974), one of neo-liberalism's economic architects, refers to the family as "marriage markets". From such an economically reductionist standpoint, public care could be seen to be inefficient, overly bureaucratic, self-serving and requiring an injection of market realism.

The imprint of neo-liberalism is stamped on social work (and across the public services) by the doctrine of managerialism (Clark and Newman, 1997). This was based around core principles of economy, efficiency and effectiveness, and a belief that these aims could be achieved by more and better management (Pollitt, 2003). In social work, managerialism became manifest in ideas of care management, whereby care could be broken down into clean-cut stages of assessment and programmed interventions that would lead to measurable and improved outcomes over specified (preferably short) periods of time (Rose, 2010). It reinforced a notion of care (and social work more generally) as something that could be reduced to a series of instrumental tasks. In residential childcare this belief was operationalized in narrow vocational qualifications frameworks, which were manifestly unsuited to the holistic and dynamic nature of care practice (Heron and Chakrabarti, 2002) and indeed the relational core of thinking and knowing (de la Bellacasa, 2012).

Another feature of managerialism was its concern for ideas of rights and protection. While on the surface warmly persuasive, these discourses are problematic. Protection betrays an essentially misanthropic take on human relationships, involving

> a very different conception of the relationship between an individual or group, and others than does care. Caring seems to involve taking the concerns and needs of the other as the basis for action. Protection presumes . . . bad intentions.
>
> *(Tronto, 1993: 104)*

Child protection became the driver of children and families social work. The manifestation of this in residential childcare was a notion of 'safe caring', which from a perspective of care and upbringing – both of which involve offering new experiences with attendant risks of things going wrong – takes on an oxymoronic quality. On the ground, a predominant concern for safety resulted in a proliferation of needless and ethically dubious recording practices (Hardy, 2013) and staff who were "so adversely affected by low morale, depression, exhaustion or burn-out that they cease caring properly for the children" (Kent, 1997).

Children's rights, as they have emerged in public policy, are equally problematic, premised on "a particular understanding of the subject as a rational, autonomous individual" (Dahlberg and Moss, 2005: 30). By this reckoning, children and adults become linked to one another, primarily through a series of contractual arrangements, which are evident in residential care in developments such as the proliferation of information booklets and complaint procedures.

Changes in the nature of social work, according to Holman,

> facilitated a different kind of social work, which [is] at once both mechanical and inspectorial – some would say macho. Social workers found themselves having to follow procedures contained in rule books which were almost the size of novels.
>
> *(1998: 124)*

Initial child protection scandals focused on the family, but as signal cases such as Cleveland and Orkney – where social workers intervened precipitously and intrusively into family life – began to raise questions about the profession's competence in this area, the spotlight turned on residential care. Partly as a result of its ambivalent relationship with social work, residential care could not count on the same cultural capital as the family and was therefore vulnerable when the spotlight of abuse fell upon it. This resulted in a series of scandals and subsequent inquiry reports. In fact, our knowledge of the nature and scale of abuse in care is rather less clear-cut than can be presented; Webster (2005), for instance, deconstructs the Waterhouse Report (2000), the foundational inquiry report into institutional abuse upon which many subsequent assumptions are based, while I question the basis upon which understandings of abuse are constructed (Smith, 2010).

The result of inadequately thought-through beliefs around abuse is to reinforce a negative perception of identity in respect of residential childcare, which in turn, legitimizes a tendency to further restrict its usage. As Webb observes: "in the face of the impracticality of its total abandonment, (organizational responses have) consigned those in what is sometimes now called 'corporate care' to an even more stigmatising experience" (Webb, 2010: 1394).

At another level, the negative publicity focused on residential childcare might be reframed and understood within a foundational aim of the neo-liberal project to maintain a state of perpetual crisis. Garrett (2008) suggests that the whole notion that the care system is 'failing' can be understood as an intensely ideological project, required within the neo-liberal frame of reference to reveal failure in order to provide a rationale for privatization. The neo-liberal reform of care started with older people's services (Scourfield, 2007). It has spread rapidly, however, to the extent that the majority of children in care (67%) now live in privately run provision (Narey, 2016).

A further feature of neo-liberalism is that it is premised on an image of the person as autonomous and self-seeking, requiring that their baser instincts be kept in check by layers of legal injunction and behavioural codes. It seeks "to remake work and to alter the aims, aspirations and affiliations of a range of professional groups and fields" (Garrett, 2008). It has injected new forms of insecurity into people's working lives. This is frequently discussed in terms of the notion of 'precariousness' or 'precaricity' reflected in, for example, the growth of short-term contracts, zero hours' contracts and the growth of 'agency' working where wages are pared to a minimum and staff have few employment rights (Garrett, 2008). In the case of residential childcare, the aspiration towards a qualified workforce has been incrementally reduced. Residential work is now 'social care', a primarily vocational rather than professional task. The lower level of qualifications required to do care jobs is offset by policing the workforce through ever-expanding inspectorial and audit functions (Humphrey, 2003). These developments have obvious implications for the development of professional identity for residential childcare, raising the question of whether it can even claim such an identity.

The consequence of this privileging of the managerial over the caring is that the moral, practical and relational aspects of care have become corrupted. Wardaugh and Wilding (1993), reflecting on the 'Pindown' regime in Staffordshire children's homes where children were subject to an extreme form of behaviour management, formulate a number of propositions which they argue contribute to the corruption of care. Corruption, they argue, can be of various kinds, but it essentially constitutes an active betrayal of the basic values on which the organization is supposedly based. Many of these, the authors argue, are compounded by managerial responses. In focussing narrowly on avoiding internal management failures, they have actually reinforced other organizational features implicated in the corruption of care, specifically those pertaining to the impact of bureaucratic structures on care practices and the consequences of feelings of powerlessness experienced by those who provide direct care. The fundamental corruption in the care system over recent decades has been a failure to care, leading to a situation where:

> the concept of care within public care for children has been rarely seen as visible . . . a narrowing of what we mean by care, a lowering of expectations of what the state can offer in terms of care. Of particular note is the marked contrast between the potential for care within families as centering on control and love, and the optimum expected from state care which is around safekeeping.
>
> *(Cameron, 2003: 91–92)*

This combination of ideology, cost and spoiled identity has contributed to a massive decline in the usage of residential childcare from a high point in the mid-1970s (Bebbington and Miles, 1981). In England, for instance, "placements in community homes fell from over 25,000 to less than 2000 between 1981 and 2000" (Kendrick, 2012, p 288).

This process of residualization has led to attempts to identify a specialist 'therapeutic' function with children and youth with identified mental health or behavioural needs and to seek, within that, to identify 'evidence-based' models of care and treatment (Whittaker, del Valle and Holmes, 2015). Specialist treatment models seem to converge around ideas of trauma, increasingly bolstered by neuroscience. This is 'scientific' method writ large, promising that if only we can find the biological roots of a problem and intervene early enough, then we can then head off difficulties further down the line. This bio-politics reflects a more general 'biologizing' of what is appropriately social scientific terrain, offering "the comforting possibility of simple solutions to complex problems" (Canter, 2012: 112). "The idea that the brain causes behavior", Canter goes on, "is easier to get across than the subtler and more complex explanation embedded in learning, interpersonal transactions and culture" (2012: 112). As I have argued, upbringing is more about learning and culture than it is about biology. Yet dominant political and professional cultures turn to the scientific, with little evidence of success. As well as being ineffective, this is also a very Western view of care. Across much of the developing world, the notion of therapeutic residential care has limited transferability from Western practice research centres to life on the ground elsewhere (Fulcher and Islam, 2016).

Towards a professional identity for residential childcare

An ontology of care

My argument thus far in this chapter is that attempts to conceptualize residential childcare through scientific and managerial lenses misconceive the nature of embodied practice. These attempts imagine care as a duty, a series of tasks devoid of emotional essence: yet care is not possible, according to MacMurray, in terms of duty and obligation but must emerge as an ethic of love (see McIntosh, 2004). Ideas of care and upbringing require a relational ontology; human beings are ethical, committed and emotional (Lynch et al., 2009). Care and upbringing cannot be seen as discrete sets of tasks that can be separated from the relationship in which they are embedded (Lynch et al., 2009). The same authors also pose a challenge to current concerns about the outcomes of care, arguing that qualities of care and solidarity produce outcomes "that can be seen and felt if not always easily measured" (2009: 38).

An epistemology of care

Scholars have begun to explore the nature of professional knowledge and practice (Bondi et al., 2011; Dunne, 1993). A key topic of debate in this connection

is whether the knowledge or judgment required for effective practice in the caring professions is reducible to the technical 'evidence-based' rationality to which
professions such as medicine (and, by extension, social work) have aspired (Bondi
et al., 2011). Bondi et al. argue that technically rational forms of knowledge are
problematic in "people professions", where deliberation is inevitably implicated in
value disputes, taking it into the moral or ethical more than the scientific realm.
Morality in this sense is not about devising or conforming to rules or codes but
learning to cultivate a moral life.

Scholars such as Dunne and Bondi et al. draw on the ancient Greek philosopher
Aristotle to support their critique of dominant models of professional education.
Aristotle identified three different forms of knowledge or intellectual virtues: *techne*,
or craft knowledge; *episteme*, or scientific knowledge; and *phronesis*, or practical reasoning, to which scholars are increasingly turning in seeking to elucidate professional practice. Dunne argues that thinking on education has tended to privilege
Aristotle's notion of *techne*. While *techne* might prove very useful and appropriate
for a craftsperson making a cabinet – a process which requires instrumental and
largely replicable skills, able to be articulated and passed on through an apprenticeship model – it is less appropriate for 'people work'. A residential care worker
cannot aspire to some unproblematic notion of 'best practice' or 'evidence-based
practice', as what is considered to be such will change according to a whole variety of circumstances involving individual personality, agency and context. What is
required in such situations might be better understood as phronetic knowledge.
An Aristotelian concept of *phronesis* is pragmatic, variable and context dependent.
It is oriented towards a virtue ethics version of the good. It is also action oriented
and is thus consonant with the practical realities of residential childcare practice.
Crucially, it involves deliberation about values being based on a value rather than an
instrumental rationality; it is about the development of a certain kind of person, "a
person disposed towards questioning and criticizing for the sake of more informed
and responsible engagement" (Sullivan and Rosin, 2008: xvi). The end point of
phronesis is praxis, a form of ethically committed action which realizes the good at
which it aims through the process of caring rather than some externally specified
aim. The 'good' of residential childcare, thus, is realized in its praxis, which must be
characterized as an ethical and worthwhile activity in itself, not just through its ends
or outcomes. Kreber (2015) identifies what a worker brings to this as "authenticity", living in accordance with one's values.

There is no algorithm through which to guide such ethically committed practice, no code of practice, no 'best practice'. Kreber (2015) suggests that what is
required is an inner capacity to cope with two distinct phenomena of our times:
epistemological uncertainty and complexity, which, together, she suggests, result in
an existential experience of 'strangeness'. Residential care workers need to become
comfortable in not knowing and to seek to flourish amid the strangeness of an
ever-changing world.

Bernstein (1983) maintains that a hermeneutic perspective is important in
praxis-oriented professions where human beings are continually engaged in the
social construction and deconstruction of their worlds. As such, hermeneutics

might also be thought to bring with it particular implications for the way we might think about residential childcare practice. Clark (2012) proposes that rather than falling back on rules or algorithms – or to use Gadamer's (2004) term, "method" –

> resolving ethically problematic situations should better be understood as a hermeneutic process demanding a repeated and progressive quest to reconcile the detailed particularities of the case with complex, competing and evolving moral imperatives.
>
> *(Clark, 2012: 115)*

It is perhaps this idea of praxis or practical knowledge that converges around a particular set of values that residential care workers need to begin to develop and talk up in respect to their professional identities.

Concluding discussion

All of my arguments up till now might be thought to suggest that residential childcare and social work possess very different essences and that this might suggest that both cannot be accommodated within what might be thought of as a 'social work identity'. This is my argument, up to a point; there are undoubted and fairly fundamental differences between 'caring about' and 'caring for', centring largely on questions of proximity, intimacy and embodiment, which are central features of care and upbringing. Indeed, developments in Scotland – where a new ordinary degree-level qualification has been agreed as a requirement to work in residential childcare – suggest that policy directions are beginning to recognize the differences between residential childcare and other forms of social work. (This development, itself, reflects a further divergence between Scotland and England, where Narey's 2016 review of residential childcare has come out against a degree-level qualification and indeed is sceptical of the need for any particular qualifications for care work.) It is in reflecting on this new development in Scotland that I come to wonder whether differences are indeed 'essentialist' or whether it is social work that has changed to become a site of technical/rational bureaucratic activity. Perhaps, it need not be like that: social work might itself reclaim some of the moral and practical (and in Scotland, the socio-educational) strands that characterized it in the years following professionalization. It is these that have been eroded to the point of virtual disappearance on the back of the managerial onslaught. As Meagher and Parton (2004) argue, ideas of care might challenge social work to reconsider its own professional identity.

Whether in or out of social work, there are particular pillars upon which any emerging identity for residential childcare must be built: it must be life space–based praxis oriented, with the attendant focus on values; relational, and within that, dispositional and broadly socio-educational rather than overtly therapeutic. It is also irredeemably embodied and practical, with all the messiness that goes along with this. It is around these areas rather than current obsessions with discrete tasks, 'what works' interventions and the quest to measure outcomes that aren't amenable to measurement, that any healthy identity might emerge. New or different qualifications are unlikely to make much difference to the identity of staff, or ultimately the experiences of children and youth, unless some of these central epistemological and indeed ontological aspects can be grappled with.

References

Ainsworth, F. (1981). The Training of Personnel for Group Care with Children. In F. Ainsworth & L. C. Fulcher (Eds.), *Group Care for Children: Concept and Issues* (pp. 225–246). London: Tavistock.

Bebbington, A. & Miles, J. (1989) The Background of Children Who Enter Local Authority Care. *The British Journal of Social Work*, 19(5): 349–368

Becker, G. S. (1974). A Theory of Marriage. In T. W. Schultz (Ed.), *Economics of the Family: Marriage, Children, and Human Capital* (pp. 299–351). Chicago, IL: University of Chicago Press.

Bernstein, R. (1983) *Beyond Objectivism and Relativism: Science, Hermeneutics, and Praxis*, Philadelphia: University of Pennsylvania Press.

Bondi, L., Carr, D., Clark, C., & Clegg, C. (2011). *Towards Professional Wisdom: Practical Deliberation in the People Professions*. Farnham: Ashgate.

Bourdieu, P. (1986). Forms of Capital. In J. Richardson (Ed.), *Handbook of Theory and Research for the Sociology of Education* (pp. 241–258). Westport, CT: Greenwood.

Bourdieu, P. (1993). *The Field of Cultural Production*. Cambridge, UK: Polity Press.

Cameron, C. (2003). An Historical Perspective on Changing Child Care Policy. In J. Brannan & P. Moss (Eds.), *Rethinking Children's Care* (pp. 80–95). Buckingham: Open University Press.

Cameron, C., Reimer, D., & Smith, M. (2016). Towards a Theory of Upbringing in Foster Care in Europe. *European Journal of Social Work*, 19(2): 152–170.

Cameron, C. & Moss, P. (2011). *Social Pedagogy and Working with Children and Young People: Where Care and Education Meet*. London: Jessica Kingsley Publishers.

Canter, D. (2012). Challenging Neuroscience and Evolutionary Explanations of Social and Psychological Processes. *Contemporary Social Science: Journal of the Academy of Social Sciences*, 7(2): 95–115.

Clark, C. (2012). From Rules to Encounters: Ethical Decision-Making as a Hermeneutic Process. *Journal of Social Work*, 12(2): 115–135.

Clarke, J., & Newman, J. (1997). *The Managerial State: Power, Politics and Ideology in the Remaking of Social Welfare*. London: Sage.

Coady, P. (2014). Relationship Boundaries in Residential Child Care: Connection and Safety in Group Care Relationships: A Practitioner Research Study Exploring Boundary Decisions of Residential Child Care Workers in Their Relationships with Young People. *Research, Policy and Planning*, 31(2): 79–91.

Dahlberg, G. and Moss, P. (2005) *Ethics and Politics in Early Childhood Education*. London: Routledge/Falmer.

De la Bellacasa, M. P. (2012). Nothing Comes without Its World': Thinking with Care. *The Sociological Review*, 60(2): 197–216.

Douglas, R., & Payne, C. (1981). Alarm Bells for the Clock-on Philosophy. *Social Work Today*, 12(23): 110–111.

Dunne, J. (1993). *Back to the Rough Ground: 'Phronesis and Techne in Modern Philosophy and in Aristotle*. Notre Dame, IN: University of Notre Dame Press.

Emond, R. (2003). Putting the Care into Residential Care: The Role of Young People. *Journal of Social Work*, 3(3): 321–337.

Fulcher, L., & Islam, T. (eds.) (2016). *Residential Child and Youth Care in a Developing World*. Claremont, South Africa: CYC-Net Press.

Gadamer, H. G. (2004). *Truth and Method*. London: Continuum.

Garrett, P. M. (2008). Social Work Practices: Silences and Elisions in the Plan to 'Transform' the Lives of Children 'Looked After' in England. *Child and Family Social Work*, 13(3): 311–318.

Gilligan, C. (1982) *In a Different Voice: Psychological Theory and Women's Development*. Cambridge, MA: Harvard University Press.

Goffman, E. (1961). *Asylums*. New York: Anchor Books.

Hardy, M. (2013). Shift Recording in Residential Child Care – Purposes, Issues and Implications for Policy and Practice. *Surveillance and Society*, 12(1): 108–123.

Harvey, D. (2005). *A Brief History of Neo-liberalism*. Oxford: Oxford University Press.

Heron, G., & Chakrabarti, M. (2002). Examining the Perceptions and Attitudes of Staff Working in Community based Children's Homes: Are Their Needs being Met? *Qualitative Social Work*, 1(3): 341–358.

Holligan, C., Hanson, L., Henderson, G., & Adams, M. (2014). The 'Care' of Children in Need in Contemporary Scotland: The Role of Positivism and Performance Indicators in Official Imaginings of Childhood and Well-being. *Scottish Journal of Residential Child Care*, 13(1). Retrieved from https://www.celcis.org/knowledge-bank/search-bank/journal/scottish-journal-residential-child-care-vol-13-no-1/.

Holman, B. (1998) *Faith in the Poor*. London: Lion Books.

Humphrey J, C. (2003) New Labour and the Regulatory Reform of Social Care, *Critical Social Policy*, 23(1): 5–22.

Kendrick, A. (2012) What Research Tells Us about Residential Child Care. In M. Davies, (Ed.), *Social Work with Children and Families* (pp. 287–303). London: Palgrave Macmillan.

Kent, R. (1997) *Children's Safeguards Review*. Social Work Services Inspectorate, Edinburgh: The Scottish Office.

Kilbrandon Report (1995). *Children and Young Persons*, Scotland. Edinburgh: HMSO.

Kreber, C. (2015). Reviving the Ancient Virtues in the Scholarship of Teaching, with a Slight Critical Twist. *Higher Education Research & Development*, 34(3): 568–580.

Lynch, K., Baker, J., & Lyons, M. (2009). *Affective Equality: Love, Care and Injustice*. Basingstoke: Palgrave Macmillan.

McIntosh, E. (ed.) (2004). *John MacMurray: Selected Philosophical Writings*. Exeter: Imprint Academic.

Meagher, G., & Parton, N. (2004). Modernising Social Work and the Ethics of Care. *Social Work and Society*. Retrieved from http://www.socwork.net/sws/article/view/237/412.

Mollenhauer, K, (1983). *Forgotten Connections: On Culture and Upbringing*. London: Routledge.

Moss, P., & Petrie, P. (2002). *From Children's Services to Children's Spaces*. London: Routledge.

Narey, M. (2016). *Independent Report: Children's Residential Care in England*, Department for Education. Retrieved from https://www.gov.uk/government/publications/childrens-residential-care-in-england. (Accessed 25 July 2016).

Noddings, N. (1984). *Caring: A Feminine Approach to Ethics and Moral Education*. Berkeley: University of California Press

Phelan, J. (2001). Notes on Using Plain Language in Child and Youth Care. *Cyc-Online*, 34. (November). Retrieved from http://www.cyc-net.org/cyc-online.

Pollitt, C. (2003). *The Essential Public Manager*. Maidenhead: Open University Press.

Rose, J. (2010). *How Nurture Protects Children*. London: Responsive Solutions.

Rowe, J., & Lambert, L. (1973). *Children Who Wait: A Study of Children Needing Substitute Families*. London: British Association for Adoption and Fostering.

Scourfield, P. (2007). Are there Reasons to Be Worried about the 'Caretelization' of Residential Care? *Critical Social Policy*, 27(2): 155–180.

Sevenhuijsen, S. (1998). *Citizenship and the Ethics of Care: Feminist Considerations on Justice, Morality, and Politics*. New York: Routledge.

Sewpaul, V. (2005). Global Standards: Promise and Pitfalls for Re-inscribing Social Work into Civil Society. *International Journal of Social Welfare*, 14(3): 210–217.

Smith, M. (2009). *Rethinking Residential Child Care: Positive Perspectives*. Bristol: Policy Press.

Smith, M. (2010). Victim Narratives of Historical Abuse in Residential Child Care: Do We Really Know What We Think We Know? *Qualitative Social Work*, 9(3): 303–320.

Smith, M. (2013). Forgotten Connections: Reviving the Concept of Upbringing in Scottish Child Welfare. *Scottish Journal of Residential Child Care*, 12(2): 13–29.

Smith, M., Fulcher, L., & Doran, P. (2013). *Residential Child Care in Practice: Making a Difference*. Bristol: Policy Press.

Stacey, C. (2005). Finding Dignity in Dirty Work: The Constraints and Rewards of Low-Wage Home Care Labour. *Sociology of Health and Illness*, 27(6): 831–854.

Steckley, L. (2012). Touch, Physical Restraint and Therapeutic Containment in Residential Child Care. *British Journal of Social Work*, 42(2): 537–555.

Steckley, L. (2013). Is Life-Space a Threshold Concept? *CYC-Online*, Issue 172: 23–29.

Steckley, L., & Smith, M. (2011). Care Ethics in Residential Child Care: A Different Voice. *Ethics and Social Welfare*, 5(2): 181–195.

Sullivan, W. M., & Rosin, M. S. (2008). *A New Agenda for Higher Education: Shaping a Life of the Mind for Practice*. San Francisco, CA: Carnegie Foundation for the Advancement of Teaching and Jossey-Bass.

Trieschman, A., Whittaker, J. K., & Brendtro, L. K. (1969). *The Other 23 Hours: Child-Care Work with Emotionally Disturbed Children in a Therapeutic Milieu*. New York: Aldine de Gruyter.

Tronto, J. (1993). *Moral Boundaries: A Political Argument for an Ethic of Care*. London: Routledge.

Wardaugh, J., & Wilding, P. (1993). Towards an Explanation of the Corruption of Care. *Critical Social Policy*, 13(37): 4–31.

Webb, D. (2010). A Certain Moment: Some Personal Reflections on Aspects of Residential Childcare in the 1950s. *British Journal of Social Work*, 40(5): 1387–1401.

Webster, R. (2005). *The Secret of Bryn Estyn: The Making of a Modern Witchhunt*. Oxford: The Orwell Press.

Whittaker, J., del Valle, J. F., & Holmes, L. (2015). *Therapeutic Residential Care for Children and Youth: Developing Evidence-Based International Practice*. London: Jessica Kingsley Publishers.

Whyte, B. (2016). Social Work in Scotland: Who Calls the Shots? *Ethics and Social Welfare*. published on-line 20 June 2016. doi: 10.1080/17496535.2016.1194547.

PART III

Professional education, socialisation and readiness for practice

13

SHAPING IDENTITY? THE PROFESSIONAL SOCIALISATION OF SOCIAL WORK STUDENTS

Julia Wheeler

Introduction

Professional socialisation is often reported as the internalisation of a set of values congruent with the culture of the profession (Zarshenas et al., 2014). It is considered to be the process whereby students develop a sense of self as members of a profession, internalize the values of their profession and exhibit these values through their behaviour. Professional socialisation is a key aspect of social work pre-qualifying training. The final practice fieldwork placement has long been viewed as one of the most crucial elements in enabling students to transfer learning on the course into practice (Parker, 2007: 765). Whilst there has been substantial research into how students develop their skills in social work education, very few studies have focused upon the student's development of professional identity and the process of professional socialisation (Clapton, 2013). Valutis, Rubin, and Bell (2012) state: "Professional education imparts values and identity as well as knowledge to students. It contributes in both intended and unintended ways to the socialization of students to the professional culture" (1047).

Understanding how social work students are socialised into the profession enables educators to improve upon the support delivered during their social work education. In addition, by raising an awareness of the process of professional socialisation, social work organisations can be better prepared in not only supporting social work students, but also in retaining the social work force (Miller, 2010: 363).

The process of professional socialisation is fascinating to observe and as a result this became the basis of doctoral studies carried out by the author. It is argued that individual students construct their professional identity over the duration of the professional education programme and in relation to significant others, such as the student group, placement supervisors and practice educators, through the process of professional socialisation. Therefore, the research sought to understand this process by interviewing final-year postgraduate students and their practice supervisors.

The context of identity formation and socialisation

In undertaking this research, Jenkins' (2004, 2008) view of social identity was regarded as particularly advantageous in exploring professional socialisation, as he offers a broad framework for understanding identity within three areas: individual, interaction and institution. Within this framework, identity is regarded as both individual and collective. These aspects are 'entangled' and interact through processes of identification (Jenkins, 2004: 16). In supporting this approach, Jenkins makes use of the work of Pierre Bourdieu and his concepts of habitus, capital and field. However, as this study was focused more upon the students' interaction with others, the work of Lave and Holland was also valuable (2001, 2009), especially their use of Social Practice Theory to create 'history in person'.

Similar to Bourdieu, Lave and Holland do not view minds as operating separately from bodies, nor from practice; instead, they claim we "shape the on-going social world", and as we move through social spaces and institutions we are "persons-in-practice" (2009: 2). Individuals adapt to the moment and the situations encountered through their practice contexts. The 'history in person' concept is similar to Bourdieu's notion of habitus in the sense that it is regarded as durable, acquires a sensibility and is recreated in what Lave and Holland term, "contentious local practice" (2001: 30). "Contentious local practice" offers a framework for understanding how individuals are historically related to their previous experiences but are also different because there is potential for conflict and tension within the horizons of everyday practice. This conflict is represented by what Lave and Holland (2001, 2009) refer to as "enduring struggles" within "contentious local practice". When applied to social work students and their experience of professional socialisation, this is a useful theoretical framework for understanding where the student brings previous experience and identity to bear, but also how these are further developed in interaction with other people (such as professionals, service users and peers) in practice settings.

To explore the socialisation process, a small-scale study was conducted in which nine postgraduate social work students and five placement supervisors were interviewed. The students and supervisors were located in a range of placement settings, from working with adults and children within local authorities to voluntary agency practice settings. All of the placement supervisors interviewed were currently working with and supporting a student on the programme. Of the five supervisors, three of the students they were working with at the time of the research had also volunteered to be interviewed.

Themes were identified following the interviews and analysis undertaken utilising grounded theory (Charmaz, 2014). Three broad themes emerged from the data. First was the relevance of the students' previous experience and their identity prior to embarking upon the programme, and the impact of this experience upon the students' professional identity and socialisation into the social work profession. Second was the importance of interaction with others during the programme, particularly those involved in the students' final placement. Third, the positive and negative impact of organisational practices emerged as a significant theme, especially the emergence of hot desking and the increasingly bureaucratic nature of workplace culture.

Student and supervisor experiences: impact of others

Within the interviews a good deal of the students' narratives were devoted to explaining their practice with service users, most offering detailed examples of practice cases. What was clear within these accounts was the significant impact working with service users and carers had on students as they developed not only their practice, but also their professional identity. The most important aspect highlighted by students was the opportunity to develop a professional 'relationship' with service users. For example, students talked about learning and developing as a result of direct work with service users. Students stressed that this 'resource time' that they were allowed as learners to work with service users might become more restricted once they were qualified, but they were currently valuing the opportunity to develop relationships. One student described this as follows:

> I think that is probably one thing I will struggle with if I go to work in a statutory setting, because I just got used to doing that real relationship like, based practice and see how valuable that is, and then the chance is that you are going to work where you don't have the time to do that.

A number of the students interviewed had first-hand experience as service users or carers, and they explored how this prior experience was valuable to their practice and how it impacted upon their professional development and ability to empathise with service users. These students explained how they struggled with whether or not they should disclose personal experiences, and how much to disclose within fieldwork placement settings:

> I think throughout the course actually, if you reveal too much of yourself in terms, your inner life, your inner kind of emotional life or what you are thinking, then maybe you kind of show yourself up to be someone who can't cope maybe, or kind of all of that.

Perhaps because of this challenge, the majority of the students raised the importance of peer relationships to their professional development. It became apparent that students' relationship with peers on the programme was particularly important as the power imbalance was substantially reduced within these relationships. For instance, other personnel within the placement and in the programme had the power to assess and potentially 'fail' students (Finch, 2015). Thus students felt 'safer' exploring difficult experiences in placement with their peers and considering how these might impact upon their professional identity and development. The crucial nature of peer relationships was also found in the research of Mosek and Ben-Oz (2011).

During the research discussed in this chapter, students explained how they sought the support of peers within the course whom they perceived to share comparable life experiences and values. Students achieved this by organising an informal network of support outside of the programme during placement, in addition to contacts developed through social media, such as Facebook or Twitter. This was explained extensively by one student:

> Actually, on both my placements, I have been in touch with other students and organised 'beer supervision' rather than 'peer supervision'! Just saw each other a bit and had a few glasses of wine, chat about what was good or bad and I think that is quite important as well. We don't have beer supervision here, as we see each other more, so more like coffee supervision but yeah we bump into each other quite a lot. That is nice because there is usually one of us who is behind on this or whatever, when you talk you find it can dissipate the problem as you are either in that place or have been.

Only two students interviewed mentioned the impact of tutors, which has been researched by other academics (Clapton, 2006; Clapton & Cree, 2008; Wilson and Campbell, 2012), although all students commented upon key teaching experiences, such as critical reflection and communication skills. Consequently, there was little to reflect upon in terms of the impact of tutors and lecturers upon students.

Despite the challenges of disclosure and being constantly assessed, students did explain the importance of placement personnel in the development of their professional identity. Often it was not just one individual who positively influenced the development of a student's professional identity; it was the team of personnel around the student in their placement workplace. This was particularly essential if the student did not find their supervisor supportive. This concurs with Bogo's (2010) research, where students sought out the support of others if their supervisor was unavailable or unapproachable. Key to this support provided by the wider team was the opportunity to observe varying styles of working and role models, which has been corroborated by earlier research undertaken by Webb (1988). Similarly, Grant et al. (2016) found a combination of peer support and 'shadowing' more experienced social workers to be significant in the professional socialisation process of newly qualified social workers.

This modelling facilitated the socialisation process and was summed up concisely by one student:

> I think, it's made me realise how it is nice to see other people work and you, I think you admire certain parts of it. You almost, you see someone doing something, oh I really want to be just like that social worker, for example.

Thus, this is not just role modelling, but also allowing students to test out different ways of learning to find their own style of working. A student went on to explain:

> I think for me as a social worker I think that's the one thing I've learnt in this placement is actually if you are true to yourself then that's how you can be the best social worker you can be. That's an impact that everyone I've seen working has had on me, I think.

This supportive team environment that the students spoke of included other types of professionals, such as youth workers, support workers, family support workers and volunteers. For example, students explained how supportive their team was in the office environment, and some students found their managers supportive and interested in their practice:

> But they are all very much, all stop me and say how are you doing and how are you managing, even before I started they said, how do you think you will deal with this? How are you going to manage? It is really nice, not a nicety, it is a professional competency, like can you manage this?

One of the students was in a setting where they did not have direct contact with social workers and their supervisor did not have a social work qualification. As the earlier study of Scholar et al. (2014) found, students were mostly positive about this type of placement experience and in fact felt incredibly well supported by their supervisor and agency. They did have contact with social workers from other agencies, and their practice educator was social work–qualified, but it was the support of their supervisor and workplace that they found significantly supported their development.

Overall, the study reported on in this chapter found that students had positive experiences of fieldwork placement personnel, who assisted in the overall development of professional identity through the process of socialisation. While students did not always talk about these professionals explicitly assisting the development of their professional identity, this did figure strongly in interviews concerning working with health professionals. For example, interacting with other professionals during placement had a significant impact, as one student explained:

> Yes, my placement is within a multi-disciplinary team, it is dominated by the medical staff, so to find the voice from a social model into dominated medical model it is a challenge sometimes. It has tested my values, personal values as well as the values of social work, in terms of if you are going on a joint visit with people like Occupational Therapists or Physiotherapists, I had a question when someone said, I don't know what social workers do.

Research conducted in other professions has identified the importance of health professionals within identity formation and socialisation (Beddoe, 2011: 28). This was highlighted by supervisors in this study, and explained by one particular supervisor:

> Well within the team we are multi-disciplinary, so and it is very health based, and we are kind of the add on. . . . So we do have to be quite boundaried ourselves as a team and clear what our role is, when often the other professionals are clear what our Social Work role is. Within the team we do a lot in terms of educating the other professions.

From this quote it appears that the process of explaining one's own bounded role enables a practitioner to be more conscious and clear about their professional identity. This is corroborated by Adams et al. (2006: 56), where they found professionals compared and differentiated themselves from other professional groups in interaction with those professionals in the workplace. Therefore, students were defining and redefining their professional identity and role in relation to one another in multidisciplinary placement settings.

Another supervisor went on to explain how the student assisted them in furthering their own professional identity as they needed to be clear with the team concerning the work and role of a student social worker. This is similar to Parker and Doel's (2013) findings, where they advocated that social work placements should be an opportunity for all parties to learn, develop and promote two-way learning processes between supervisors and students.

Fieldwork placement supervisors

The importance of the students' placement supervisor was a prominent feature of the interviews. Working with supervisors was regarded as a mostly positive experience for students, with only a few exceptions. However, one student found that the relationship with a supervisor took some time to develop:

> I think personality comes down to it quite a lot, so I get on really well with her, but she is a really quiet individual. At first, for me she was so quiet I lacked confidence in her ability, and it has taken me a while to kind of peel back that shell and actually find someone that's knowledgeable and that relationship has improved a lot and the respect from me has come and the ability to question has come, but it has taken two months to get to that point.

One of the reasons this student cited for slow development of their relationship was a difference of perspective in the application of theory. The student's supervisor was a trained counsellor and utilised these skills within her work, whilst the student opted for a different theoretical perspective, mostly adopting a task-orientated approach. This need for congruence with the supervisor resonated with other students as they described the sharing of personal qualities with supervisors as compatible values, motivations and political stances. The latter was voiced by one student as follows:

> Yes, I'm never sure as we are fairly similar and coming from a similar political place and also in terms of how we would practice, such as the signs of safety, narrative and all those kind of influences in the background. So I'm never sure I feel that influence is more because they are similar to me and so not had to change in that sense.

On one hand, in a negative sense, students who had a difficult relationship with their supervisor felt this more keenly than those with positive experiences. One student described a particularly challenging relationship with a supervisor:

> There was a lot going on, and I kind of had this sense that I was a burden. So although I was very busy, doing all the learning and e-learning that they recommended, keeping myself busy, but I was very much isolated at that point.

On the other hand, students who had supportive and positive relationships with their supervisors found them to be essential at times when they were experiencing difficulties in placement:

> I think if it wasn't for the support of my supervisor I would have been, I don't know, maybe crumbled by now. But I can see that, everything I do they are very supportive, and in the sense of making me feel confident in myself to be assertive.

This success was also due in part to the quality of the relationship the student had with their supervisor:

> I think my relationship with my supervisor is quite a strong one actually, I don't know if that is because before I went on the placement there was some issues in my personal life, that I had to be quite transparent about at the time before I got there. With that, she then appropriately I felt shared some stuff about herself as well, when she was starting out as a practitioner and I feel that within that it has been quite an accepting kind of, you can be who you are, but still be a competent professional. I feel that, there is just an openness to discuss that sort of thing and then move on.

This demonstrates the importance of supervisors sharing their own previous experience and 'sense of self' with students, to encourage the student to also 'make use of self' and prior experiences. This would also generate feelings of trust and confidence as well as respect for the supervisor's experience. This is supported by the research of Barretti (2007) and Bogo (2006), in which they concluded that students found that the key ingredients in establishing a positive relationship were the supervisor's personal qualities.

The importance of support from supervisors is widely found in much of the literature concerning supervisors and practice educators (Davidson, 2011; Gelman and Lloyd, 2008; Giddings, Vodde, and Cleveland, 2004; Koeske and Kanno, 2010). Supervisors themselves highlighted a number of alternative ways in which they supported students through the socialisation process, such as through critical reflection and role modelling in addition to supervision. Supervisors often spoke about challenging students and enabling them to question their practice. To achieve this, a range of tools to encourage students to explore their identity and values were utilised. Supervisors understood how support was positive in assisting the development of a student's professional identity. One supervisor explained this as follows:

> It helps them to increase their skill base and their ability to understand human behaviour and some of the difficulties that some of the service users' groups do kind of face. I think that helps them in their confidence, in doing the work and their understanding of human behaviour, which I think all kind of impacts on development of your professional identity.

From a student's perspective, one student described the impact of this support in building confidence to practice:

> I can see, I never had confidence to, probably deal with a complex situation, on the phone or face to face. Dealing with that, and talking to my colleagues and talking to my supervisor, or to my line manager as well, it gives me that confidence to say yes I can do it.

Supervisors also explained some interesting means of managing the tensions in supporting students as learners within the placement environment. They accounted for ways in enabling students to successfully negotiate agency procedures and to develop resilient styles that evolved at times of "enduring struggles" as noted by Lave and Holland (2001). For instance, one supervisor believed that a way of navigating these practices was for the student to 'conform' to what they perceived as the agency identity:

> I think the organisation gives very clear boundaries of what they expect a student to meet and how their professional identity at a corporate level is mostly constructed by the expectation of that agency. So you will dress a certain way, you will not have lip rings and so on. So the agency, it does construct them, and their professional identity.

Here the supervisor refers to students conforming to agency dress codes as a way of promoting corporate identity. The conformity described here supports the earlier research by Scholar (2013: 366), where she argued that agency dress codes were a means of the agency imposing organisational control and agency values. This supervisor went on further to explain:

> I really work with the students then, also for my own practice, I have to know, I have to check out that their values match those of the agency. It's almost like you do a mini 'fit for practice' again, I have to check that out . . . but I also see the student as an extension of me.

The "student as an extension of me" supports the view that comparable styles of working help form a more positive relationship. However, this quote takes it a step further, suggesting that students also need to share and conform to the agency culture. This is congruent with research concerning newly qualified social workers in which graduates explained that they experienced their values being compromised as they attempted to 'fit' within the organisation (Donnellan and Jack, 2010).

Although students conform to this perception of agency identity, this is something of an act (or as Leigh terms it, a "credible performance"; see Chapter 14 in this volume), as they present themselves as employable by the agency and thus potentially compromise their personal identity. Fook, Ryan and Hawkins (2000) similarly contend that students adapt their personal identity to navigate the agency's, so that they can become "mutually exclusive" (158). Students are often caught in the middle ground of having to prove they are ready and 'fit' for practice, and wish to be viewed as employable (Tham and Lynch, 2014), despite how they might feel about the agency systems and supervisor's expectations.

Supporting students does not always require a conformist stance. The majority of supervisors took an entirely different stance when working with students, one which promoted the student's confidence, independence for learning and assertiveness. Enabling students to develop the confidence to challenge the agency systems was considered important. As one supervisor argued:

> I also don't understand this but some supervisors have a blind loyalty to the Local Authority. Which I don't understand, as I am happy with students, maybe because I am union representative as well, to completely slam the idea of key performance indicators. When I get an email to say fantastic you have achieved 90%, this is completely meaningless – and I have that discussion with them [the student]. But some supervisors are horrified when I do that. I am not saying anything radical.

In fact, all of the supervisors in this study, despite differing styles of supporting the student, shared the view that resilience is crucial to developing professional identity (Kinman and Grant, 2014, Beddoe, 2013). Students consistently reported that key to this resilience and management of agency practices is the positive use of supervision and the support of the supervisor. One student mentioned:

> I'm making healthy choices and being open about it and letting people know where I'm at and I think that has been a really good thing. I feel that it has

been used in the way, I think you could have the best supervisor in the world but if you haven't got the courage to use them, then it doesn't matter as you soldier on, on your own. But I do think my attitude has changed. I was the student in the first year that said I wouldn't get any benefit out of supervision, because I feel my attitude has been the boss is here, keep your head down. Now I feel I have a good working relationship and made me understand my own working.

Surprisingly for some students, placement supervisors (who supervise the student's workload during placement) undertaking the training as practice educator (who assesses the student in practice and supports the student to make links with theory) also had exceptionally positive experiences. Students were surprised because initially they thought there would be detrimental challenges with the same person undertaking both roles. In particular, they were concerned about the amount of power this person would have in their placement, especially concerning assessment of practice. Contrariwise, they found that their supervisor/practice educator had an enhanced understanding of both practice realities and the learning needs of students, including the course requirements. This was particularly pertinent for a student who had a split placement and found their supervisor/practice educator was extremely knowledgeable:

She is direct and she does also seem to know everything about everything. When I ask something she can always answer, she worked on the practice educator before, which is really useful. So I have a supervisor who has worked in both teams, and understands the processes and differences between the two teams.

Impact of the organisation

Organisations are often keen to support students and graduates in light of the high vacancy rates and to improve upon the retention of social workers (Collins, 2008, also Chapter 11 in this volume). Rajan-Rankin (2014: 2427) states that while there is concern about retention, less is known about the 'process' by which a student social worker learns to manage and regulate their emotions. He points to the importance of organisational responsibility for enabling this process rather than leaving it to individual practitioners. The organisational culture could promote flexible support for social workers (Hotho, 2008), rather than enforcing rigid and inflexible institutional procedures. This in turn would improve upon the retention of newly qualified social workers. Hussein et al. (2014) found that newly qualified social workers required good support within the workplace if they were to be retained. This means fostering good staff morale and providing appropriately supportive supervision (Tham, 2007). Creating a supportive environment and workplace culture for students is crucial and should be facilitated by placement personnel. One supervisor in this study explored the organisational culture and the importance of how identity formation was supported within the agency:

> Within the wider organisation, we do have a reasonably strong Social Work identity. We have a Social Work Education lead and he does quite a good role of representing us and we have had a Social Work conference that he has organised. He is proactive and he stands up for Social Work amongst the other professions. Sounds like them and us, but it is not.

This supervisor was based in a more health-orientated setting, and it seems her organisation wanted to retain clear roles and a sense of purpose. Alternatively, a student who was also based within a predominantly health setting stated:

> But I think there is still more to be done in terms of raising the profile of social workers, what does social workers and the profession of social work and the identity of social work, what does it mean in other teams, especially the medical people.

So whilst the supervisor's account promotes the idea that agency support had assisted social workers in health settings to develop a clearer professional identity, this was not the experience of a student who was in a different local authority setting. It is likely that these two organisations promoted very different learning cultures for social workers.

One particular controversial practice highlighted in all the student interviews was the issue of hot desking. This has been negatively commented upon in the media by bodies such as British Association of Social Work and Community Care. Conversely, two students within the sample stated that hot desking was useful in sitting next to different social workers and professionals in order to observe varying styles of working. However, the majority of students described how these working conditions had a negative impact upon their learning and development. Students stated that their own 'space' was important in promoting effective working conditions. For instance, students spent a good deal of time seeking out available desk space and computers to complete assessments. This extended quote demonstrates the issue:

> I don't like it, only because I like to have my space that I can go into in the morning. I like to sit within the team, because I can hear what my agency supervisor is doing and I think in terms of the person, you feel out of it if you are not sat with your team. You sit with other teams and sometimes you notice you get a funny look because you are sat in someone's seat. So I think that can be, not hugely uncomfortable, as I'm not the kind of person, where it would affect me too much. But you do definitely see it across the whole floor. I definitely prefer just to have my own desk and have my drawers, rather than shuffling about every day, trying to get my stuff together.

Some students worked in teams where flexible working was promoted, including home working. This was partly due to the introduction of hot desking, but also because they worked in large rural geographical areas where home working was more practical and time efficient. This led to a reduced team presence in the office. It also had the negative effect in promoting feelings of isolation in the team that were especially felt when supervisors were working from home. It was apparent that the organisational cultures have a significant impact upon students and their development as practitioners.

Concluding discussion

The majority of the students interviewed explained how they were significantly influenced and supported by personnel in placement. This reflected particularly on shared comparable values, experiences and motivations, and at times political stances and theoretical perspectives. Supervisors were portrayed by students as key to this development if they were open to sharing their own life experiences with students. Peers figured significantly within the interview responses, but also the student's interaction with service users was crucial in their learning development as a social worker. Therefore, it is not enough for the supervisor or key placement personnel to be merely supportive and offer good-quality supervision; they also need to display comparable values and qualities to the student's.

In terms of socialisation, the interaction a student has with other professionals is pivotal; it is clear that professional identity develops when students have the opportunity to explain their role, values and theoretical perspectives to other professionals such as health professionals. In doing so, students develop confidence in their role and identity as a social worker and are able to defend this as necessary. Students and practitioners interviewed explained that they have needed to negotiate different settings and situations in practice. As a result of this, students were very much concerned with how they were perceived by other professionals, as well as those who would be assessing them. Students within predominantly health care settings strived to explain their role and professional identity to health practitioners, which in turn assisted them in feeling more confident.

The placement organisation and context also has a significant role to play in supporting and developing a social work student's professional identity. The narratives collected from students and supervisors illuminate that challenging working practices such as hot desking are manageable if students are supported and encouraged by their supervisors and other placement personnel. The styles of supervisors varied from expecting students to conform to actively promoting independence and confidence in challenging the organisation. All the supervisors within the sample agreed that students need to develop resilience and emotional intelligence to manage these challenges and tensions they will encounter in social work. This in turn has an impact on the retention of newly qualified social workers.

This chapter has emphasised the significance of both informal and formal levels of support offered by placement personnel and the workplace as crucial to student success and positive socialisation into the profession. Students explained how they need to observe different ways of working and be encouraged to develop their own practice style, rather than conforming to a rigid set of agency expectations. However, this is increasingly difficult to achieve with trends towards more regulated and risk-averse workplaces.

References

Adams, K., Hean, S., Sturgis, P., & McLeod C. J. (2006). Investigating the factors Influencing Professional Identity of First Year Health and Social Care Students. *Learning in Health and Social Care*, 5(2): 55–68.

Barretti, M. A. (2007). Teachers and Field Instructors as Student Role Models. *Journal of Teaching in Social Work*, 27(3–4): 215–239.

Beddoe, L. (2011). Health Social Work: Professional Identity and Knowledge. *Qualitative Social Work*, 12(1): 24–40.

Beddoe, L., & Davys, A. et al. (2013). Educating Resilient Practitioners. *Social Work Education*, 32(1): 100–117.

Bogo, M. (2006). Field Instruction in Social Work. *The Clinical Supervisor*, 24(1–2): 163–193.

Bogo, M., & Mishna, F. et al. (2010). Emotional Reactions of Students in Field Education: An Exploratory Study. *Journal of Social Work Education*, 46(2): 227–243.

Charmaz, K. (2014) *Constructing Grounded Theory* (Second edition). London: Sage.

Clapton, G. (2013). Minding the Gap: Assisting the Transition from the Academy to the Profession. *Social Work Education*, 32(3): 411–415.

Clapton, G., & Cree, V. E. (2006). Grasping the Nettle: Integrating Learning and Practice Revisited and Re-imagined. *Social Work Education*, 25(6): 645–656.

Clapton, G., & Cree, V. E. et al. (2008). Thinking 'Outside the Box': A New Approach to Integration of Learning for Practice. *Social Work Education*, 27(3): 334–340.

Collins, S. (2008). Statutory Social Workers: Stress, Job Satisfaction, Coping, /Social Support and Individual Differences. *British Journal of Social Work*, 38(6): 1173–1193.

Davidson, C. (2011). The Relation between Supervisor Self-Disclosure and the Working Alliance among Social Work Students in Field Placement. *Journal of Teaching in Social Work*, 31: 265–277.

Donnellan, H., & Jack, G. (2010). *The Survival Guide for Newly Qualified Child and Family Social Workers: Hitting the Ground Running*. London: Jessica Kingsley.

Finch, J. (2015). 'Running with the Fox and Hunting with the Hounds': Social Work Tutors' Experiences of Managing Failing Social Work Students in Practice Learning Settings. *British Journal of Social Work*, 45(7): 2124–2141.

Fook, J. M., & Ryan, P. D. et al. (2000). *Professional Expertise: Practice, Theory, and Education for Working in Uncertainty*. London: Whiting & Birch.

Giddings, M. M., & Vodde, R. et al. (2004). Examining Student-Field Instructor Problems in Practicum. *The Clinical Supervisor*, 22(2): 191–214.

Grant, S., Sheridan, L., & Webb, S. A. (2016). Newly Qualified Social Worker's Readiness for Practice in Scotland. *British Journal of Social Work*. doi: 10.1093/bjsw/bcv146. First published online: March 12, 2016.

Holland, D., & Lave, J. (2001). *History in Person: Enduring Struggles, Contentious Practice, Intimate Identities*. New Mexico: School of American Research Press.

Holland, D., & Lave, J. (2009). Social Practice Theory and the Historical Production of Persons. *An International Journal of Human Activity Theory*, 2: 1–15.

Hotho, S. (2008). Professional Identity – Product of Structure, Product of Choice: Linking Changing Professional Identity and Changing Professions. *Journal of Organizational Change Management*, 21(6): 721–742.

Hussein, S., & Moriarty, J. et al. (2014). Organisational Factors, Job Satisfaction and Intention to Leave among Newly Qualified Social Workers in England. *Social Work Education*, 33(3): 381–396.

Jenkins, R. (2004). *Social Identity*. London: Routledge.

Jenkins, R. (2008). *Social Identity* (Third edition). London: Routledge.

Kinman, G., & Grant, L. (2014). *Developing Resilience for Social Work Practice*. London: Palgrave.

Koeske, G. F., & Kanno, H. (2010). MSW Students' Satisfaction with Their Field Placements: The Role of Preparedness and Supervision Quality. *Journal of Social Work Education*, 46(1): 23–38.

Lloyd, C. M., & Gelman, C. R. (2008). Field Notes: Pre-Placement Anxiety among Foundation Year MSW Students: A Follow-Up Study. *Journal of Social Work Education*, 44(1): 173–183.

Miller, S. E. (2010). A Conceptual Framework for the Professional Socialization of Social Workers. *Journal of Human Behavior in the Social Environment*, 20(7): 924–938.

Mosek, A., & Ben-Oz, M. (2011). Baccalaureate Social Work Education: A Developmental Perspective. *Journal of Teaching in Social Work*, 31(1): 89–109.

Parker, J. (2007). Developing Effective Practice Learning for Tomorrow's Social Workers. *Social Work Education*, 26(8): 763–779.

Parker, J., & Doel, M. (2013). *Professional Social Work*. London: Sage.

Rajan-Rankin, S. (2014). Self-Identity, Embodiment and the Development of Emotional Resilience. *British Journal of Social Work*, 44: 2426–2442.

Scholar, H. (2013). Dressing the Part? The Significance of Dress in Social Work. *Social Work Education*, 32(3): 365–379.

Scholar, H. et al. (2014). Learning to Be a Social Worker in a Non-traditional Placement: Critical Reflections on Social Work, Professional Identity and Social Work Education in England. *Social Work Education*, 1–19.

Tham, P. (2007). Why Are They Leaving? Factors Affecting Intention to Leave among Social Workers in Child Welfare. *British Journal of Social Work*, 37(7): 1225–1246.

Tham, P., & Lynch, D. (2014). Prepared for Practice? Graduating Social Work Students' Reflections on Their Education, Competence and Skills. *Social Work Education*, 33(6): 704–717.

Valutis, S., & Rubin, D. et al. (2012). Professional Socialization and Social Work Values: Who Are We Teaching? *Social Work Education*, 31(8): 1046–1057.

Webb, N. B. (1988). The Role of the Field Instructor in the Socialization of Students. *Social Casework*, 69(1): 35–40.

Wilson, G., & Campbell, A. (2012). Developing Social Work Education: Academic Perspectives. *British Journal of Social Work*, 43(5): 1005–1023.

Zarshenas, L., Sharif, F., Molazem, Z., Khayyer, M., Zare, N., & Ebadi, A. (2014). Professional Socialization in Nursing: A Qualitative Content Analysis. *Iranian Journal of Nursing & Midwifery Research*, 19(4): 432–438.

14

CREDIBLE PERFORMANCES

Affect and professional identity

Jadwiga Leigh

Introduction

Goffman's work has been widely used to develop our understanding of interactions in studies of organization but less so when exploring concepts of affect and emotion in social work. This chapter draws on material from an ethnographic study of a child protection statutory agency to explore how narrative performances carried out between social workers convey an affective dimension in which professional identities are partly shaped. The chapter begins by introducing Goffman's work, then goes on to explore how his perspective has been used to inform studies of social work organizations. The chapter examines a variety of practitioners' performances to explain how affect takes shape in certain situated social activities and how this subsequently evokes emotive encounters amongst workers. The term 'situated activity' was developed by Goffman to define affect as a 'somewhat closed, self-compensating, self-terminating circuit of independent actions' (1963: 96). To elaborate this concept further Wetherell (2012) has convincingly argued that situated affective performances construct identities, reputations and subjectivities because they not only craft meaning but they also build social orders, histories and institutions. Micro-organizational affective performances remain largely unarticulated in social work research as many studies tend to focus on ways in which practice can be improved. Yet there is a significant overlap between the identity of the social worker and how their practice is carried out because a large part of social work takes place in an organizational context (Bissell, 2012). In part, at a theoretical level, the chapter reflects the 'affective turn' in contemporary sociological thinking (Clough and Halley, 2007). This chapter concludes with a discussion of the implications of such activities for social workers so that consideration can be given to this in future. This quote from Goffman eloquently captures the journey of identity formation by linking it directly to notion of credibility:

> The self then as a performed character is not an organic thing that has a specific location whose fundamental fate is born, to mature, to die; it is a dramatic effect arising diffusely from a scene that is presented and the characteristic issue, the crucial concern is whether it will be credited or discredited.
>
> *(Goffman, 1959: 252–253)*

Being seen as credible is a characteristic trait that is performed when we are in interaction with others. Manning (2000: 284) once suggested that credibility was 'the quality of being believable' and that this quality was 'integral to both trust and deception'. Drawing on Goffman's work, Manning further argued that the 'production of credibility' was a way in which people made their actions convincing to other people (2008: 284). Over the course of his human behaviour observation studies, Goffman developed the idea that people are able to 'cook up reality' to reconcile the differences they feel emerge between experiences of trust and deception (Goffman, 1963: 445). In other words, Goffman believed that people use the same mechanisms to appear trustworthy as they do when attempting to conceal deceit.

In this chapter, I draw from the conception of producing credibility in this way by applying it to the discipline of social work. I demonstrate that if social workers are to be seen as credible by those they work with, some level of deception is often required. This is because being seen as a credible practitioner is an aspect of practice that can enable a social worker to feel respected for the work that they do. Bubandt and Willerslev (2015) have referred to the nexus between empathy, sociality and deception as 'tactical empathy' as it appears to underlie much of the everyday forms of fakery that Goffman (1959), Bourdieu (1984) and Hastrup (2004: 46) have previously referred to. 'Faking it' with others therefore requires actors to fine-tune forms of empathic deception in order to maintain social dignity through pretence and other everyday forms of impression management (Bubandt and Willerslev, 2015: 9; Harrington, 2009; Miller, 2003). This form of fakery is important because not establishing a creditable identity can significantly affect the way others relate to a social worker as a professional (Pithouse, 1998). The crucial concern for a practitioner, as a performed character, is whether their professional 'self' will be credited or discredited by others (Goffman, 1959).

What captured Goffman's attention was the way in which people strove to make their performances convincing. Forming impressions is part of the dramatic processes of social interaction. It involves ritual observation because when an individual enters the presence of others they commonly seek to acquire information as it helps them to define the situation and enables others to know in advance what to expect (Goffman, 1959). These interactions reflect a sort of order, as Goffman recognized that actors enmeshed in interactions set out claims for 'recognition, status, prestige or even notice' (Manning, 2008: 680). Goffman's (1963, 1967) abiding concern therefore was with the interaction order which focused on the structure, process and products of social interaction.

The interaction order is imperative in credibility work because whilst we form impressions of others, we are also aware that they do the same with us and we act accordingly. It is through our appearance, or 'personal front', that we manage others' impressions of us, influence their definitions of situations and, in turn, affect their conduct (Goffman, 1959: 24). Goffman described this activity as a 'performance', a sequence of 'gestures, postures, verbalizations or actions' seen and responded to by others which are always embedded in surrounding social systems (Manning, 2008: 680). Maintaining credibility once it has been achieved involves the individual using various kinds of resources as well as developing a willingness to abide by rules of conduct (Manning, 2000). However, Goffman also recognized that if an individual was to arrive at an authentic self, then some grounding was required because the self can be 'so fragile and vulnerable' (Kim, 2003: 78).

Being respected by others is considered to be the hallmark of a positive professional identity because it emphasizes the importance of reputation and credentials for practitioners (Ashford and Mael, 1989). In fact, Webb (2016: 359) has even suggested that labelling a social worker 'unprofessional' is a powerful shaming device because it brings the practitioner's credibility, reputation and professionalism into question. Developing a reputation and maintaining it in social work is not just something professionals wish to achieve, but it's also a social activity that has powerful repercussions as well as affective and emotive dimensions.

The difference between affect and emotion

Some scholars have focused on the concept of affect to develop a vitalist and process-based perspective (see Adkins and Lury, 2009; Ahmed, 2004; Blackman and Venn, 2010; Hardt, 2007), or they have focused on the potential of becoming (see Massumi, 1996). It is agreed that affect can be considered a psychosocial concept because it interferes with our emotions and our interactions with others (Brennan, 2004). Shaviro (2016) neatly summarises the difference between affect and emotion:

> If emotions are personal experiences, then affects are the forces (perhaps the flows of energy) that precede, produce, and inform such experiences. Affect is pre-personal and pre-subjective; it is social, or even ontological, before it is strictly individual. Affect isn't what I feel, so much as it is what *forces me* to feel. Affect in this sense is not necessarily conscious; but conscious experience may well issue from it.

However, Wetherell (2012: 3) contends that ordinary 'basic emotion' terms such as sadness, anger, fear, surprise, disgust and happiness do not adequately describe the variety of affective performances, scenes and events that take place in life. Instead, she proposes that social analysis should focus on the 'affective practice' of an individual and their wider group so that researchers can attempt to understand how people are moved, and attracted to or pained by certain social interactions (2012: 78). She settles therefore on the concept of 'affective practice' as the most promising way forward for understanding affect, as it tries to follow what participants do and feel. It is this particular perspective of affect that will be drawn on in this chapter when attempting to explore the accounts of different social workers' interactions inside a specific organization. Part of this chapter's purpose is to contribute to further investigation of this concept, because affect could be central in helping researchers understand the precariousness of neo-liberal workplaces (Gill and Pratt, 2008; Hardt, 1999; Negri, 1999). This emphasis can contribute to a more 'reflexive exploration of both the discursive and affective implications' of conflict in the social work workplace (Stavrakakis, 2014: 33). Thus, it may help readers to better understand how social workers relate to the influential norms and discourses which circulate within their organization.

Credibility, self and child protection social work

Exploring the context in which the field of child protection social work is currently situated is important if we are to consider the professional identity of its practitioners. Freidson (1986: 230) once described 'professionalism' as the impact a profession had on its members. He recognized that professionals' attitude and their commitment to their career became that of their own identity because professionals represent their areas of practice; they represent their profession through who they were and what they did.

The narrative method of identity construction is what some believe emerges from the telling of one's own story. Mishler once remarked, 'we speak our identities' (1999: 19). However, Riessman felt that this then overlooked what remained unsaid, inferred, shown and performed in gesture, action and association. Riessman (2008: 312) instead suggested that in narrative identity work, narrators can show, without just using language, a way to make claims about the 'self'. Identity is therefore constructed and accomplished performatively through the stories we tell about our lives.

The cultural narratives surrounding child protection have emerged amidst complex ethical issues related to a beleaguered history marked by insecurity and anxiety. Social workers have, as a result, had to reconstruct their own professional identity within this active, sociopolitical climate. This is evident from the literature that explores the role organizations play and the impact workplace culture can have on the self and credible performances. The organizational ethnographic work of White (1997) and Pithouse (1998) is relevant in revealing that social work is a profession which is firmly subject to the power of hierarchical bureaucracies. Maintaining a good reputation is not simply the concern of managers; it is an activity which is widespread and affects workers throughout the organization, from the front-line social worker to the Area Director and on to elected councillors. Producing credible performances to impress others is therefore an organizational issue and one which develops from the cultural routines, linguistic practices and storytelling sessions which all take place within social work (White, 1997).

Yet external organizational influences also present social work teams with pressing and conflicting issues to consider, especially as uncertainty and blame is more pronounced than ever before (Pithouse, 1998). This has led some to argue that the identity of social work has been 'threatened' and 'spoiled' (1998: 2). Over the years, the acceptable political game of bashing social workers and the 'unduly vindictive and sensational attention' from the media has led to the development of defensive organizational practices which have, in turn, prompted many to develop the 'watch your back' narrative (White, 1997). Managers believe that if cases are scrutinized effectively, poor practice can be identified and subsequently eliminated. This has prompted the development of a 'them' and 'us' mentality between managers and social workers and in turn led to social workers feeling discredited and undervalued (Gibbs, 2009: 295).

Trying to prove to others that one is a 'credible practitioner' is an activity of social work that can take place in many different forms. However, it is not just an activity that takes place inter-agency but one which also dominates interactions with others outside of the agency. Broadhurst et al. (2010) found that social workers were making active practice errors, such as taking shortcuts, in an attempt to manage large workflow pressures as well as meet performance targets. This led to a 'prevailing performance culture' as social workers were being held accountable for errors in a system which focused inherently on 'unfavourable audits' (2010: 366). What the authors also noted was the affective and emotive impact this process had on individuals as they often described feeling anxious, stressed and fearful.

Credibility therefore appears to be an activity which many strive for in social work, but the way it is acquired varies and is dependent on the interaction taking place. What is widely recognized, however, is that the wider culture influences the organization within which these interactions take place. Being considered a 'credible practitioner' is an aspect of social work practice that is often clouded by the fear of making mistakes or feeling inadequate.

Cultural norms therefore play a significant role when individuals seek approval and acceptance because they determine whether practitioners should be rewarded with social status or receive punishment (Leigh, 2013). Social workers learn to hide their distress as a means of achieving credible performances. The notion of feeling not 'good enough' is barely tolerated by society at large and even less so in professional organizations such as social work (Gibson, 2014). While it is recognized that the challenges many social workers face are often characterized by fear, shame, anxiety and distress, further analysis of these studies indicate that professional credibility also plays an important role in practice and organizational issues. Indeed, making a good impression in the minds of others enables social workers to feel valued and accepted as professionals (Greenwald and Harder, 1998).

Introducing the case

In order to understand how such performance cultures can affect social workers, managers and senior managers the remaining part of this chapter will explore three extracts of data drawn from a twelve-month ethnographic study of a children and families social work statutory agency situated in England. The organization, which

I will call for confidentiality purposes the Dimes Ashe department, held responsibilities for early intervention and the prevention of child abuse.

The department consisted of four safeguarding teams which had in total thirty-six social workers, ten middle managers (team managers and assistant team managers) and three senior managers (two service unit managers and one assistant director). The agency dealt with both children in need (low-level intervention) and child protection referrals (when a child is at risk of significant harm). All the managers, from the Assistant Team Manager tier up through the managerial hierarchy to the Assistant Director, were qualified social workers.

The importance of appearing credible

When an Ofsted inspection[1] visit is expected, it can create many feelings of anxiety for all staff of a statutory child protection agency: the rating an agency receives for their social work performance is important for a number of reasons. In the Dimes Ashe department achieving a rating of 'good' or higher was deemed very important. However, what became clear in this study was that many managers were never completely sure of which cases may be considered by Ofsted as a good piece of casework.

However, what did become apparent during the quality inspection audit was the amount of preparation invested into putting on a good performance for the Ofsted inspectors when they did arrive. For example, it was decided in advance which families would be invited in talk to the inspectors about the service they had received, which social workers would take part in the feedback focus groups and also which cases would be presented as success stories. All of these performances were purposefully staged to present the appearance that the agency functioned well. However, the problem with trying to impress Ofsted with staged performances is that the 'authentic' performances are often not seen or appreciated (see Webb's Chapter 16 in this volume and Goffman, 1959). This is because no one is really sure what Ofsted considers good practice. This uncertainty can make some managers feel nervous or worried that they will be reprimanded by inspectors for encouraging social workers to be creative with certain cases. Ella, a qualified social worker with five years' experience, explains this in more detail.

Ella:	I did put the [name of family] one forward but Claire pulled it and said 'No' (shouting) . . . even though I thought (points to chest) it was a fantastic example of multi-agency working but she pulled it (shrugs shoulders).
Jadwiga:	Why did she pull it?
Ella:	I think it was because MAPPA (Multi-Agency Public Protection Agencies) were still involved (shakes her head)
Jadwiga:	But that's the beauty of it. . . .
Ella:	(laughs) It is not our decision it is MAPPA's we are ready for closing (points to chest) but for MAPPA, MAPPA still want convincing that it

Jadwiga: How did that make you feel?

Ella: I was quite disappointed really (sounds upset) . . . because she had already arranged it with my parent so I had already told the parent and asked her (shakes her head) and she said 'Yeah, yeah definitely I think it has been great the support I have been given from all the agencies. I think as a group of agencies I have really been supported' (shakes her head and laughs) and she was really keen to come and share that so then I had to tell her that we didn't need her (shakes her head).

Jadwiga: What I think is interesting about that case is the risk element that we don't normally have on the other cases – it is the only one I have seen where risk has been allowed to take place.

Ella: And that is what Claire is worried about – what will Ofsted think of 'that risk'? (raises voice)

Jadwiga: What are you going to do?

Ella: I've a good mind to tell the inspectors during the feedback discussion (almost shouting) but then again I probably won't (lowers voice).

The case Ella is describing here related to a family whose children were subject to child protection under the category of 'emotional abuse'. The children's father was addicted to alcohol and when inebriated he was violent towards his wife in the presence of his children. When Ella was allocated the case, she recognized that the children's mother and the children needed significant support for the trauma they had experienced. However, she also understood that when the father was not drinking or being violent he was actually a good father. Ella believed therefore that she could build on the father's strengths and meet the wishes of the children. The children wished for their father to stop drinking, for him to stop hurting their mother and for them to stay together as a family. Ella worked hard to build a good working relationship with the family but she recognized she could not do this alone. She therefore collaborated with other agencies so that appropriate support could be provided for all involved and the issues could be resolved for both children and parents. Together, they had turned the situation around successfully. It was a case that Ella was proud of, one that could have been celebrated as it had positive outcomes for the children and their parents.

However, although Claire (Ella's manager) had initially wanted to show Ella's case to Ofsted, she became nervous when she learned that MAPPA (Multi-Agency Public Protection Agencies) still held concerns. At this point it becomes apparent that even though both Ella and Claire wish to impress Ofsted with their proficiency and integrity, both differ in their view of what it is that Ofsted may find impressive. Claire was not sure that this case would establish a favourable definition of social work practice to inspectors because the father had received a twelve-month custodial sentence and because MAPPA (the responsible authority tasked with the management of registered sex offenders, violent and other types of sexual offenders, and offenders who pose a serious risk of harm to the public) wanted to remain involved for longer to ensure that the risks were indeed managed well. Indeed, Goffman (1959) recognized that often the personal front of the performer was used to conceal a more authentic performance which had occurred. In this case, Claire's manipulation of the cases that Ofsted did see was done to foster a more desirable impression of her team's work, one which in her view was less 'risky' and perhaps more likely to meet the expectations of inspectors.

From Ella's perspective, the element of risk may have been a concern for MAPPA but not necessarily for Ofsted, which she felt would have been more interested in the way in which she had carried out the work to reach the family's desired outcomes. Yet social work teams rely on dramaturgical cooperation from teammates, one that is dependent on fostering a given definition of the situation. Although Ella is 'disappointed' with her manager's decision, she is still nonetheless not prepared to reveal the details of the case to inspectors. This is perhaps because she fears letting her manager down or perhaps because she has now been placed in a position which relies on her maintaining a particular impression before them. As a loyal teammate, Ella does not wish to discredit her manager and therefore becomes a team 'accomplice' in ensuring that Ofsted are presented with a particular vision of the team's practice and that they remain unaware of the good but risky practice that is being taken in other cases (Goffman, 1959: 88).

Being seen as a creditable practitioner is an important part of professionalism in social work practice (Leigh, 2013). But what is evident in this context is that the definition of credibility is different for different members of the same team. Even though these differences are present, it is apparent that for Ella being a loyal team member was also important. This further supports Goffman's notion that those who participate in a particular situated activity become members of a team when they 'cooperate together' to 'present their activity in a particular light' (Goffman, 1959: 106). The term 'situated activity' is a thematic hook that Wetherell (2012:78) uses but which is originally derived from from Goffman's work on interaction rituals and encounters. Goffman defined a 'situated activity system' as a somewhat closed, self-compensating, self-terminating circuit of independent actions (1963: 96). It is this concept that Wetherell (2012) uses particularly well when exploring moments of affective action – moments during an interview when an ordinary action of a participant produces something distinct because of the emotions they experience at that time.

In the interview extract with Ella, I emphasize the bodily movements that she made because the element of interaction often disappears from view in transcription. Yet, words are often accompanied by movement, and many have acknowledged that 'affect is lodged within embodied sequences of action' (Goodwin, 2006: 40). The movements that Ella makes in her interview accentuate how this interaction with her manager made her feel. At first it is evident that Ella is annoyed that Claire has pulled her case, and the decision to do so conflicts with Ella's belief that it was a good example of how agencies collaborate effectively to showcase for Ofsted. The disbelief that Ella experiences is apparent when she shakes her head and laughs sarcastically. The word that Ella actually uses is 'disappointed', yet her bodily actions during the interview demonstrate that she was more than just disappointed; as the story unfolds, it emerges that she may have felt discredited by Claire when she got cold feet and changed her mind. Affect therefore plays more than just a creative form of collective activity; it supplies the texture of certain practices and renders these as highly involving and highly invested (Wetherell, 2012).

Establishing credibility through paperwork

The next extract is taken from an interview with an Assistant Director, Tim. It starts with the author exploring what credibility means and how Tim thought it should be performed by social workers. Here Tim tries to explain how the concept of credibility has changed its meaning as social work practice has also had to change in recent years.

Jadwiga: So how has it changed from when you were in practice?

Tim: Well, back then, there was a lot more face-to-face contact with people. We had the reputation of going into families and literally working with them, building relationships with them. To a certain extent now we have been reduced to proving our credibility with a certain set of tasks (coughs) – you know doing an initial assessment which is prescribed by the national assessment framework as to what needs to be in it (laughs). And then we have ICS with its tick boxes which doesn't seem to be treating social workers like professionals to me (coughs). It is the government saying (puts on a stern face and wags his finger) 'I don't trust you enough to bring your abilities, training to this, to write in a blank sheet of paper, I'm going to ask you direct questions on this'. I mean you wouldn't expect a doctor to do that (dry laugh). You would say (tilts head to one side, tone lowers) 'Here is a problem, here is a set of symptoms what do you think?' I mean, they might use a few headings but they will be headings of their own making (laughs and shakes his head).

It is evident that, for Tim, the reputation of doing professional practice is an important part in forming a creditable identity. However, what troubles him is the way in which social workers now have to prove their worth: it is no longer through the relationships that they build with the families they work with but rather the way in which they complete their assessments of that family that matters. What annoys Tim even more is that the assessments social workers need to complete have been rigidly structured; they consist of 'tick boxes' and 'direct questions'. Therefore, Tim feels that these Pro formas do not allow social workers to perform in the way that other professionals do.

To explore this concept further, Tim uses the example of a doctor and compares what might be expected of a doctor's practice with what is expected from a social worker's practice. By comparing the two, Tim argues that in performing social work practitioners should have the same rights as other professionals who have a good reputation, those who are able to tacitly use their learned knowledge and have professional autonomy when working with people who need support.

The bodily movements and gestures which accompany Tim's words also emphasize how much Tim is affected by this particular issue. This is a narrative which is presented by someone who has personally experienced an identity change. Tim had qualified as a social worker thirty years earlier, and this part of his story documents how Tim is convinced that when he was in practice spending more time with families was an activity social workers were credited for. It ends cynically, with a dry laugh and a wagging of the finger, as he attributes this change in practice to bureaucracy, an arduous formality he believes has been forced upon the profession by the government.

Goffman (1959) noted that there was always a natural back-and-forth movement between cynicism and sincerity for individuals. However, he also warned the observer to always be mindful that the individual may put on a front for their own self-protection. Goffman (1963: 319) used the concept of 'role distance' to describe the space between an individual and a role, including the identity which accompanies that role. Role distance allows the individual leeway to accept a role in their own way and to neglect the other self that is typically considered to be part of the role (Kim, 2003).

It is difficult to gain an understanding of how role distance can occur when the reader is provided with short interview extracts. Yet it emerges in this context because Tim reveals distance from his own role through his affective performance. Although he uses the term 'we' to indicate that he is part of the group that has been affected by the changes, he concludes both statements with a cough – a gesture which may appear meaningless at first but with further exploration could be seen as a discrete action used to conceal the part he has played in implementing the changes. Performance management is after all an activity which has affected the entire public sector: targets must be met, whatever the particulars of that local context (Broadhurst et al., 2010).

As an Assistant Director, part of Tim's role was to make sure that all teams were performing effectively. This often took form in the emails he sent to team managers expressing disappointment when teams were not returning completed assessments within the timescale. Even though Tim is explicitly expressing a distaste for the form filling exercise that social workers have been reduced to in an interview with a front-line social worker/ researcher, he is still responsible for ensuring that social workers tick the boxes and properly answer the standardized questions he dislikes. Therefore, it is only when trying to convey his understanding of the abstract and ambiguous world in which social work is situated that Tim inadvertently reveals he too plays a significant part in contributing to the meaningless chore that social workers have been tasked with.

The implementation of assessment tools

This final extract is taken from observations of a team meeting where the team manager, Dan, was trying to assess whether anyone on his team had yet used the new risk assessment tool that the organization had tried to implement.

Dan: And that home conditions assessment tool, has anyone used it yet?

Cheryl: Why? Do we have to use it? Is it so we can tick another box? (laughs)

Dan: (laughs) Because it's useful. (sighs) We are not mandated to do it and people are not being forced to do this.

Cheryl: (shrugs shoulders) Well I just wondered whether there was some target that we needed to reach.

Anne: (laughing) Well there normally is so why not this time? I tried to use it the other day but the final grade said that the child was at serious risk of harm when it was obvious that was so not true (laughs loudly).

Dan: No I know and I don't think it's even the case that we have to use this one and we could use another graded one. I just think it's very tricky (sighs) but it is coming as they are trying to train everyone on it and there will be more training pushed out and then everyone will be on it because in the long run we'll have a better reputation (nods and smiles). (serious tone) If we're not doing it we'll lose credibility with the others and inspectors won't be impressed either.

Although it may not be obvious to the reader from this particular extract, Dan was actually well liked by all his team. Social workers often spoke of how lucky they felt they were to have him as a manager because they appreciated his loyalty and guidance. Dan not only knew how to make his team laugh but he was also the kind of manager who would make sure that his team felt supported. The good relationship he had with his team may become more apparent if we now revisit the extract. Although it begins with Dan attempting to be serious when trying to determine whether his team has used the new assessment tool, it emerges that Dan was putting on a front in order to try and create the impression that he was taking the new managerial directive seriously.

Yet Dan's attempt at being serious evokes sarcasm from Cheryl who sees an opportunity to express her distaste for what might be another performance management target, and this prompts Anne to join in and support her. In addition, we learn that Anne has used the tool and in doing so found it was flawed, an issue she has clearly spoken to Dan about previously as he acknowledges this comment with 'I know'. This makes Dan's task of convincing the team that it is a worthy tool to implement more difficult.

There is another agenda at play in this dialogue that appears towards the end of this extract. Although Dan is trying to remain jovial with his team, his affective performance (the expressed sighs and the adoption of a serious tone) reveals that he is evidently under pressure from others to implement this new procedure. Goffman

(1963: 210) once suggested that people used the same mechanisms to appear trust-worthy as they did when attempting to conceal deceit; in this context we see Dan 'working the system' as he tries to persuade the team to adapt to the new procedure. He does this by using an incentive he hopes will change their mind: the reward of credibility. However, Goffman (1967) was ever conscious of the inherent discrep-ancy between the self and its role: he believed that the role could never completely overwhelm the individual. Instead, the individual was forever manipulating the role and was never faithful to it. In this extract we see Dan experience conflict between his collective identity of 'being a social worker and part of a team' and his indi-vidualist managerial role involving both meeting the needs of his peers and also a performance-driven system.

Concluding discussion

Goffman's observations of how credibility can be accomplished, in combination with Wetherell's astute eye for affective dispositions, have enabled us to explore three narratives performed by different social workers. In doing so, we've examined in detail just how micro-organizational affective practices emerge and unsettle the professional self of three individuals. Goffman, as made clear at the beginning of this chapter, urges that the professional self is not an organic trait: it is a dramatic character performance which arises from social interactions and staged scenes. In this context, those who took centre stage attempted to manage others impressions with an affective performance.

However, in this particular context, by exploring the more nuanced details of performativity, we have learned that accomplishing credibility in social work is not a straightforward process which is simply attained by putting on a good per-formance. It is an activity which can unsettle thoughts and feelings as it demands that the social worker questions their values and loyalties to others. These affective dimensions have significant implications for the future of social work practice for a number of reasons.

To begin with, although it is widely recognized that being respected is consid-ered to be the hallmark of professional identity, what this means in reality appears to have become confused in contemporary practice settings. Rather than showing others that working closely with families and taking risks can be worthwhile activi-ties, these narrative performances demonstrate that the desire to be well regarded by external spectators often means that creative social work practice is concealed (Riessman, 2008). This further strengthens Goffman's (1959) view that the authen-tic self is fragile and vulnerable as we see how these managers are reluctant to challenge the performance culture they find themselves situated in. Instead, in an attempt to be seen as credible in the eyes of external others, they feel it is necessary to partake in some level of deception.

Such performances can lead to scenes of internal conflict as practitioners chal-lenge managers' decisions. This could lead some to conclude that there is a 'them' and 'us' culture present (Gibbs, 2009). However, by examining the affective element of each performance it is evident that it is far more complex than this: these managers appeared conflicted by the decisions they made, the games they played and the activities they encouraged their social workers to take part in. Three key observations stand out. First, although maintaining a good reputation is deemed important for social workers, accomplishing an identity they can be proud of in a performance culture is often compromised in favour of the agency's reputation. Second, challenging the performance culture rather than being a slave to it was seen to be important. Third, although there appears to be a 'them and us' culture, it is far more complex than this suggests. Perhaps this hints at a professional identity that is not only fluid but also in tension.

Note

1 Ofsted is the Office for Standards in Education, Children's Services and Skills in the UK. It inspects and regulates services that care for children and young people, and services providing education and skills for learners of all ages.

References

Adkins, L., & Lury, C. (eds.) (2009). Special Issue: The Empirical. *European Journal of Social Theory*, 12(1): 5–20.

Ahmed, S. (2004). Affective Economies. *Social Text*, 22(2): 117–139.

Ashford, B. E., & Mael, F. (1989). Social Identity Theory and the Organization. *Academy of Management Review*, 14: 20–39.

Bissell, G. (2012). *Organisational Behaviour for Social Work*. Bristol: Policy Press.

Blackman, L., & Venn, C. (eds.) (2010). Affect. *Special Issue: Body and Society*, 16(1): 7–28.

Bourdieu, Pierre. (1984). *Distinction: A Social Critique of the Judgment of Taste*. Cambridge: Harvard University Press.

Brennan, T. (2004). *The Transmission of Affect*. Ithaca, NY: Cornell University Press.

Broadhurst, K., Wastell, D., White, S., Hall, C., Peckover, S., Thompson, K., Pithouse, A., & Davey, D. (2010). Performing 'Initial Assessment': Identifying the Latent Conditions for Error at the Front-Door of Local Authority Children's Services. *British Journal of Social Work*, 40(2): 352–370.

Bubandt, N., & Willerslev, R. (2015). The Dark Side of Empathy: Mimesis, Deception, and the Magic of Alterity. *Comparative Studies in Society and History*, 57(1): 5–34.

Clough, P. T., & Halley, J. (eds.) (2007). *The Affective Turn: Theorizing the Social*. Durham: Duke University Press.

Freidson, E. (1986). *Professional Powers*. Chicago: Chicago Press.

Gibbs, J. (2009). Changing the Cultural Story in Child Protection: Learning from the Insider's Experience. *Child and Family Social Work*, 14(3): 289–299.

Gibson, M. (2014). Social Worker Shame in Child and Family Social Work: Inadequacy, Failure, and the Struggle to Practice Humanely. *Journal of Social Work Practice*, 28(4): 417–431.

Gill, R. & Pratt, A. (2008) In the Social Factory? Immaterial Labour, Precariousness and Cultural Work. *Theory, Culture and Society*, 25(7–8):1–30

Goffman, E. (1959). *The Presentation of Self in Everyday Life*. New York: Doubleday, Anchor Books.

Goffman, E. (1963). *Stigma*. London: Penguin.

Goffman, E. (1967). *Interaction Ritual: Essays in Face to Face Behavior*. New York: Doubleday, Anchor Books.

Goodwin, M. H. (2006). *The Hidden Life of Girls: Games of Stance, Status and Exclusion*. Malden, MA: Blackwell.

Greenwald, D., & Harder, D. W. (1998). Evolutionary, Cultural and Psychotherapeutic Aspects. In P. Gilbert & B. Andrews (Eds.), *Shame, Interpersonal Behaviour, Psychopathology, and Culture* (pp. 225–245). Oxford: Oxford University Press.

Hardt, M. (1999). Affective Labour. *Boundary*, 26(2): 89–100.

Hardt, M. (2007). What Are Affects Good for? In P.T. Clough & J. Halley (Eds.), *The Affective Turn: Theorizing the Social* (pp. ix–1). Durham, NC: Duke University Press.

Harrington, B. (2009). *Deception: From Ancient Empires to Internet Dating*. Stanford: Stanford University Press.

Hastrup, K. (2004). *Action: Anthropology in the Company of Shakespeare*. Copenhagen: Museum Tusculanum.

Kim, K. (2003). *Order and Agency in Modernity: Talcott Parsons, Erving Goffman, and Harold Garfinkel*. Albany: University of New York Press.

Leigh, J. (2013). The Process of Professionalization: Exploring the Professional Identities of Child Protection Social Workers. *Journal of Social Work*, 14(6): 625–644.

Manning, P. K. (2000). *Erving Goffman and Modern Sociology*. Cambridge: Polity Press.

Manning, P. K. (2008). Goffman in Organizations. *Organization Studies*, 29(5): 677–699.

Massumi, B. (1996) 'The Autonomy of Affect', in P. Patton (Ed.), *Deleuze: a Critical Reader* (pp. 217–239). Blackwell, Oxford.

Miller, W. I. (2003). *Faking It*. Cambridge: Cambridge University Press.

Mishler, E. G. (1999). *Storylines: Craft Artists' Narratives of Identity*. Cambridge, MA: Harvard University Press.

Negri, A. (1999). Value and Affect. *Boundary*, 26(2): 77–88.

Pithouse, A. (1998) *Social Work: The Social Organisation of an Invisible Trade*. Aldershot: Ashgate.

Riessman, C. K. (2008). *Narrative Methods for the Human Sciences*. London, England: Sage.

Shaviro, S. (2016). Affect/Emotion. Retrieved from http://www.shaviro.com/Blog/. (Accessed 20 September 2016).

Stavrakakis, Y. (2014). Debt Society: Psychosocial Aspects of the (Greek) Crisis. In K. Kenny & M. Fotaki (Eds.), *Psychosocial and Organization Studies: Affect at Work* (pp. 33–58). Basingstoke: Palgrave Macmillan.

Webb, S. A. (2016). Professional Identity in Social Work. In M. Dent, I. L. Bourgeault, J. L. Denis & E. Kuhlmann (Eds.), *The Routledge Companion to the Professions and Professionalism* (pp. 355–370). London: Routledge.

Wetherell, M. (2012). *Affect and Emotion: A New Social Science Understanding*. London: Sage.

White, S. (1997). *Performing Social Work: An Ethnographic Study of Talk and Text in a Metropolitan Social Services Department*. (Unpublished PhD thesis). University of Salford.

15

MAKING PROFESSIONAL IDENTITY

Narrative work and fateful moments

Maura Daly and Martin Kettle

Introduction

In Scotland the issue of professional identity was brought into sharp relief by the publication of *Changing Lives: Report of the 21st Century Social Work Review* (Scottish Executive, 2006). As Webb (Chapter 1 in this volume) identifies, this report reflects the problems that beset social work and focuses particularly on issues of professional identity. *Changing Lives* states: "There is an urgent need for social work to clarify its professional identity in order to establish clear roles for individual social workers" (2006: 39). Since the publication of that report, the challenges to professional identity have been deepened by the enactment of the Public Bodies (Joint Working) (Scotland) Act 2014, which establishes partnership working arrangements between health and social care, and puts in place management arrangements that make lines of accountability and professional leadership more diffuse. In turn it is argued that this diffuseness brings professional identity into sharper relief (Baxter, 2011).

This chapter explores the development of professional identity through reflective accounts written by a cohort of social work students at the end of their graduate programme. In introducing this chapter, three benchmarks need to be outlined. First, the chapter is concerned less with the identity of the social work *profession* than with the identity of social work *professionals,* although they are inextricably linked (Wiles, 2013). This is not intended to privilege one at the expense of the other, but rather to focus on the emerging professional identity of qualifying social workers. Second, the chapter is written in a Scottish context. There are differences in the context between the jurisdictions of the UK; for example, at the time of writing the review of the Scottish social work education is nearing completion. What is clear is that its unitary nature encompassing work with children and families, adults and people in the criminal justice system is likely to be maintained (SSSC, 2015) as opposed to the dual review process undertaken in England with reviews for children and families separate from reviews for adults (Croisdale-Appleby, 2014; Narey, 2014) and the development of 'fast-track' approaches to social work education in different specialisms (see for example, Baginsky and Manthorpe, 2014; Maxwell et al., 2016; Warner et al., 2015). Having said that, it is important to acknowledge that the notion of "becoming a social worker" resonates at a global level across professional education systems (Cree, 2013). Third, as authors, we are not positioned outside of narrative identity work ourselves. (Kanuha, 2000; Kettle, 2014; Taylor, 2011). Almost inevitably, our own narrative identity work will creep into the picture. However, we have done our best to bracket our professional experience (Tufford and Newman, 2010) and to follow Wolcott's (2001: 67) exhortation to, "put yourself squarely in the picture, but don't take centre stage". In that sense we are "working the hyphen" (Cunliffe and Karunanayake, 2013; Fine, 1994) between insider and outsider. This chapter will now set out the context for the study and offer a brief outline of the approach taken to the study, its findings and the implications for practice.

Research context

The context for the study is a module entitled Making Professional Identity, which is taught over the second year of a Master's programme in Social Work. The central theme of the module is the development of the professional self with the opportunities to explore issues that include power, authority, accountability and professional boundaries (Smith, 2008; Tew, 2006). Central to the development of the module was the objective of providing a space for students to explore, talk about and work through issues arising from their placement and their developing sense of professional identity.

The module is assessed by way of a critically reflective account on how students' professional identity has developed over the life of the programme. Whilst noting limitations to the use of (Taylor, 2013) and scepticism towards (Macfarlane and Gourlay, 2009) critical reflection, this mode of assessment is seen as providing an opportunity for students to provide a coherent account of the development of professional identity. However, as well as providing a basis for assessment, these artefacts can also be seen as sources of data, offering insights into the narrative identity work undertaken by students.

Three intersecting theoretical areas informed the development of the module and feed through into the analysis of the accounts: (i) the work of Anthony Giddens on identity and the reflexive self in late modernity (Giddens, 1991), in particular, his notion of fateful moments as being pivotal in identity transformation; (ii) the importance of narratives and associated narrative identity work (Ibarra and Barbulescu, 2010); and (iii) the importance of professional selves as provisional or becoming (Scanlon, 2011). These three aspects come together to provide the theoretical lens through which students' accounts are examined. This chapter will explore these three aspects before turning to an exploration of the findings.

Giddens and the reflexive self

The work of Giddens (1991) on the relationship between self and social structure in late modern society has been particularly influential in the development of this chapter, as has its importation in social work more broadly (Ferguson, 2001, 2003, 2013; Dent, Chapter 2 in this volume). Whilst the influence is strong, it is not beyond critique. From within social work, the work of Giddens and Ferguson has been criticised for overemphasising the agency of individual practitioners (Garrett, 2003, 2004). However, in summarising the debate between Ferguson and Garrett on the virtues of Giddens, Houston (2004) contends that social workers are constrained but never completely conditioned, and this chapter follows him in contending that as reflexive practitioners students are capable of exercising agency around their emerging professional identity.

Further, in Giddens' (1991) exploration of identity formation, he identified the importance of "fateful moments", which he defines as when "business as usual" is disrupted and new perspectives are adopted, at "times when events come together in such a way that an individual stands at a crossroads in their existence or where a person learns of information with fateful consequences" (1991: 113). For Giddens the key element of a fateful moment is that it demands that the individual considers the consequences of particular choices and actions and so engages in an assessment of risk. In doing this they are likely to be engaged in identity work. Further, these transition points are seen by Giddens as being potentially empowering. According to Giddens, a fateful moment can be within the control of an individual, even deliberately created, but may also come about as a result of circumstances beyond the individual's control. Previous students would frequently identify what were variously referred to as 'fateful' or 'light-bulb' moments, and there was deemed to be value in exploring these moments in greater detail.

Professional identity as narrative

Positioned centrally in this chapter is the notion of the development of professional identity as narrative. Space does not permit a full exploration of the "narrative turn" in social science research (Clandinin and Connelly, 2000; Riessman, 2008) or different strands of narrative research (Roberts, 2002). This chapter will adopt the simple definition offered by Connelly and Clandinin (1999: 2) in their work on the development of professional identity as "stories to live by". This permits a framing of narrative identity as "a person's internalised and evolving life story, integrating the reconstructed past and imagined future to provide some degree of unity and purpose" (McAdams and McLean, 2013: 233), and it is the notion of identity as both coherent and evolving that makes its exploration of particular relevance for this chapter. Constructs used in research on narrative identity include agency, the degree to which people feel able to effect change; meaning making, which is the level to which people are able to take learning from an event; and resolution, which is about how it is possible to achieve closure. Each of these three constructs are of relevance here.

Connelly and Clandinin (2000) suggest that to enter a professional knowledge landscape is to enter the place of stories, but at the same time stories have history and take shape as life unfolds. They are underscored by the dynamic, shifting and multiple identities that professionals acquire. Connelly and Clandinin argue that these "stories to live by . . . are expressions of an embodied knowledge of the landscape, of space and time, of borders, cycles and rhythms" (2000: 113). Importantly, though, Ibarra and Barbulescu (2010) take Ashforth's notion further to develop a process model, arguing that a concept of identity as narrative is especially critical for professionals in transition. It is suggested that these self-narratives are powerful instruments that constitute a transition across gaps between old and new roles and identities (Ashforth, 2001). Importantly, though, Ibarra and Barbulescu take the notion further to develop a process model of what they refer to as "narrative identity work", which they define as: "social efforts to craft self-narratives that meet a person's identity aims. By self-narrative we mean a narrative or story – terms we use interchangeably about the self" (2010: 137). Importantly, then, narrative identity transformation doesn't just happen but needs to be worked at. This chapter will proceed to explore some of the nature of that work, the 'making' of identity.

In terms of identifying the effectiveness of narrative identity work, Ibarra and Barbulescu (2010) identify two clusters of outcomes for this work to be deemed to be successful. First, authenticity, which relates to at the most basic level being seen as true to oneself, with behaviour and self-concept aligned (see Webb, Chapter 16 in this volume). Ibarra (1999) identifies a source of emotional discomfort where people are unable to construct a coherent narrative, leaving them feeling inauthentic. Bringing this into the context of criminal justice social work, Fenton (2015) writes about the concept of ethical stress and disjuncture, which is the stress experienced when practitioners cannot base their practice upon their values, and this dealing with and managing that ethical stress is part of the process that forms part of the *work* of narrative identity formation (Osteen, 2011). Second, there are outcomes related to validation. Whilst on a social work programme at a macro level validation comes from passing the course, it will be argued that a deeper validation comes from having a narrative that is shared with, endorsed by, and indeed challenged by, students, workplace colleagues and in particular practice educators (Doel, 2010; Dunk-West, 2013).

Professional identity as becoming

The final aspect of the theoretical underpinnings of this chapter is the provisional nature of professional identity. This is a consistent theme throughout the literature (Scanlon, 2011). As Dent and Whitehead (2002: 11) put it, "Identity is neither stable, nor a final achievement" (see Dent, Chapter 2 in this volume). Ibarra (1999) suggests that it is its provisional nature that allows professionals, particularly those in professional education, to exercise agency. She argues that people adapt to new professional roles by having the opportunity to experiment with images that serve as trials for identities that are not yet fully elaborated. Scanlon (2011), in writing about becoming a professional, draws on Wenger's (1998) concept of trajectory, which suggests that this is an acceptance of the 'ongoing-ness' of developing a professional self.

However, supplementary to the notion of becoming, of identity as fluid, is what Munro (2004) refers to as identity as "punctualized", where identity is standing in advance, "To be on call when needed: on time, every time! Every time, that is, when it is demanded" (Munro, 2004: 305). This relates closely to Applebaum's concept of the stop, which:

> lives in the interstices of action, an ordinary recluse. It shuns the spotlight, yet exerts a definite and important control over what takes place. Furthermore, it gives a key to a deeper engagement in a meaning that unfolds our lives. . . . *The stop is the advent of an intelligence of choice.*
>
> *(1995: xi; author's emphasis).*

This connects back to Giddens' conceptualisation of the fateful moment, and to agency, and points to narrative identity work being done in the continuity of the narrative production, but also at key points within that narrative.

Where the three strands of the theoretical underpinnings come together is in the notion of "emplotment", which is the process by which narratives link temporal events by directing them towards a conclusion (Ricoeur, 1984). Ibarra and Barbulescu (2010) contend that a coherent self-narrative needs to make sense sequentially: asking students to undertake their narrative identity work retrospectively clearly invites and encourages coherence. Students develop coherence by identifying two primary devices for building narrative coherence as being plot structure and protagonist agency – and this is where there is synergy with the work of Giddens. What Ibarra and Barbulescu describe as the "second act" "typically ends with a turning point, climax or catalytic event" (2010: 141), and this closely aligns with Giddens' notion of fateful moments. Ibarra and Barbulescu's second device for the establishment of narrative coherence is protagonist agency: here the narrator adopts a protagonist's stance to account for any apparent discontinuity in the identity-making story. This phenomenon occurs throughout the analysis of the accounts, to which this chapter will now turn.

Research methodology

As already discussed, the data for this chapter consist of reflective accounts written by student social workers at the end of their postgraduate education programme. A sample of these assignments was gathered and analysed using thematic analysis (Braun and Clarke, 2006, 2013). There are disadvantages to this approach, in particular that these accounts are written within academic conventions as well as retrospectively, so that there are pressures to construct a narrative that is coherent and produces positive closure. Further, it is not possible to interrogate the ambiguities and subtexts of each narrative. It is also important to acknowledge the influence of both the teaching and the assignment guidance. However, students were not overly constrained by the assignment task, and often went beyond the taught material. In addition, this was an opportunity to explore data without their production being unduly influenced by the researcher.

University ethical approval and informed consent from the student authors of the assignments were obtained. Further, to limit the possibility of students feeling in any way pressured to agree to participation, the seeking of consent was delayed until after students had their final results. More than half of those students who were approached (16 of 29) agreed for their accounts to be included in the sample. In the presentation of findings, all students have been given pseudonyms.

Research findings

This chapter will now turn to an exploration of the narrative identity work undertaken by student social workers, addressed through three themes that emerged from the data, namely (i) early identity work, (ii) fateful moments and (iii) relationships with power and authority.

Early identity work

A key finding revealed a very limited appreciation of professional identity for students, or indeed of what it meant to be professional, prior to starting the programme. Although Glenda described writing about her professional attitude in the early days of the course, she was able to acknowledge that,

> Quite what I meant by a 'professional attitude' I am still unsure to this day.

The engagement with what it means to be a professional was a complex one, with some students gaining confidence from growing into a professional role. There was also a recognition that professionalism is a disciplinary mechanism, and there was reference to Powell's (2010) conception of professional identity as something that can also act to constrain social workers.

Accounts often explored students' pushing at the boundaries of professionalism. They demonstrated acute awareness of the potential limits placed by professionalism. Daniel expressed it thus:

> If the parameters of 'what professional social work is' becomes something that actively prohibits and works against social justice, then I may not identify myself as a 'professional' social worker.

Here we find Daniel prioritising his commitment to social justice over claims to professionalism. This engagement with the notion of 'professionalism' clearly indicates that narrative identity work sometimes began before students embarked on the education programme. Their accounts were generally contextualised with some biographical material that explored why students had found themselves on a Masters in Social Work. Perhaps unsurprisingly, family was very important, with the majority of accounts making reference to positive family experiences for which they were appreciative. There was also a growing sense of wishing to work in a helping context, with the move into social work seen as a natural destination. However, for some students identity was forged in their community, and not always for positive reasons (Jenkins, 2014). Emily located her motivation for embarking on the programme directly in her experience of exclusion:

> I knew what it felt like to come up against walls, to be at intersects, and working with people who also experienced structural differences – often different from mine – felt like a natural progression.

Undergraduate study and employment were also very clear drivers for studying social work, for moving beyond an academic understanding of structural inequalities and an expressed desire to be part of a solution. As Peter explained:

> I found there was only so many times I could write essays about one in five people in Scotland living in poverty before I decided that I needed to try and do more than just write about it.

In particular, students who had studied sociology or other social sciences at the undergraduate level described a deepening of understanding of structural issues, sometimes describing an involvement in voluntary work. Justin, for example, volunteered both on a helpline and in working with refugees. As he put it,

> the first provided a path to a direct helping relationship with people; the second, a direct view into social exclusion and patterns of injustice and inequality.

For some students, early identity work was done in their paid employment, which was often as support workers for third-sector organisations. Fateful moments were identified by Nat who described an incident with a young man in a residential setting who became very aggressive. He put it neatly:

> I was shocked and shaken, but not deterred.

Students typically look back on those incidents with a metaphorical shake of the head at the naivety of their younger selves, often related to a lack of a clear perspective within which to locate their experience.

Joining the programme itself was identified in the accounts as being a pivotal moment and a place where identity work was being done, as with Nat:

> In 'becoming' a social worker (Scanlon, 2011) I first had to become the social work student, leaving the certainties of employment in a residential childcare setting.

Initially, there was a stage of convincing themselves that this identity was something worthwhile; but once this was achieved, then there was an important aspect of joining a group of "proto-social workers" (Marcia). For some students the joining of the programme strengthened their professional identity and gave them a common understanding. Being able to share experiences, challenges and successes increased a sense of belonging and was seen as empowering. However, that wasn't the case for everyone. Ben described how he needed support during this transition and clung tenaciously to his old third-sector support worker identity and how this provided "psychological stability in the transition process of synthesising a new professional identity".

The sites of early identity work can be seen as being a combination of family, community, paid employment, academic study and the transition to the education programme. However, more intensive identity work began after the course was started. There were two sites for this work – the classroom setting and practice placements – but the bulk of the identity work was undertaken in a placement context. The remainder of this chapter will focus on that area, looking first at the area of fateful moments before turning to an exploration of the third theme of power and authority.

Fateful moments

Intersecting points where students were required to pause and re-evaluate their thinking – and by implication their identity – were frequently identified in the accounts as key places where narrative identity work was done. They were variously identified as 'light-bulb moments' or 'pivotal moments'. Although precipitated by a range of causes, there were two contexts in which identity work was done: first, the event itself; and second, the awareness of the event being captured, either retrospectively in these accounts or as an active component of the supervisory relationship.

These pivotal moments can be seen as having a number of different sites. For the purposes of analysis, these can be divided into two main types. The first is external, where the moment was brought about by factors in work that was being asked of the student, and this group divides into issues of decision, case and agency (in the organisational sense), which further divides into those driven by service users, colleagues or other agencies. The second group comprises what will be referred to as 'insight moments', which could occur in isolation, but were often crystalized and captured during supervision.

The first site of fateful moments related to the work that students were being asked to undertake. For those students experiencing statutory social work for the first time, fateful moments could come about by being asked to undertake home visits and undertake an assessment. This process identified students as representatives of the agency and placed them in a position where they felt they were being forced to either make judgements about families or possibly act as gatekeepers to resources. Marilyn, working in a community care team, expressed anxiety about "getting it wrong" and the service user possibly not getting the services needed.

Particularly in a children and families' context, there was identity work done about crossing the intimate threshold of family life and engaging families in discussion about the well-being of children. Ferguson (2011: 18) refers to this as "growing the child protection skin". Emily describes how she developed much greater awareness of how intrusive it must be for service users to have strangers assessing them in their own homes. She captured her doubt sharply:

> Who am I to do this? Who was I to walk into the house of a parent, to occupy that space of authority, and to judge their living conditions and how they raised their children?

Moving beyond the home visit, fateful moments sometimes involved decisions implicit in the social work task that was allocated or that came about as a result of developments in the case that was being worked. Denise gives two examples of the former: one when she was asked to undertake an assessment of whether two siblings, currently in separate foster care placements, should be reunited; and another when she was asked to assess whether a young person in long-term foster care should be returned to her mother. In neither of these instances did the student carry sole responsibility for the decision, but their information carried considerable weight by virtue of the intensive nature of the work undertaken. The accounts for both of these cases identified an acute awareness of the literally life-changing decisions that were being made and the issues of self-doubt that arose as a consequence. As Denise put it:

> Once I had met Ann and her foster carers, I was required to make a decision on the most suitable accommodation. I really struggled accepting the positional power I had in this situation.

Decisions arising from developments in the case were about triggering legal processes: for example, where consideration was being given to the initiation of breach proceedings in relation to a community payback order. One instance, when a recommendation about a case was made by Nat and supported by the practice educator but overruled by management, had a significant impact on him:

> The experience left me feeling dejected and despondent, and I wondered why I would wish to continue in this profession, experiencing barriers myself. However, I actually feel stronger as an emerging professional.

In terms of pivotal moments arising from work with service users, these were dependent upon the students' ability to both capture and reflect upon the moment.

For example, Emily discovered that a mother was not being honest with her about contact with her ex-partner, with subsequent implications for the safety of children. This contrasted with attitudes that she developed in her previous third-sector employment:

> This was an important moment wherein I questioned my professional identity and had to interrogate my approach. In my other work with survivors of domestic abuse and sexual violence, it was essential that women were always believed by workers.

It was working through with the service user to understand the pressures on her that contributed to the lack of honesty where the real identity work was carried out.

Direct work with service users generated a range of fateful moments. For Stella this moment was a growing awareness of the multiple risks associated with parental substance misuse and the responsibility that came along with that. For Samantha this moment came in a challenge from a family, who

> expressed their views that I was too young to be a social worker as I was not feisty enough and didn't tell them what to do.

Identity work also came about as a consequence of growing anxiety around work tasks. Yvonne described not being able to switch off at the end of the day, taking work home with her in her head and losing sleep. By using Karpman's (Hawkins and Shohet, 2012) drama triangle, we can better understand Yvonne's comment:

> I was able to instantaneously identify that I take on the role of the rescuer (Kinman et al., 2014) which involves the need to 'save' the service user from vulnerabilities and adversities.

This led to reflection on how her identity was shaped, how it should be adjusted and what additional strategies might be developed.

A recurring theme was, as one account put it, a "hyper-criticality" of being more critical of practice than was warranted. Charlene's supervisor put it very bluntly. "What planet are you on?" the supervisor asked before going on to advise her not to give herself a hard time: there would be plenty of other people to do that for her. Situated in a third-sector organisation with limited support, Nat described his resolution thus:

> Caught between this hyper-criticality and a lack of positive modelling, practical guidance and supervision I took a 'true-to-self' strategy; finding comfort in pre-existing and familiar professional repertoires.

Finally, in terms of precipitating identity work, were professionals from other disciplines. Students' accounts explored how they were challenged, either by a lack of cooperation in relation to information sharing or by criticism. Kylie had provided a lock-safe box for parents to keep drugs in, but was vigorously challenged by another professional for colluding with the parents' drug use. This example from Kylie represents a sense of identity emerging through the challenge of another professional.

This section has explored the notion of pivotal moments and their role in narrative identity work. Pivotal moments required students to be open to having the experience, capture that experience, reflect upon it and then be able to assimilate the experience. A further important site for narrative identity work was students' exercise of power and authority; it is to this theme we now turn.

Power and authority

Although intersecting with pivotal moments, students' experiences of exercising, and observing the exercise of, power and authority was so central to the development of their professional authority that it warrants dedicated discussion. Students experienced many complex aspects of power, engaged with its complexities and demonstrated a nuanced understanding of the parameters. As Emily put it:

> Understanding power as monolithic runs the risk of denying people agency; of failing to recognise the ways in which people resist oppressive systems.

Numerous examples described experiencing a paradox of feeling powerless, yet being perceived as powerful by service users or other professionals. Emily was also able to see that it

> was dangerous to be very comfortable with power, but it was equally dangerous to be so uncomfortable with it.

This grappling with the nuances and paradoxes of power in a social work context was one that formed a significant part of the work that students reported.

Narrative identity work was also undertaken through observation rather than direct involvement. An instance of this was Ben's discussion of lateness, where he draws on Smith's (2008) discussion of the "power of late". Ben observed that social workers in placement were regularly late for home visits, and received no sanction for this. He refused to assimilate this into his identity:

> While the client, if late, is constructed negatively as non-engaging with services. This aspect of social work behaviour I rejected as unacceptable. In my practice I avoided lateness and made every effort to be punctual for visits.

This power of lateness was particularly acute for students placed in a criminal justice setting, where persistent lateness could result in sanctions up to and including a community payback order being breached. This setting was seen as constraining the limits of discretion. As Justin put it:

> I felt that my identity was quite literally spelled out for me in the criminal justice setting, with rigid government policy documents detailing good practice.

Students' identity work was often done around the limits of discretion and positional power, and negotiating the limits of that discretion. Nathan, in his work in a statutory children and families setting, described how he was:

> the latest embodiment of a system that had placed C on the child protection register, on a supervision order, almost removed him, and had intruded upon family life repeatedly.

In resisting this, Nat sought to explore the limits of discretion, negotiating with the family around the terms of the supervision order, and recognising and working collaboratively with the limits of power and "going beyond care versus control to an exploration of the spaces in between". Similarly, Owen saw negotiation of power as working at the boundaries of discretion, and that his identity as a social worker was predicated on maintaining a working relationship, even in the face of hostility and aggression from service users. He was able to see that one of the performative aspects of power came about in case records, as they represented the official version of events and were typically something over which service users had little control. In supporting a service user to access her records he was able to facilitate her gaining more control over her situation.

The accounts contain numerous instances of nuanced exploration of power, using it judiciously, and using it with the aspiration of "good authority", defined by (Ferguson, 2011: 120) thus:

> Power in and of itself is not oppressive. It can be and sometimes is in how it is unethically exercised. But, equally, it is a positive and necessary resource, depending entirely on whether how it is used constitutes 'good authority'.

Peter also referred to the use of 'good authority' and explored how he developed in a children and families' placement, growing in confidence in overcoming feelings of unease. He

> had to gain access to people's 'private spaces' (bedrooms, kitchen cupboards, fridges) in order to build a holistic picture of risk/concern.

The accounts showed a preference for using "power together" as opposed to "power over" (Tew, 2006). This did not mean that students shied away from exerting power when it was required. Karen, on placement in a criminal justice setting, was faced with a decision to instigate breach of a community payback order of a service user's non-compliance, but in reaching that decision she carefully explored whether she had done everything within her power to ensure cooperation by making appointments that were convenient for the service user.

In concluding this exploration of the use of power in a social work context, it is apparent that a detailed critical engagement with power – with all its paradoxes and nuances – was central and that narrative work involves negotiating the space between power and powerlessness (Duschinsky et al., 2016).

Concluding discussion

This chapter has used reflective accounts by student social workers as data to explore narrative identity work. Whilst limitations to this approach have been acknowledged, it has highlighted the potential for this method as a way of gaining access to the work that emerging practitioners undertake in the formation of professional identity.

The chapter provides good evidence that emerging practitioners have significant insight into their trajectories, and in that sense they reflect Ingold's (2011) conceptualisation of practitioners as "wanderers, wayfarers, whose skill lies in in their ability to find the grain of the world's becoming and so to follow its course whilst bending it to their evolving purpose" (211).

Thus, for those of us involved in social work education, supporting students to develop their wayfaring skills is a positive contribution to their agency. Narrative identity work is very much a continuing project. It seems appropriate to leave the last word with Emily, who quotes Freire (1996: 60): "Those who authentically commit themselves to the people must re-examine themselves constantly".

References

Applebaum, D. (1995). *The Stop.* Albany: State University of New York Press.
Ashforth, B. E. (2001). *Role Transitions in Organizational Life: An Identity-based Perspective.* Mahwah, NJ: Lawrence Erlbaum Associates.
Baginsky, M., & Manthorpe, J. (2014). *The Views of Step Up to Social Work Trainees – Cohort 1 and Cohort 2.* London: Department for Education.
Baxter, J. (2011). *Public Sector Professional Identities: A Review of the Literature.* Milton Keynes: Open University.
Braun, V., & Clarke, V. (2006). Using Thematic Analysis in Psychology. *Qualitative Research in Psychology,* 3: 77–101. doi: 10.1191/1478088706qp063oa.
Braun, V., & Clarke, V. (2013). *Successful Qualitative Research.* London: Sage.
Clandinin, D. J., & Connelly, F. M. (2000). *Narrative Inquiry: Experience and Story in Qualitative Research.* San Francisco: John Wiley and Sons.
Connelly, F. M., & Clandinin, D. J. (1999). *Shaping a Professional Identity: Stories of Education Practice.* London, Ontario: Althouse Press.
Cree, V. (ed.) (2013). *Becoming a Social Worker: Global Narratives.* Abingdon: Routledge.
Croisdale-Appleby, D. (2014). *Re-Visioning Social Work Education: An Independent Review.* London: Department of Health.

Cunliffe, A. L., & Karunanayake, G. (2013). Working within Hyphen-Spaces in Ethnographic Research: Implications for Research Identities and Practice. *Organizational Research Methods*, 16: 364–392. doi: 10.1177/1094428113489353.

Dent, M., & Whitehead, S. (2002). Introduction: Configuring the New Professional. In M. Dent & S. Whitehead (Eds.), *Managing Professional Identities: Knowledge, Performativities and the 'New' Professional* (pp. 1–11). Abingdon: Routledge.

Doel, M. (2010). *Social Work Placements: A Traveller's Guide*. Abingdon: Routledge.

Dunk-West, P. (2013). *How to Be a Social Worker: A Critical Guide for Students*. London: Palgrave Macmillan.

Duschinsky, R., Lampitt, S., & Bell, S. (2016). *Sustaining Social Work*. London: Palgrave McMillan.

Fenton, J. (2015). An Analysis of 'Ethical Stress' in Criminal Justice Social Work in Scotland: The Place of Values. *British Journal of Social Work*, 45: 1415–1432. doi: 10.1093/bjsw/bcu032.

Ferguson, H. (2001). Social Work, Individualization and Life Politics. *British Journal of Social Work*, 31: 41–55. doi: 10.1093/bjsw/31.1.41.

Ferguson, H. (2003). In Defence (and Celebration) of Individualization and Life Politics for Social Work. *British Journal of Social Work*, 33: 699–708. doi: 10.1093/bjsw/33.5.699.

Ferguson, H. (2011). *Child Protection Practice*. London: Palgrave McMillan.

Ferguson, H. (2013). Anthony Giddens. In M. Gray & S. Webb (Eds.), *Social Work Theories and Methods* (Second edition, pp. 25–35). London: Sage.

Fine, M. (1994). Working the Hyphens. In N. K. Denzin & Y. S. Lincoln (Eds.), *Handbook of Qualitative Research* (pp. 70–82). Thousand Oaks, CA: Sage.

Freire, P. (1996). *Pedagogy of the Oppressed*. London: Penguin.

Garrett, P. (2003). The Trouble with Harry: Why the "New Agenda of Life Politics" Fails to Convince. *British Journal of Social Work*, 33: 381–397. doi: 10.1093/bjsw/33.3.381.

Garrett, P. (2004). More Trouble with Harry: A Rejoinder in the 'Life Politics' Debate. *British Journal of Social Work*, 34: 577–589. doi: 10.1093/bjsw/bch067.

Giddens, A. (1991). *Modernity and Self-Identity: Self and Society in the Late Modern Age*. Cambridge: Polity Press.

Hawkins, R., & Shohet, P. (2012). *Supervision in the Helping Professions* (Fourth edition). Maidenhead: Open University Press.

Houston, S. (2004). Garrett Contra Ferguson: A Meta-Theoretical Appraisal of the 'Rumble in the Jungle'. *British Journal of Social Work*, 34: 261–267. doi: 10.1093/bjsw/bch025.

Ibarra, H. (1999). Provisional Selves: Experimenting with Image and Identity in Professional Identity. *Administrative Science Quarterly*, 44: 764–789. doi: 10.2307/2667055.

Ibarra, H., & Barbulescu, R. (2010). Identity as Narrative: A Process Model of Narrative Identity Work in Macro Work Role Transition. *Academy of Management Review*, 35: 135–154. Retrieved from http://www.hbs.edu/faculty/Lists/Events/Attachments/129/Ibarra%20Paper.pdf.

Ingold, T. (2011). *Being Alive: Essays on Movement, Knowledge and Description*. Abingdon: Routledge.

Jenkins, S. (2014). *Social Identity* (Fourth edition). Abingdon: Routledge.

Kanuha, V. K. (2000). 'Being' Native versus 'Going Native': Conducting Social Work Research as an Insider. *Social Work*, 45: 439–447. doi: 10.1093/sw/45.5.439.

Kettle, M. (2014). Reflecting upon Child Protection - the Professional Doctorate Journey. *Higher Education, Skills and Work-Based Learning*, 4: 184–195. doi: abs/10.1108/HESWBL-10–2013–0016.

Kinman, G., McMurray, I., & Williams, J. (2014). Enhancing Self-Knowledge, Coping Skills and Stress Resistance. In L. Grant & G. Kinman (Eds.), *Developing Resilience for Social Work Practice* (pp. 148–168). London: Palgrave McMillan.

Macfarlane, B., & Gourlay, L. (2009). The Reflection Game: Enacting the Penitent Self. *Teaching in Higher Education*, 14: 55–59. doi: 0.1080/13562510903050244.

Maxwell, N., Scourfield, J., Zhang, M. L., de Villiers, T., Hadfield, M., Kinnersley, P., Metcalf, L., & Tayyaba, S. (2016). *Independent Evaluation of the Frontline Pilot: Research Report*. Cardiff: Cardiff University.

McAdams, D. P., & McLean, K. C. (2013). Narrative Identity. *Current Directions in Psychological Science*, 22: 233–238. doi: 10.1177/0963721413475622.

Munro, R. (2004). Punctualizing Identity: Time and the Demanding Relation. *Sociology*, 38: 293–311. doi: 10.1177/0038038504040865.

Narey, M. (2014). *Making the Education of Social Workers Consistently Effective: Report of Sir Martin Narey's Independent Review of the Education of Children's Social Workers*. London: Department for Education.

Osteen, P. J. (2011) Motivations, Values, and Conflict Resolution: Students' Integration of Personal and Professional Identities. *Journal of Social Work Education*, 47: 423–444. doi: 10.5175/JSWE.2011.200900131.

Powell, S. (2010). Hide And Seek: Values in Early Childhood Education and Care. *British Journal of Educational Studies*, 58(2): 213–229.

Ricoeur, P. (1984). *Time and Narrative* (Vol. 1). Chicago: University of Chicago Press.

Riessman, C. (2008). *Narrative Methods for the Human Sciences*. London: Sage.

Roberts, B. (2002). *Biographical Research*. Buckingham: Open University Press.

Scanlon, L. (2011). Becoming a Professional. In L. Scanlon (Ed.), *Becoming a Professional: An Interdisciplinary Analysis of Professional Learning* (pp. 13–32). Dordrecht: Springer.

Scottish Executive. (2006). *Changing Lives: Report of the 21st Century Social Work Review*. Edinburgh: Scottish Executive.

Scottish Social Services Council (SSSC). (2015). *Review of Social Work Education: Statement on Progress 2014–2015*. Dundee: Scottish Social Services Council.

Smith, R. (2008). *Social Work and Power*. London: Palgrave McMillan.

Taylor, C. (2013). Critically Reflective Practice. In M. Gray & S. Webb (Eds.), *The New Politics of Social Work* (pp. 79–97). London: Palgrave McMillan.

Taylor, J. (2011). The Intimate Insider: Negotiating the Ethics of Friendship When Doing Insider Research. *Qualitative Research*, 11: 3–22. doi: 10.1177/1468794110384447.

Tew, J. (2006). Understanding Power and Powerlessness: Towards a Framework for Emancipatory Practice in Social Work. *Journal of Social Work*, 6: 33–51. doi: 10.1177/1468017306062222.

Tufford, L., & Newman, P. (2010) Bracketing in Qualitative Research. *Qualitative Social Work*, 11: 80–96. doi: 10.1177/1473325010368316.

Warner, G., Little, M., Baker, V., & Wrigley, Z. (2015). *An Impact Evaluation of Social Work and the Frontline Programme: Study Protocol*. Dartington: Dartington Social Research.

Wenger, E. (1998). *Communities of Practice: Learning, Meaning, and Identity*. Cambridge: Cambridge University Press.

Wiles, F. (2013). Not Easily Put into a Box: Constructing Professional Identity. *Social Work Education*, 32: 854–866. doi: 10.1080/02615479.2012.705273.

Wolcott, H. (2001). *Writing Up Qualitative Research* (Second edition). London: Sage.

16

PROFESSIONAL IDENTITY AS A MATTER OF CONCERN

Stephen A. Webb

Why is professional identity a matter of concern for so many different professions and especially for social work? The extent to which the Scottish *Changing Lives: Report of the 21st Century Social Work Review* dramatically concluded that "the 'crisis' in social work is mainly *a matter of professional identity* that impacts on recruitment, retention and the understanding of the profession's basic aims" (2006: 4, my emphasis added). Anecdotally, this concern seems to be ubiquitous across social work, particularly with senior policymakers, professional bodies, management, pressure groups and activists.

What does it mean to say that professional identity is a matter of concern? Here I want to pick up from and extend upon where I left off in the opening chapter. If you recall, the significance of "mattering" in considerations of professional identity was underlined. This chapter is intended to critically synthesise the various chapter contributions throughout the volume using the lens of matters of concern.

So we may ask, What is a matter of concern, and what makes it different from say a moral panic or controversy? Here is the first suggestion: professional identity is a matter of concern because it involves something inherently unsettled, to be investigated and explicated. The second insight follows from this: issues of professional identity permeate working life and exist across all elements in social work, to a large extent. In this sense identity is overrun by the issues rather than simply reproduced by individual practitioners (Andersen et al., 2015). By overrun or overtaken, the crucial insight here is that the agency of the social worker, as argued in this chapter, is enacted and derived from many interfering sources, rather than possessed by individual practitioners. Moreover, social work is always a matter of concern; it cannot be mastered instrumentally, proven in scientific facts or achieved without the collaboration of many actors. It is always unsettled, rarely resolved in any straightforward way. Thus, professional identity in social work is always networked and always social, always connected. It is always entangled. Bruno Latour (2004) has proposed a methodology that is useful in guiding an operative, critical approach to the issues facing social work. Latour proposes the notion of "matters of concern" in distinction to the more common scientific category of "matters of fact." While matters of fact, in Latour, are developed without consideration of desire (moral, ethical or other), matters of concern embrace and are centred in those desires. While matters of fact exist without context, in an attempt to uncover the indisputable, matters of concern gather context(s) into themselves (Ripley, Thun, and Velikov, 2009). Ivakhiv goes so far as to claim: "Everything begins with matters of concern. Such matters are always, as they have ever been, matters that involve us, touch and brush up against us, envelop us, or otherwise call on us to respond to them" (2014: 3).

Concerns have worked their way ever deeper into our lives, to the point that even the primal act of eating and anticipation of the next weather forecast become matters of concern. How then are we best to approach these matters of concern surrounding professional identity? Here I want to begin by examining some of the dominant tendencies evident in perspectives offered on professional identity, many of which have been outlined in this book. These I feel give us a strong sense of why identity is such an embattled concept, so unsettled and an enduring matter of concern. Throughout the volume the contributing authors have identified reoccurring concepts, patterns of thought and various strong methodological emphases. Whether these be dispositional attributes of practitioners (commitment, vocation and performance), rich context (inter-professional partnerships, risk work and health care settings), expressions of meaning (narrative, embodied knowledge and reflexive experience) or professional aggregations (collective vs. individual; identity vs. identification), each in their different way conveys regular patterns of understanding for this tricky concept. But they also contradict, pull apart and coexist uneasily with each other in important ways. In this chapter, the book is concluded by closely examining the underlying logic which sits behinds these different accounts and issues. How is professional identity, as a matter of concern, sustained and reproduced by various logics and assumptions? In this context we can make good use of insights developed in the burgeoning organisational theory literature on "institutional logics" (Thornton, Ocasio, and Lounsbury, 2012).

As a matter of concern, professional identity in social work has an institutional value and logic which foregrounds any analysis. This is why, and most importantly, we need to consider how – in spite of the diversity of approaches, political struggles and competing value claims – there is a certain normative dimension to the way we make sense of professional identity. Conveyed in the chapters of this book, there is an institutional logic to professional identity in social work which displays a certain ontological order and status (i.e. which gives way to a more lucid definition of what professional identity is as a phenomenon and what it is not). Refining the ontology of concepts such as professional identity is a good way to make clearer what it means for social work, and how it can be articulated with other concepts, such as professional socialisation, resilience and workplace recognition. As Friedland explains:

> An institutional logic presumes that institutional meanings, on the one hand, and individual or organisational interests and powers, on the other, are inter-dependent. An institutional value, or substance, finds the ontology of the central object or state of being through which normatively enforced practices are organised and hence constitute the resource through which powers are afforded and upon which these practices depend.
>
> *(2013: 35)*

Friedland says in a review article that institutional logics "undo the conceptual heterogeneities separating the rational and the non-rational, the technical and the cultural, the material and the ideal" (2012: 385). He contends that understanding how each institutional logic is "ordered around regimes of practice, constituted by specific constellations of rule, role and category" (ibid.) that provide helpful insights into how professional identity becomes a matter of concern for social work. Questions of value and worth sit at the centre of this push to translate the institutional logics perspective into a reconsideration of issues of professional identity. Again turning to Friedland, he says, "Institutional logics, I would argue, return us to that element from which the new institutionalism fled: value" (ibid., 386). There are several logics of value inherent in matters of concern with professional identity or identity work in social work. These include the four logics of:

- Productionist rationality;
- Sentimental politics of authenticity;
- Dynamic stabilisation as a mode of professional reproduction; and
- Regimes of justification, worth and recognition.

The following sections in this chapter deal with each of these institutional logics in turn. The purpose is to investigate these "orders of worth" as well as the limitations and dangers associated with conceiving of professional identity as a matter of concern. The four logics interlock in the institutional arrangements of social work and its professional regulation, in patterns of education and socialisation, and in the mechanisms of practitioner optimisation. It is apparent that a certain connectedness exists between these different logics, especially since notions of value, evaluation and worth are ever-present throughout. This reflects the reproductive qualities associated with professional identity in the demand for and formation of mobile and active subjects – social work practitioners. In the wider context of late modernity, Rosa et al. explain:

> In this process, the late-modern individual becomes a "perpetuum mobile" of its own kind: an actor who not only cares for him-/herself but also for the economic and social reproduction of the system, and who can never be sufficiently active and mobile nor ever show sufficient initiative.
>
> *(2016: 7)*

Productionist rationality

The first institutional logic in play relates to operativity and production. Here we can invoke the classical lineage of ideas relating to Aristotle's view of "production-ist" as conceived as things which are "formed matter". Several chapters in the book have alluded to what might be termed a "productionist rationality" in considerations of professional identity. Deleuze and Guattari acknowledge the key role of production in late capitalist modernity:

> Hence everything is production: *productions of productions,* of actions and of passions; *productions of recording processes,* or distributions and of co-ordinates that serves as points of reference. . . . This is the first meaning of process as we use the term: incorporating, recording and consumption within production itself, this making the term production of one and the same process.
>
> *(1983: 4)*

Thinking of everything as production, including anxieties and other "subject" identity experiences, creates a common language with which to talk about professional identity. The mantra of "becoming a social worker" characterised as a journey is crucial to this respect (see Daly and Kettle, Chapter 15 in this volume). Different relationships and contexts hold open or foreclose, encourage or dissuade, different possibilities for becoming in social work (Van Dooren, 2016: 45).

In respect to the operativity of identity formation and identification, these are regarded as "having-to-be". Case study material in the book consistently shows that professional identity is a prerequisite: not something that simply exists but *has to be* brought into being. There is a tacit requirement to produce it, in a manner akin to Aristotle's "giving form to matter". It appears that there is no opt-out for students or practitioners in giving form to matters of professional identity. Anecdotally, one colleague reported to the author, we are here to "support students to develop their own identity - we can't do the 'identity work' for them". The assumption is identity is waiting to happen; it simply needs to be kick-started and supported. But more than this, professional identity is implicitly viewed through the lens of self-actualisation, an achievement. The (unspoken) expectation is that students and practitioners will labour on it. Professional identity is the actualisation of having-to-be, with the practitioner self as the container which needs to be filled. This operativity translates as an imperative of duty or morality of office to be achieved by the practitioner. The prerequisite of a professional identity is already decided (by educators and field practitioners) in a preliminary way in educational or workplace contexts. Let's be clear here: it is reckoned to be accumulative, linear and progressively affirmed. The parallel with Kant's concept of ethics is striking, if not surprising, given that social work has always flirted with his moral code (Webb, 1989). Professional identity becomes a duty-to-be or, in Kantian terms, it "is always in progress and yet always starts from a beginning, it is an ideal and unattainable, while yet constant approximation to it is duty" (1996: 537). Perhaps this proximity to duty is the reason why the International Federation of Social Workers maintain that "An ethical code also contributes to the strengthening of professional identity" (2006: 4). The British Association of Social Workers (BASW, 2014) defines professionalism as "identifying as a professional social worker" and the Standards for Employment of Social Workers in England asks how employers can "recognise and support the professional identity of social workers within your organisation" (Local Government Authority, 2014). However, it is this productionist "having-to-be" in the formation of professional identity, I would suggest, which gives it the force and veracity to incur a mattering of concern. The case study material provided in several chapters show how sanctions are likely to incur for those inoperative social work students who don't show concern around matters of identity formation during professional education.

Sentimental politics of authenticity

Throughout the literature there is a tacit ideal of authenticity of a professional self that can be organized to convey the values and mission of social work. I call this the sentimental politics of authenticity. This is the second institutional logic identified which brings together the interplay of meaning and structure in professional life. Leigh (Chapter 14 in this volume) showed that interaction in social work demands a sort of professional performance. She worries that the business of credibility management is put front and centre stage. If we take performance and authenticity to be antithetical, then much of professional life will be deemed inauthentic. A deficit of authenticity becomes a matter of concern for social work. In attacking the ills of the present, authenticity invokes tradition and taps into the shared identity of a social work profession. Educators and senior practitioners are regulators of this for newly qualified social workers. They test for authenticity-driven converts in relation to the social work mission and values. An affected folksiness is almost a necessity to "be a professional practitioner". Tracing a new form of inwardness from Weber onwards, Erickson and Price (Chapter 6 in this volume) tell how the inner voice is important because it guides practitioners about the right thing to do. This idea has entered deep into the social work psyche, which has long held on to the view that being in touch with our feelings is a means to acting authentically. Erickson and Price imply that taking an instrumental stance to the professional self means losing the capacity to listen to the authentic inner voice. It strikes me that the huge industry which has grown around the virtues of the reflective practitioner is somehow related to this (Webb, 1996). Reflection should reveal the professional ideal of authenticity and the essentialist goals of a self-realised, self-fulfilled practitioner. Reflection gives more sentimental force to the professional culture of authenticity in social work (Taylor, 1991). The preoccupation with authenticity, and the technique of reflection used to achieve it, move considerations of professional identity beyond static and fixed identities (see Dent, Chapter 2 in this volume) to embrace an attentiveness to the way in which practitioners themselves exert their own agency in remaking what counts as "professional behaviour" (see Daly and Kettle, Chapter 15 in this volume).

What at first glance may appear nebulous is an interesting article by Van Dooren (2016) which explores how identity is imagined and managed in a bird conservation programme to produce "authentic" crows. It throws up some interesting insight and parallels about how we can think of authenticity for social work. What counts for the crows in conservation programmes seems to also count for the training of social workers. Like many social work education programmes, the training of crows values behavioural stasis for the simple reason that behaviour is a key part of the identity of the species. Behaviour is regarded as a developmental achievement for securing an essential professional identity. For both the training of crows and social workers, authenticity functions in professional contexts to position particular identities as "false or derivative, and others [as] true and original" (2016: 39). These identities are always being performatively reiterated in reflective diaries, learning and supervision logs, and case notes. However, professional identity understood as performative is not an essence but a "doing", as Jensen succinctly shows in Chapter 4 in this volume. Authenticity, then, is a performative materialisation of the "ideal social worker" (see Daly and Kettle, Chapter 15 in this volume). I've hinted at a darker side to authenticity politics, which is confirmed by McQueen's comments on identity claims: "Such claims are often cloaked in a language of 'authenticity' which leads to demands for conformity amongst individual members of the group in order to gain acceptance and approval" (McQueen, 2011).

Conformity, control, regulation and disciplinary practice – all involving power relations – reflect what has been referred to as the darker side of thinking about professional identity.

Dynamic stabilisation as a mode of professional reproduction

The third logic which attenuates matters of concern to professional identity relates to reproduction qualities in what is termed "dynamic stabilization" (Rosa et al., 2016). Through the logic, professional identity is cast as dynamic with respect to professional growth, innovation and change, on the one hand, and quite robust, durable and stable in terms of professional affiliation on other hand. Dynamic stabilisation frames professional identity as involving more than just permanent processing or continuous operation, as discussed in the productionist rationality section. It derives its veracity in growth, augmentation and innovation, not just from processual reproduction. This dynamism, in turn, entails an intrinsic logic of escalation, continuous improvement and acceleration. The dynamic is developmental for the social worker because it commits practitioners to perpetual "progress" toward new challenges, projects and affiliations in the making of professional identity. Identity takes on dispositional qualities of resilience; it is defined by Rajan-Rankin (2013) as "a dynamic process wherein individuals display positive adaptation despite experiences of significant adversity or trauma" (2426). Regulation crucially plays into this, whereby social workers increasingly face regular quality checks of their professional competence, confidence and commitment. "Fitness to practice" is the important benchmark where action is taken if a registered social worker falls below the regulator standards. The most obvious example of the dynamic stabilisation logic is the continuing professional development (CPD) agenda – a central requirement for professional registration – which refers to learning activities that professionals engage in to develop and enhance their abilities. Throughout the CPD policy literature, practitioners – and particularly newly qualified social workers - are hailed to "maintain", "assert" and "embrace" their professional identities. As indicated in Chapters 1 and 5 in this volume, there is a persistent concern about erosion of professional identity in social work, especially in the face of health and social care integration. Coming increasingly under the jurisdiction of medicine and allied health, social work may find itself restricted in virtually every aspect of its work. CPD is often regarded as one mechanism to effectively offset this scare. In the UK the introduction of the new assessed and supported year in employment (ASYE) programme and probationary period is another example. The ASYE is a 12-month programme for assessing newly qualified social workers (NQSWs). We can detect ways in which professional identity is deployed as a benchmark construct to measure the impact of CPD and AYSE activities. The Health and Care Professions Council (HCPC) typically uses practitioner cases examples to justify the AYSE. Following is an example which highlights the link between professional development and identity.

> I found the ASYE workshops very helpful in developing my professional identity as a Social Worker. The first workshop (which took place 2 months prior to this registration period) was based on this subject and gave me a wider view of Social Work including a historical and international perspective. During the session we revisited our values and what sustains and motivates in the role.
>
> *(Health and Care Professions Council, 2014)*

The British Association of Social Workers (BASW) maintains that "social workers need to demonstrate professional commitment by taking responsibility for their conduct, practice and learning, with support through supervision" (BASW, 2012: 3). It makes the development of professional identity a key benchmark in its CPD policy (2012). The UK *Skills for Care* (2014) manual talks about the necessity to "develop more robust professional identities" through reflective practice. In Chapter 11 (in this volume), Collins drew attention to the significance and ubiquitous nature of "affective" commitment and resilience as benchmarks of good standards in social work. He says that practitioners "with low affective commitment are seen to be more liable to difficult behaviour at work, absences and higher turnover rates" (p. 152). In this figure of the "active social worker" sits the reproductive logic of "self-optimisation", with the imperative of growth, actualisation and expansion inherent in all appeals to professional identity. In this context professional identity is effectively privatized as a matter of concern (Rosa, 2016: 7). The extent to which managerialist policy assumes social work identity to be fundamentally individualistic is certainly a worthy area for future research.

Regimes of justification, worth and recognition

Taylor is keen to stress just how important recognition is, referring to it as "a vital human need" (1994: 26) and stating that misrecognition "can inflict a grievous wound, saddling its victims with a crippling self-hatred" (ibid.: 26; also see McQueen, 2011). The struggle for worth and recognition in social work is intimately bound up to matters of concern around professional identity. How does social work engage with relevant stakeholder groups (other professions, the public, media and politicians) when its legitimacy comes under threat? Social work mobilises orders of worth in order to publicly justify its professional status and on occasion repair its professional reputation. If it is successful it stabilises the professional collective and achieves a "legitimacy repair" (Patriotta, et al., 2011). Justifications in such contexts requires specific professional competencies of worth with regard to the construction of convincing accounts and arguments. A robust but dynamic professional identity is one device that is deployed in this justificatory process with social work. Boltanski and Thévenot's theory of justification can be used to account for the ways in which professional identity is actively mobilised to engage with discourses and objects to maintain the legitimacy of social work and relevant practitioner activity. They conducted numerous empirical studies in the 1980s to illustrate how practitioners mobilise various rationales to advocate their positions, build convincing arguments or demonstrate how a situation is fair or unfair (Patriotta, et al., 2011).

Two areas providing fertile ground for examining struggles for worth, legitimacy and recognition in relation to professional identity are: (i) forms of knowledge in practice; and (ii) inter-professional partnerships and collaboration. Both aspects have been addressed in this book. Hardesty's Chapter 8 describes two conflicting epistemological imperatives wired into the practitioners' job, the scientific and the embodied standpoints; and Beddoe's Chapter 9, along with Emprechtinger and Voll's Chapter 10, focuses on inter-professional collaboration in different types of social work settings. All three chapters provide compelling accounts of the issues at stake for professional identity using in-depth case material. In relation to legitimation and forms of knowledge in practice, Dent and Whitehead (2002) argue:

> for professional status to be legitimised, it has to be based on 'scientific knowledge, and/or validated by 'scientific knowledge. In other words, the professional must succumb to the pressure to be measured against so-called 'objective' criteria in scientific mode before they can assume their elevated position.
>
> *(8)*

Legitimation confirms and cultivates professional identity. But more importantly, perhaps, in terms of relations of power, claims for specialised formal knowledge are essential. In Abbot's terms this is why "the ability of a profession to sustain its jurisdictions lies partly on the power and prestige of its academic knowledge" (1988: 53). But the status of and claims for knowledge are not so clear-cut in social work. Hardesty, in Chapter 8, reaches stark conclusions about the tensions between contradictory forms of knowledge. Her empirical research shows there are:

> incommensurate demands upon workers to be simultaneously perspectival, empathic, and producers of disembodied objective knowledge compel workers to legitimate their identity through techniques of objectification. As part of this process of justification they cut away the nuances and value judgments that inform the many evaluations they make while doing frontline practice (see Boltanski and Thévenot, 1991). Therefore, objectivity obscures, even while it is lauded as the harbinger of unbiased and transparent practice.
>
> *(p 118, this volume)*

In 2001 I wrote a highly cited article about the impact of evidence-based practice suggesting that the tendency to separate processes into "facts" and "values" implicit in evidence-based procedures undermined professional judgement and discretion in social work. In a similar fashion to Hardesty, it was claimed that the evidence-based preoccupation with positivistic methods and determinate judgement entraps social workers within a mechanistic form of technical rationality (Webb, 2001: 57). This preoccupation with the "what works" agenda of implementation science is only likely to further hinder the development of rich, interdisciplinary research agendas in social work using innovative social sciences.

Whilst not wishing to rehearse the arguments put forward by Beddoe and Emprechtinger and Voll in earlier chapters, it is important to emphasise how issues relating to inter-professional practice constitutes a significant matter of concern for social work. As indicated above this is often couched in the "erosion of professional identity" debate. The example below gives a sense of the sorts of sentiment this stokes up for both researchers and practitioners.

> We demonstrate that a key cause of failure in IPP (inter-professional practice) can be attributed to inter-professional conflicts based on threats to professional identity, and provide insight into how professional identity faultlines have the potential to be activated and conflict induced when there is differential treatment of professional groups, different values between professions, assimilation, insult or humiliating action and simple contact within the team.
>
> *(McNeil et al., 2013: 291)*

Assimilation is regarded as a real threat. Edwards et al. (2002) argued professionalism is based on epistemological and social criteria, broadly interpreted as knowledge and autonomy. In England, the closure of the College of Social Work in 2015 led many commentators to suggest this severely undermined the professional autonomy of social work. Returning to the Scottish *Changing Lives Report* (2006), discussed at the beginning of this chapter, we can easily detect a palpable concern when the authors suggest that:

> professional identity should be based more on core values and principles in order to distinguish the nature of the social worker's contribution from that of individuals working within other agencies and to protect against the threat of boundary erosion as the result of development in other professions. Issues of recruitment and retention to social work are inextricably linked to the issue of professional identity.
>
> *(http://www.gov.scot/Publications/2005/12/1994633/46360)*

These core values and principles are inevitably reflective of both a social justice and ethics of care agenda. How women in a gendered profession, such as social work, construct their professional identity in response to workplace interpersonal interactions and core values are clearly important considerations. Is it likely that female practitioners generally see their identities as compatible with an ethics of care? Starting with Latour's notion of "matters of concern", discussed in this chapter, this inspires Maria Puig de la Bellacasa (2011) to develop the concept of "matters of care". Drawing on feminist knowledge politics she suggests that a focus on matters of care adds a "critical" edge to care that Latour's politics of things tends to disregard. She stresses:

> the capacity of the word 'concern' to move the notion of 'interest' towards more affectively charged connotations, notably those of trouble, worry and care. Understood as affective states, concern and care are thus related. Care, however, has stronger affective and ethical connotations.
>
> *(2011: 89)*

Bellacasa goes on to contend that "Understanding caring as something *we do* extends a vision of care as an ethically and politically charged practice, one that has been at the forefront of feminist concern with devalued labours" (ibid., 90, my emphasis added). One popular formulation of care opposes it to knowledge. Others, however, argue that knowing requires caring about what and how one knows (Friese, 2013). How we enact care in relations with students, colleagues and service users and how care circulates as a gendered performance remains an important consideration for any analysis of professional identity. Martin et al. (2015), however, warn against the laudatory and romantic visions of care, the sentimental politics discussed above. In their research workshops they explore the darker side of care and its implicit relation to power.

> Care is a selective mode of attention: it circumscribes and cherishes some things, lives, or phenomena as its objects. In the process, it excludes others. Practices of care are always shot through with asymmetrical power relations: who has the power to care? Who has the power to define what counts as

care and how it should be administered? Care can render a receiver powerless or otherwise limit their power. It can set up conditions of indebtedness
or obligation. It can also sediment these asymmetries by putting recipients in
situations where they cannot reciprocate.

(2015: 3)

In the final few paragraphs, I wish to draw attention to emergent areas for research
and possible future directions for a concentrated study of professional identity in
social work. As a concept it suffers from a well-known problem in sociology, of
being regarded, simultaneously, as structuring and structured. On the one hand,
practitioners are thought to have lively agency in forming their own identity, on
the other hand, it is argued that professional identity is interiorized and structured
for practitioners by wider contexts, such as the workplace, professional associations
and government austerity measures. Various authors in this volume have pointed
out that attention to "identity work" is likely to yield good results. Identity work
can be thought of as an act of producing and is constitutive. This, however, presents
a significant methodological challenge and concerns about coherence in the study
of professional identity. How can local, situated accounts of professional identity
sensibly be tied to questions of macrostructure? Bourdieu (1990: 69) illustrates the
problem: "It is because agents never know completely what they are doing that
what they do has more sense than they know". As we've seen above, considering
institutional logics as social structures allows us to reassert that they exist independently of practitioners' perceptions and examine how they condition their actions.
It is along these lines that Summerson Carr (2015) offers fascinating insights in her
study of care workers having to deal with bedbugs in service users homes.

Yet rather than viewing agency as a property and potentiality of human individuals more or less constrained by "structure," as a crass version of practice
theory would have it, seasoned *U-Haven* professionals tended to see agency –
or, the capacity to effectively act – as the sum total of complex, non-linear
transactions among program participants, staff, drugs, monthly checks, visitors, medications, policy mandates, psychotic symptoms, aspects of the built
and crumbling environment and, of course, bedbugs.

An understanding of professional life as ecological, stressing the dynamic reciproc-
ity between materiality and affect, human actors and their environments, and to
conceive of action as performative adaptations to complex networked relations,
may well be the way forward for studies of identity. And who knows, even inter-
species relationships! The anthropological lines of research pursued by Summerson
Carr strike one as some of the most innovative and creative in considerations of
expertise and professional life.

One area which certainly demands closer attention is the intra-professional
group differences and relations to matters of concern with professional identity.
While Smith (Chapter 12) has valuably focused on residential childcare; Keddell

and Stanley (Chapter 7) on child protection workers; and Beddoe (Chapter 9) health social workers, there is much greater scope for detailed analysis focusing on identity differences across various social work contexts. I have in mind here mental health, work with the elderly, working with people with disability, criminal justice social work and work with asylum seekers and refugees. How does the specific service user context impact on professional identity as a matter of concern? This type of analysis would allow us to elaborate about the capacity for integration of disparate experiences and identification that works to join or separate social work practices. It would also enable us to more fully appreciate relations of power within and across different professional groupings in social work. As several chapters in this book have shown, the work of the French sociologist Bourdieu is likely to be particularly lively and instructive here. The breaking down of the constituents of the structuring elements of professional identity requires a focused attention to field and networks, or better still, perhaps, the "habitus" concept which Bourdieu develops (Silva, 2016). The concept of habitus as intrinsically fragmented in professional life, in a process of liminality of "liminality" (working life in transitions and in-betweens with increasing "spaces of possibles", e.g. hot desking and flexi working) turning professional identity more problematic and troubled. Wetherell (2012) points to the need to approach intersectionality in relation to the analysis of habitus as a professional field. She considers affect, as "embodied meaning-making", as a notion close to that of habitus. Because no singular affective habitus exists, she thinks in "affective intersectional" ways to identify the constituents of the affecting forces that form identity. Similarly, Leigh, in Chapter 14, developed this emphasis, arguing the "turn to affect" is important for social work and it embraces an ontological concern with corporeal and material affective reactions only partially connected to ideas, organisations and professional discourse.

A final provocative thought to finish the book. Can you imagine what a fully formed professional identity might look like? Are you able to think the consummate, final product? Have you witnessed a professional identity that has reached its end point in "becoming a professional social worker"? I doubt it. There is an ontological problem at stake here with the assumption that professional identity has the character of "being in". What it tells us is something about the impossibility of an identity coinciding with itself. There can never be a completed professional identity of a social worker or anyone else for that matter. Does this suggest we should ditch the identity model completely? Nancy Fraser thinks the identity model of recognition is deeply flawed and "that it lends itself all too easily to repressive forms of communitarianism, promoting conformism, intolerance and patriarchalism" (2000: 110). But that is a story for another day.

References

Andersen, L. B., Danholt, P., Halskov, K., Brodersen, N., & Lauritsen, P. (2015). Participation as a Matter of Concern in Participatory Design. *Co-Design*, 11(3–4): 250–261.

BASW. (2012). *Professional Capability Framework – ASYE Level Capabilities*. Birmingham: BASW.

BASW. (2014). *The Code of Ethics for Social Work*, Birmingham: BASW.

Bellacasa, M. P. (2011). Matters of Care in Technoscience: Assembling Neglected Things. *Social Studies of Science*, 41(1): 85–106.

Boltanski, L., & Thévenot, L. (1991). *On Justification: The Economies of Worth*. Princeton: Princeton University Press.

Bourdieu, P. (1990). *The Logic of Practice*. Stanford, CA: Stanford University Press.

Deleuze, G., & Guattari, F. (1983). *Anti-Oedipus: Capitalism and Schizophrenia*. Minneapolis: University of Minnesota Press.

Dent, M., & Whitehead, S. (eds.) (2002). *Managing Professional Identities: Knowledge, Performativities and the 'New' Professional*. London: Routledge.

Edwards, A., Gilroy, G., & Hartley, D. (2002). *Rethinking Teacher Education: Collaborative Responses to Uncertainty*. London: Routledge Farmer.

Fraser, N. (2000). Rethinking Recognition. *New Left Review*, 3, May/June: 107–120.

Friedland, R. (2012). Review of the Institutional Logics Perspective: A New Approach to Culture, Structure, and Process. *Management*, 15: 583–595.

Friedland, R. (2013). God, Love and other Good Reasons for Practice: Thinking through Institutional Logics. In E. Boxenbaum & M. Lounsbury (Eds.), *Institutional Logics in Action*, (pp. 25–50). Bingley: Emerald Group Publishing.

Friese, C. (2013). Realizing Potential in Translational Medicine: The Uncanny Emergence of Care as Science. *Current Anthropology*, 54(7): 129–138.

Health and Care Professions Council. (2014). *CPD Profile*. London: HMSO

Ivakhiv, A. (2014). On Matters of Concern: Ontological Politics, Ecology, and the Anthropo(s)cene. In *UC Davis Environments and Societies Paper* (pp. 1–16). Burlington: University of Vermont.

Latour, B. (2004). Why Has Critique Run Out of Steam? From Matters of Fact to Matters of Concern. *Critical Inquiry*, 30(2): 225–248.

Local Government Authority. (2014). *The Standards for Employers of Social Workers in England*, London: HMSO.

Martin, A., Myers, N., & Viseu, A. (2015). The Politics of Care in Technoscience. *Social Studies of Science*, 45(5): 625–641. doi: 10.1177/0306312715602073.

McNeil, K., Mitchell, R., & Parker, V. (2013). Inter-professional Practice and Professional Identity Threat. *Health Sociology Review*, 22(3): 291–307.

McQueen, P. (2011). *Social and Political Recognition*. Internet Encyclopaedia of Philosophy. Retrieved from http://www.iep.utm.edu/recog_sp/.

Patriotta, G., Gond, J-P., & Schultz, F. (2011). Maintaining Legitimacy: Controversies, Orders of Worth, and Public Justifications. *Journal of Management Studies*, 48(8), December. doi: 10.1111/j.1467–6486.2010.00990.x.

Rajan-Rankin, S. (2013). Self-Identity, Embodiment and the Development of Emotional Resilience. *British Journal of Social Work*, 44(8): 2426–2442.

Ripley, C., Thun, G., & Velikov, K. (2009). Matters of Concern. *Journal of Architectural Education*, 62(4): 6–14.

Rosa, H., Do, K., & Lessenich, S. (2016). Appropriation, Activation and Acceleration: The Escalatory Logics of Capitalist Modernity and the Crises of Dynamic Stabilization. *Theory, Culture & Society*, 34(1). Published online before print July 29, 2016. doi: 10.1177/0263276416657600.

Silva, E. B. (2016). Habitus: Beyond Sociology. *The Sociological Review*, 64(1): 73–92.

Skills for Care. (2014). *Critically Reflective Action Learning: Improving Social Work Practice though Critically Reflective Learning*. Leeds. Retrieved from http://www.skillsforcare.org.uk/Learning-development/Learning-and-development.aspx.

Summerson Carr, E. (2015). Occupation Bedbug: Or, the Urgency and Agency of Professional Pragmatism. *Cultural Anthropology*, 30(2): 257–285. Retrieved from http://dx.doi.org/10.14506/ca30.2.08.

Taylor, C. (1991). *The Ethics of Authenticity*. Cambridge: Harvard University Press.

Taylor, C. (1994). The Politics of Recognition. In Amy Gutmann (Ed.), *Multiculturalism: Examining the Politics of Recognition* (pp. 25–73). Princeton: Princeton University Press.

Thornton, P. H., Ocasio, W., & Lounsbury, M. (2012). *The Institutional Logics Perspective: A New Approach to Culture, Structure, and Process*. New York: Oxford University Press.

Van Dooren, T. (2016). Authentic Crows: Identity, Captivity and Emergent Forms of Life. *Theory, Culture & Society*, 33(2): 29–52.

Webb, S. A. (1989). A Political Critique of Kantian Ethics in Social Work. *British Journal of Social Work*, 19(1): 491–506.

Webb, S. A. (1996). Forgetting Ourselves? Social Work Values, Liberal Education and Modernity. *Studies in the Education of Adults*, 28(2): 224–240.

Webb, S. A. (2001). Some Considerations on the Validity of Evidence-based Practice in Social Work. *British Journal of Social Work*, 31(1): 51–79.

Webb, S. A. (2006). *Social Work in a Risk Society*. London: Palgrave Macmillan.

Wetherell, M. (2012). *Affect and Emotion: A New Social Science Understanding*. London: Sage.

INDEX